D0763992

NEIGHBORHOODS
IN URBAN AMERICA

Kennikat Press
National University Publications
Interdisciplinary Urban Series

Advisory Editor
Raymond A. Mohl

NEIGHBORHOODS IN URBAN AMERICA

edited by
RONALD H. BAYOR

National University Publications
KENNIKAT PRESS // 1982
Port Washington, N. Y. // London

Manufactured in the United States of America

Published by
Kennikat Press Corp.
Port Washington, N.Y. / London

Library of Congress Cataloging in Publication Data
Main entry under title:

Neighborhoods in urban America.

(Interdisciplinary urban series) (National
university publications)
Bibliography: p. 247

1. Neighborhood—Case studies. 2. Community
organization—Case studies. 3. Community power—
Case studies. 4. Community development, Urban—
United States—Case studies. I. Bayor, Ronald H.,
1944- . II. Series.
HT153.N44   307.7'6   81-3785
ISBN 0-8046-9284-X   AACR2

For my parents Mac and Lillian Bayor,
and my wife Leslie

CONTENTS

PREFACE

As neighborhoods have grown more important in the political and social life of the city, there has been a resurgence of interest in them among specialists in urban studies. Many universities now offer courses either with a neighborhood component or entirely devoted to an analysis of neighborhoods. However, the literature on neighborhoods is scattered and therefore difficult to study or use in the classroom. Since no anthology on neighborhoods was available, this volume was developed to correct that situation. The selections, of which all but one have been previously published, provide a wide-ranging interdisciplinary look at the field for those interested in the research and teaching of neighborhood topics.

For suggestions on both the structure of this volume and the articles to appear in it, I would like to thank Bayrd Still of New York University, Seymour J. Mandelbaum of the University of Pennsylvania, Kenneth T. Jackson of Columbia University, Jay A. Weinstein of the Georgia Institute of Technology, and Robert K. Whelan of the University of North Florida. I appreciate too the encouragement of Raymond A. Mohl of Florida Atlantic University and academic editor of Kennikat Press's urban series.

Thanks are also due to Jon J. Johnston, acting head of the department of social sciences at the Georgia Institute of Technology, and to the Georgia Tech Foundation for their assistance in completing this project. My gratitude also goes to those who typed this volume—Jane Wilson, Genie Vidal, and Vickie Majors.

Most of all, I would like to thank my wife Leslie for her interest in and encouragement of this work, and my daughters Jill and Robin for their patience and understanding during periods when this volume consumed all my time.

NEIGHBORHOODS
IN URBAN AMERICA

ABOUT THE CONTRIBUTORS

Ronald H. Bayor is associate professor of history at the Georgia Institute of Technology.

Caroline Golab is assistant professor of history and city planning at the University of Pennsylvania.

Mark Goldman is a professor of urban history at Empire State College in Buffalo.

Edgar M. Hoover, at the time his book was written, was professor of economics at the University of Pittsburgh.

Marsha Hurst is assistant professor of government at the John Jay College of Criminal Justice, City University of New York.

Jane Jacobs is a former associate editor of *Architectural Forum* and a well-known writer on architectural and city planning issues.

Suzanne Keller is a professor of sociology at Princeton University.

Chia-ling Kuo is an anthropologist who, at the time her book was written, was associated with an urban research project at the City College of New York.

Bob Kuttner is on the staff of the Senate Committee on Banking, Housing, and Urban Affairs.

Gilbert Osofsky was professor of history at the University of Illinois, Chicago Circle.

William L. Riordan was a reporter for the *New York Evening Post* when he conducted the interviews with Plunkitt.

Roger D. Simon is now associate professor of history at Lehigh University.

Clarence N. Stone is professor of political science at the University of Maryland.

Raymond Vernon, at the time his book was written, was professor of international trade and investment at the Harvard University Graduate School of Business Administration.

Sam Bass Warner, Jr., is presently professor of history at Boston University.

Douglas Yates is professor of political science at Yale University.

INTRODUCTION

"Neighborhood power," "local community control," "neighborhood schools" are all slogans which appear with increasing frequency in today's newspapers, indicating an era of neighborhood activism. The importance of neighborhoods as the basic unit for understanding and solving many urban problems was acknowledged recently by the National Commission on Neighborhoods, a study group created by Congress in 1977 as part of the National Neighborhood Policy Act.

The present emphasis on neighborhoods is a product of forces, attitudes, and issues which came together in the 1950s and 1960s but which go back further into American History. In the nineteenth century, with cities as fragmented collections of small communities, the neighborhoods had more autonomy and importance. As the cities began to centralize their political power and expand their boundaries during the Progressive period, the neighborhoods lost some of their identity and independence through such factors as non-partisan elections and at-large voting. Although the thrust of the Progressive movement in the cities was toward centralized control, there were individual Progressives who supported the neighborhood concept. For example, John Dewey was interested in the reestablishment of neighborhood ties and community feeling.

A neighborhood focus continued with the work of such individuals as Clarence Perry, a city planner who in 1923 supported the development of cities through a neighborhood unit system. In this idea, the city's neighborhoods would be built and planned according to certain specifications and designed to engender a sense of community. Politically the neighborhoods were the center of concern for the settlement house workers and later for such community activists as Saul Alinsky who worked in the Back of the Yards area in Chicago.

While the neighborhood concept had been kept alive during years of centralized city life, by the 1950s the neighborhood had only a weak voice in city affairs. However, the changes were coming soon. During the 1950s controversies over urban renewal began the process of awakening neighborhood advocates. In areas slated for renewal protests from neighborhood ad hoc committees emerged. The renewal controversy enhanced an already growing dissatisfaction with the responsiveness of an overly centralized city government. Coupled with a deterioration in city services and an acknowledged urban crisis, neighborhood groups appeared with more frequency. Also, there were reactions on a citywide basis. For example, in Pittsburgh the private, non-profit Allegheny Council to Improve Our Neighborhoods-Housing, Inc. (ACTION-Housing, Inc.) was established in 1957 to work in that city's communities. Some city governments also responded. In New York as early as 1951, twelve community planning councils were created for the borough of Manhattan. Although advisory, these councils, later boards, indicated a new concern with providing local citizen involvement in decision-making and were eventually expanded citywide during the next decade with enhanced powers.

The 1960s brought a continued sense of urban decline but also the civil rights movement, which was interested in the rights of the urban poor. On the neighborhood level, the civil rights crusade eventually took the form of community control in black areas. But in white neighborhoods also there were demands for community control, particularly in relation to community services. The school decentralization controversy in New York in the late 1960s further increased the neighborhood's power and visibility as did the creation in New York of an Office of Neighborhood Government in 1970.

The federal government's entry into neighborhood issues began seriously during the 1960s with President Lyndon Johnson's War on Poverty and Model Cities programs, which permitted local citizen participation in community decision-making. For example, in 1964 Congress, in setting up community action agencies to provide federal anti-poverty services in low income areas, mandated local citizen involvement through the election of community action boards. Although not always successful in actually enhancing the neighborhood's policy-making position, these programs indicated a shift in the federal government's attitude toward citizen participation which continued into the 1970s. Recently the federal government's concern with neighborhoods was illustrated by the creation of a National Commission on Neighborhoods and an assistant secretary at HUD for neighborhoods, voluntary associations, and consumer protection.

Today some cities, such as New York, have a well-developed neighborhood program which brings local community representatives into various decision-making roles. There are now also nationwide neighborhood lobbying groups such as the National Association of Neighborhoods and National People's Action. In many parts of the country neighborhoods have become the focus of urban concern and policy, as noted by the interest in such areas as Society Hill in Philadelphia, Brooklyn Heights in New York, Inman Park in Atlanta, and Bunker Hill in Los Angeles.

Studies of neighborhoods have paralleled their growing importance politically through the years. The first neighborhood studies to emerge came out of the settlement houses in New York and Chicago. However, community analysis became an important area of academic interest because of Robert Park and the Chicago School of Sociology. Park initiated urban sociological studies of Chicago with his article "The City: Suggestions for the Investigation of Human Behavior in the Urban Environment," published in the *American Journal of Sociology* in 1915. The Chicago sociologists began analyzing various aspects of the city— cultural life, spatial patterns—by concentrating on different communities within the city or what they referred to as the natural areas (natural in the sense that the city would inherently follow a certain pattern of division). Park, along with Ernest Burgess, Harvey Zorbaugh, Louis Wirth, and Roderick D. McKenzie, began to develop the ecological, zonal theories of city growth by studying urban neighborhoods. Burgess's concentric zone theory of urban development, which divided the city into five zones (central business district, or CBD, zone in transition, zone of workingmen's homes, residential zone, commuter zone), was followed by other theories of urban growth which also focused on the city's neighborhoods.

Homer Hoyt in 1939 stated his sector theory, which emphasized city development in sector or wedge shapes based on transportation facilities (corridors) emanating from the central business district. High income neighborhoods, for example, will expand outward along transportation lines from the CBD with the poorer neighborhoods developing near the CBD. In 1945 geographers Chauncy Harris and Edward Ullman offered a multiple-nuclei theory which tried to explain irregular patterns of urban structure. The city had a number of growing points, a number of nuclei, because of historical, situational, or other factors.

The theoretical discussion of urban growth and spatial patterns begun by the Chicago School opened up an inquiry into neighborhoods which still continues. Their focus on neighborhoods as a way of understanding the city is very much a part of present urban studies.

This volume illustrates the varied directions that neighborhood studies have taken. It is an attempt to bring together a number of important neighborhood articles and excerpts from books drawn from the fields of history, sociology, political science, geography, and city planning, and based on a number of cities.

The book is divided into five sections, each highlighting a significant aspect of neighborhood concern. Chapter 1, "The Neighborhood and the City," analyzes the neighborhood's relationship to and function within the larger urban area as well as the physical and social makeup of neighborhoods. Chapter 2, "Neighborhood Groups," examines ethnic neighborhoods and spatial patterns. "Government and Neighborhood," chapter 3, relates the historical sources and present problems of decentralization and community control by looking at nineteenth- and twentieth-century neighborhoods and issues. In chapter 4, "Neighborhood Cycles," the evolutionary patterns evident in the aging of neighborhoods, with a particular concentration on slum formation, are described. Chapter 5, "Neighborhood Renewal and Rehabilitation," continues the discussion of the previous chapter and notes the various strategies for neighborhood renewal and the different approaches for dealing with neighborhood residents. A bibliographic essay offering a selected look at the literature of the field concludes the book.

Maps, graphs, illustrations, most tables, and all but content or discursive notes have been deleted, along with references to them, from the articles and excerpts reprinted in this anthology. Full documentation, including maps, graphs, illustrations, and tables, can be found in the original work. I urge readers who wish to pursue the material presented in these reprints to read the originally published studies. The only article written expressly for this anthology and published here for the first time is my own, "The Neighborhood Invasion Pattern."

1

THE NEIGHBORHOOD
AND THE CITY

This first chapter analyzes the neighborhood's place within the life of the city. Neighborhood identity, the physical and social components of a neighborhood, and the function and role of neighborhoods for the nineteenth century and today are discussed.

Suzanne Keller's essay defines neighborhood, noting its physical and social components. She also comments on identifying these areas in cities by studying such factors as boundaries, use of facilities, and sentimental attachments. Her concluding remarks question the importance of these local areas in the cities of today.

In the next selection Jane Jacobs examines the uses of city neighborhoods and their role in the modern city. She analyzes why some neighborhoods function well and others do not. Looking at three types of useful urban neighborhoods with different functions (the city as a whole, street neighborhoods, and districts) and the interrelations between them, Jacobs discusses the physical planning of the city and neighborhood stability.

Mark Goldman's study of the Black Rock area of Buffalo, New York, notes the changes occurring in the neighborhood–city relationship at the end of the nineteenth century. Once the center of urban life, the individual neighborhoods became just a part of the city. Trying to maintain its identity and sense of community while also fitting into the unified city, Black Rock, by the turn of the century, as a result of technological, economic, and political changes, was on its way to being entirely absorbed within the centralizing city. The process of change and its effect on both neighborhood and city are studied.

THE NEIGHBORHOOD
SUZANNE KELLER

The term "neighborhood," most investigators agree, is not without its ambiguities. Essentially, it refers to distinctive areas into which larger spatial units may be subdivided, such as gold coasts and slums, central and outlying districts, residential and industrial areas, middle class and working class areas. The distinctiveness of these areas stems from different sources whose independent contributions are difficult to assess: geographical boundaries, ethnic or cultural characteristics of the inhabitants, psychological unity among people who feel that they belong together, or concentrated use of an area's facilities for shopping, leisure, and learning. Neighborhoods combining all four elements are very rare in modern cities. In particular, as we shall see, the geographical and the personal boundaries do not always coincide.

The common elements of most definitions of neighborhood are territory and inhabitants. Ruth Glass describes a neighborhood as "a distinct territorial group, distinct by virtue of the specific physical characteristics of the area and the specific social characteristics of the inhabitants."[1] It is easy, she observes, to find neighborhoods that are distinct territorial groups, but it is difficult, especially in cities, to find neighborhoods whose inhabitants are also in close social contact with one another. In rural areas, neighborhoods in both senses were easier to locate. Their characteristics have been summarized as follows: places with a name known to their inhabitants and smaller in size than a community, have common facilities such as a general store, a grist mill, or a school, and marked by social relations that include the exchange of assistance and friendly visiting. These are still the chief dimensions considered in urban studies. Ideally, residents of different neighborhoods are marked by a particular pattern of life—the subculture of their district—whose norms will reflect the type of terrain occupied, the dominant type of land usage, the social traditions, and the general socioeconomic structure of the area. All of these elements operate within "flexible but real geographic bounds."

Although there is some agreement on the core elements of the concept of neighborhood, "there is great variability in the totality included in it." Since the physical and the social components of neighborhoods are those chiefly stressed, let us consider each in turn.

PHYSICAL COMPONENTS

The neighborhood, viewed as an area or a place within a larger entity, has boundaries—either physical or symbolic and usually both—where streets, railway lines, or parks separate off an area and its inhabitants or where historical and social traditions make people view an area as a distinctive unit. Usually these two boundaries reinforce each other: the physical unity encourages symbolic unity, and symbolic boundaries come to be attached to physical ones.

In either case, a neighborhood is marked off from other neighborhoods in some distinctive and recognizable manner and thus has an ecological relation to the rest of the community. The location of the neighborhood and the qualities associated with it give it a certain value in the eyes of its residents and the community at large. This value is based on whether the area is conveniently or inconveniently accessible to essential activities such as work, shopping, schooling, and recreation. The rating of each neighborhood is a function of the availability of these services and of their importance to the individuals affected.

Some physical characteristics of a neighborhood, such as the layouts of streets, houses, and landmarks, are independent of its ecological characteristics. Concentrations of buildings, land use and facilities and their accompanying impact on densities, dwelling conditions, the presence or absence of light, air, and green open spaces, give an area a spatial and aesthetic identity and texture. The quality of such basic services as water supply, police and fire protection, and sanitation determine both the level of comfort and the reputation of an area. Here, too, the neighborhood is in some significant respects judged by the standards of a larger area whose capacities and preferences it reflects in miniature.

Neighborhoods are formed only under certain social and ecological conditions. One can hardly speak of neighborhoods in most villages since these are so small and familiar to their inhabitants that the whole community might be considered one neighborhood. With growth in size, the number of people, or the variety of services, the whole becomes subdivided into subareas with characteristic functions and local significance. Neighborhoods and their particular configurations of services, activities, and people thus exist precisely because a city or town has been so subdivided. The nature of these subdivisions, their uniformity and variety, are determined by the nature of the totality and its degree of specialization in work, tastes, and standards of life.

SOCIAL COMPONENTS

Within its physical and symbolic boundaries, a neighborhood contains inhabitants having something in common—perhaps only the current sharing of a common environment. This gives them a certain collective character, which affects and reflects people's feelings about living there and the kinds of relationships the residents establish. It also contributes to the reputation of an area, which even more than its potential for fellowship and convenience may weigh significantly with its more status-conscious residents and determine their relative contentment with the area as a place in which to live.

Sociologists are more likely to stress the importance of the symbolic and cultural aspects of neighborhoods and take the physical features more or less for granted. What particularly interests them is the meaning attributed to an area by its occupants and users. Spatial and physical attributes strike them as necessary but not as sufficient conditions for the existence of neighborhoods. In contrast, physical planners tend to consider the physical aspects as primary. The sociological conception of neighborhood emphasizes the notion of shared activities, experiences, and values, common loyalties and perspectives, and human networks that give to an area a sense of continuity and persistence over time. Residents of a neighborhood are seen to share a special and somewhat unique destiny arising from their ecological position in the city, their ties of past and present, and their general orientations toward the area and to one another. It is clear that the sociological conception is best realized in the more traditional rural communities or in certain social and cultural enclaves within a larger urban area.

Summarizing the two prominent conceptions of neighborhoods, we arrive at the following, sometimes incompatible, dimensions:

1. A physically delimited area having an ecological position in a larger area and particular physical characteristics arising from natural geographic conditions and from a particular configuration of activities and usages. The work of the "Chicago School" refers to these as "natural areas."

2. An area containing such facilities as shops, clubs, schools, houses, and transportation that may be used by those living in the area or by outsiders. In the latter case, a neighborhood has a special functional role in the organization of a town or city. Investigators do not always distinguish between these two types of usages—by residents and by outsiders. Some consider usage of neighborhood facilities as an index of the existence of neighborhood only if this usage is exclusively confined to residents. Yet, if outsiders use a particular neighborhood for recreational, business, or cultural purposes, this itself may be a significant determinant of neighborhood identity.

3. An area representing certain values both for the residents and for the larger community. Such values as cleanliness, quiet, safety, social solidarity, political cohesion, ethnic or religious compatibility, aesthetic quality, and social prestige have different priorities for different individuals and groups and are present in different measure among the subareas of a community.

4. A field or cluster of forces working in and on an area to give it a special atmosphere. An immigrant ghetto, a middle class suburb, or a skid row area has a special aura that affects how the area looks and how people look at the area. In part, this is an inscrutable phenomenon, and like the personality of an individual, it cannot be reduced to the composite elements since it is an outcome of their interrelations. Each individual and activity contributes to this collective effect even while they are subordinate to it. Areas thus have collective records on crime, delinquency, residential stability, wealth, morale, and morality. Neighboring is only one of the activities and components contributing to this collective record.

All of these somewhat different aspects have been included in that one term—neighborhood. No wonder that this complicates systematic discussion and inquiry.

METHODS FOR ASCERTAINING THE PRESENCE OF NEIGHBORHOODS

The existence of separate neighborhoods in urban areas has been studied in two principal ways, using either objective or subjective indicators. Using the objective method, the investigator identifies and locates physically distinct areas on the basis of statistical and census data, physical reconnaissance of the terrain, and information supplied by informants deemed especially knowledgeable about the area. Thus, Glass, in her pioneering efforts, plotted distributions of selected indicators of such area characteristics as net population densities, age and conditions of dwellings, ethnic and religious composition of the inhabitants, occupations, and figures on school attendance. She then noted where these overlapped. By tracing boundaries around areas of concentrated or overlapping distributions, she was able to identify twenty-six potential neighborhoods. More recently, a study in West Philadelphia, seeking to locate subareas for more intensive analysis asked twenty-one well-informed local persons to "name the areas which they thought of as neighborhoods." Newspapers, historical accounts, and organizational records provided supplementary information. Eventually, it was possible to identify sixteen areas ranging in population from 10,000 to over 40,000 persons.

An alternative approach utilizes information about where the people of a given area shop, work, and play, and the spatial distribution of these activities provides the basis for the drawing of boundaries. In earlier investigations of village neighborhoods, for example, areas were marked off according to the uses of village centers; usually this left some marginal areas unaccounted for and therefore unclassifiable. Instead of asking adults where they shop or work, one may ask school children attending particular schools where their parents go for certain services and then plot their answers in relation to their individual residences. A variant of this technique is to obtain the addresses of clients, members, or customers from village stores, schools, weekly newspapers, and churches, and then plot these service areas to see whether and where they overlap.

Another main approach asks respondents themselves to indicate the boundaries and extent of their neighborhoods. Often this method is used in conjunction with the first and serves as a check on its utility.

ASSESSMENTS OF FUNCTIONING NEIGHBORHOODS

Even the most ardent partisans of the neighborhood as a purely spatial phenomenon would agree that the location of geographically demarcated areas is no proof of the existence of actual neighborhoods. Some additional information is usually considered necessary to ascertain whether the residents in such areas also perceive them to be distinct social and symbolic units. Thus, Glass, having identified twenty-six distinct territorial groupings, went on to consider whether these also exhibited a given degree of concentrated social activity. This involved a comparison of the geographic units with the "catchment areas" of the following facilities and services for degrees of boundary coincidences: the catchment areas (that is, the spatial distribution of members) of all elementary and secondary schools, of youth and adult clubs, of post offices, and of greengrocers and shops for sugar registration.

In an intensive study of three West Philadelphia subareas previously identified as possessing some neighborhood potential, the following dimensions were studied further to see whether this potential was being realized: identifiability of the area; identification with the area; presence of friends and relatives within the area; use of local stores, churches, and recreational facilities; attitudes toward the area; and presence of organized local groups for the handling of local problems. Another investigator participating in this broad inquiry into local neighborhood life selected twelve subareas by means of social area analysis, a technique used to locate distinctive subareas of larger census tracts. This investigator asked one hundred randomly selected respondents in each of these subareas to identify the subarea by name and boundaries and to evaluate the area as a place to live. The study, in not preselecting its neighborhoods, has an advantage over those that do. There does not exist an inadvertent concentration on areas of known neighborhood potential. As a result, however, this study, as well as the one by Glass (which it resembles in some respects), found very little overlap between potential neighborhoods and actual neighborhood identity, use, and participation.

A knowledge of the prevalent social character of an area, ascertained by various indexes of living conditions, residential stability, and population characteristics, may be used as clues to its neighborhood potential.

If we know, for example, that a given area has a high concentration of home owners of particular income and educational levels in skilled manual occupations, we might estimate their neighboring activities to be low on the basis of what we generally know about neighboring in such groups. Or, the presence of certain facilities may reveal the sort of population with which we are dealing. Pawnshops or secondhand stores may signal the presence of low income groups; selected churches and schools, that of high income ones. In fact, Baltzell suggests charting the presence of certain schools and churches as a convenient way to trace the neighborhood migrations of fashionable society and thereby the rise and decline of fashionable upper class neighborhoods.

Information about boundaries, use of facilities, or relations among neighbors in particular areas does not tell us how adequate, suitable, or desirable such local areas are. For this, objective standards or yardsticks are required. Since such standards are lacking, relative comparisons (for example, ranking areas according to the presence of certain facilities) and understandardized subjective judgments are most frequently used, but neither of these permit us to generalize. The two questions most frequently used to tap neighborhood satisfaction are: (1) Do you consider this neighborhood of yours a good place to live? and (2) Do you intend to remain in this neighborhood permanently? The answers to these questions, whose precise meaning is not always clear, are then correlated with other characteristics of the respondents, the area, or both. Sometimes, instead of a single question, several questions are used, and an index is constructed. Or a more refined attitude scale with several ratings for each item may be devised. Individuals may also be asked to describe their conception of an ideal neighborhood or to choose among several photographs of neighborhoods the one that they prefer. A series of "games" has been designed that probe into people's wishes and attitudes regarding neighborhood facilities and services. For example, respondents are "given" fixed sums of money and are asked to imagine what facilities and settings they would choose for a house they had won, or they are asked to select among a series of density figures and commuting patterns those they prefer. In analyzing how they "spend" the money at their disposal, their values and preferences are thus revealed.

ESTABLISHING BOUNDARIES OF NEIGHBORHOODS

The extent of neighboring in an area is an unreliable clue to neighborhood boundaries in a rapidly changing urban area since not all people rely on neighbors; if they do, they have contacts with very few of them. If neighborhoods were to be defined by people's attachments to neighbors, the areas delimited thereby would be too small and variable to provide either general standards or areas sufficiently large for systematic planning purposes. Moreover, person-to-person neighboring is at best only a partial datum. People may not engage in neighboring and yet make use of local areas in other ways. Most investigators and planners would, therefore, include a wider area in their conception of neighborhood. But how wide? If it is possible to have neighborhoods in which little or no person-to-person neighboring occurs, then how are these neighborhoods to be demarcated?

Various attempts to solve these problems have so far not met with any great success. In the aforementioned study by Glass and her co-workers, only five of the twenty-six physically distinct subareas showed any overlap between physical and institutional or service boundaries. This suggests that the utilization of various urban facilities is dispersed and "not carried out within the boundaries of distinct territorial groups." The five that did exhibit a concentration of social activities within the territorially delimited area did so for all the reasons that planners regard as undesirable in a neighborhood—isolation, social class homogeneity, and poverty.

Such physically clear-cut dimensions as size of area or size of population also prove unreliable indicators. Glass found that the population of the twenty-six territorial entities was quite irregular, ranging from very few to more than 10,000 people. Similarly, the *barrios* of San Juan also vary greatly in size.

Subjective demarcations are likewise unreliable guides—when people are asked to draw the boundaries of their neighborhoods, few of them draw identical ones. And when asked to state the name of their neighborhood, they often do not use the one officially used by outsiders for the area or district. In two southern cities of the United States, for example, fewer than one of ten respondents thought of "this part of town" as "having any particular boundaries or limits." And only three-tenths "supplied some kind of neighborhood name in response to the question: 'If someone you meet elsewhere in Greensboro asks you where you live, what do you tell him?'" The author concluded that people have a rather imprecise notion of neighborhood as a smaller part of the city. When asked to designate a name for an area, people do not always use the most widely known or used name even though they may recognize it if they hear or see it. In the West Philadelphia study, referred to earlier, it was found that the area name used by the informants, neighborhood associations, and social workers was not universally known by the inhabitants of the area, seven-tenths of whom considered the area simply as part of West Philadelphia in general. In a racially mixed area in the same city, a particular name was adopted for its prestige value, thus representing a "case of the extension of a prestigious name to a less prestigious area." In contrast to these findings, Ross reports that two-thirds of the residents of an old-established area of Boston were able to supply the conventional name of the area, and four-fifths were able to name three of its four natural boundaries. But only three-tenths of the 379 residents interviewed in Stevenage, a British New Town organized into six "neighborhoods" of about 10,000 inhabitants each, were able to give the proper name of their neighborhood despite the fact that the Stevenage Development Corporation had placed great emphasis on stimulating neighborhood identity.

It appears, then, that people do not generally identify the subareas they live in by name or district boundaries unless such areas are either geographically or socially isolated or have a definite class or historic identity. People do, however, identify by name and boundaries fairly small subsections of their areas, often including no more than the street on which they live. These may more properly comprise neighborhoods as they see them.

Many studies suggest, however, that even small subsections may be quite differently perceived by residents reporting on their experiences and activities there. Even a single street may be cut up into tight little islands where exclusive and often antagonistic groups form separate units, manifesting neighborly kindness and generosity within them but distance and hostility between them. Under certain conditions, one finds a public opinion of the street that controls personal behavior both inside and outside the home and lays down local standards of taste and conduct to which the residents must conform. West Philadelphia residents when asked to describe their "neighborhood," would indicate:

the street and block on which they live. . . . These areas are usually no larger than a single block of facing houses between two cross streets. When we asked respondents what area they really knew, they usually limited themselves to a small area, seldom exceeding two to three blocks adjacent to their own house.

Similarly, in Stevenage, previously cited as an example of residents not knowing the names of their neighborhoods, respondents named their housing estates instead, suggesting that if they identified with a residential area at all, it was likely to be much smaller than the designated neighborhood, containing a population nearer 2,000 than 10,000. Gans provides other supportive evidence when he notes:

[The] concept of the West End as a single neighborhood was foreign to the West Enders themselves. . . . The residents divided it—the area—up into many sub-areas, depending in part on the ethnic group which predominated, and in part on the extent to which the tenants in one set of streets had reason or opportunity to use another.

These small, "natural" neighborhoods find their limits where personal relations stop. This makes their boundaries fluid, though still recognizable to those familiar with local customs, and responsive more to psychological and social factors than to physical ones, recalling Simmel's observation that nearness and distance have more to do with the state of one's soul than with the nature of space itself.

These examples suggest that physical factors appear to be significant only in conjunction with social factors and do not seem to exert an independent influence on neighborhood identification. In fact, physical factors may even be subordinate when respondents subdivide their street according to the social status characteristics of the various inhabitants. As Gans has noted, the strong local identification of the first generation ethnic immigrants was not related to common residence on the block or in the slum but to family and ethnic ties. The social texture of a block may be highly significant in other groups also. One detailed study shows this to be the case among British manual workers who lived in three separate blocks of twelve houses each. Each family was interviewed by one investigator. The blocks were remarkably similar in social composition, consisting of young families of manual workers who had lived on the block for more than a year. Closer scrutiny revealed some block-by-block differences. Thus, Block One included both a clerk and a member of the factory staff among its residents, whereas Block Two included only workers at the shop floor level, and Block Three contained more suburban families with a slightly wider range of occupations among the husbands and a larger number of children per family. Of the 36 families, only 11 stated that they had good neighborly relations involving mutual assistance; 14 had little contact with neighbors but were not critical of them; and 11 had either no contact or unwanted contact. The variations by block were considerable. In Block One 9 out of the 12 families had either no or poor neighborly relations, whereas in Blocks Two and Three the majority had either neutral or positive relations with their neighbors. Ten of the families were strongly critical of the housing estate and wished to move away, another 10 were somewhat critical, and 16 were satisfied and intended to stay. The families on Block One were most dissatisfied. This study shows very clearly how complicated are people's interrelations within a very small space indeed.

Even people as similar in objective social characteristics as these were found to be quite heterogeneous in their responses to their immediate neighbors.

Today people are much more differentiated in their tastes, loyalties, and habits than is often assumed. In one working class district in central Oxford, for example, a local population of about 1,000 families supported sixteen public houses, "a sign that, left relatively free from municipal control, the size of these informal groups ... is very small." This fragmentation of local loyalties contrasts strikingly with the single community center provided in the new housing estate, which these residents disdainfully rejected.

As a result of the small subdivisions informally defined by urban residents, it is not surprising that people are vague or uninformed about the boundaries either officially established or geographically obvious to outsiders. Most people see and know only a portion of the area near them and they vary as to how big a portion that is. The demarcation of boundaries on this basis might be a first step in the ascertainment of functioning neighborhoods. Demarcation by use and sentiment are additional steps.

USE OF NEIGHBORHOODS

If a local area does not have great geographical or territorial distinctiveness, its inhabitants, nevertheless, may make concentrated and distinctive use of shops, schools, parks, and cinemas. This may not result in greater local pride or symbolic identity, nor indeed in greater neighborliness or emotional attachments to the area, but it may serve to link the inhabitants to one another and to the area indirectly through a sharing of these local facilities. This is surely the crux of most planners' justification for designing spatial subdivisions in a large urban area whose convenience and accessibility would help promote local utilization of services and indirectly encourage other local attachments and loyalties.

The concentrated use of local services and facilities varies widely according to the economic and cultural characteristics of the residents, the types of facilities and their adequacy, the accessibility of nonlocal facilities, and the degree of isolation of the area, economically, ecologically, and symbolically.

Of the many factors that may affect the local use of local facilities, we may distinguish between those factors concerning the inhabitants and those concerning the area, its services, and accessibility. The importance of social, economic, and ethnic status has been noted repeatedly. In general, persons in low income neighborhoods are more likely to require shops and services close to their homes. In part this reflects their inadequate economic resources, but in part it may also reflect cultural and ethnic preferences. As Warner and Srole showed more than two decades ago, immigrant and ethnic minorities not only patronize local shops, churches, and clubs that cater to their special needs and habits, but their acculturation process may be traced thereby. Status-consciousness may likewise inhibit or encourage the use of local resources. For example, in one working class housing estate the immediate neighborhood was avoided because of the existence of a rough crowd at the end of one road.

Taste, access to transport, and sphere of activity must be taken into account when considering the facilities available. The adequacy of local facilities clearly affects whether or not people go outside their immediate district for the things they want or need. In Stevenage, prior to the completion of its town center, the day of the week made a great difference in the use of either local or town facilities. Although 85 percent of the inhabitants said they had shops within ten minutes walking distance, only 16 percent made use of these on weekends, whereas during the week, 60 percent made use of them. The possession of an automobile may alter the perception of distance so that people who are within easy driving distance of certain facilities may consider them conveniently located. Or, people may use a not too distant shopping area that is in the direction of the town center rather than one nearer to them in the opposite direction. The importance of physical distance decreases as various social, economic, and technological elements exert their influence. Families whose main wage earners work outside the local area, tend to make less use of local facilities than families both living and working within the area. Here again, we note the variable role of physical distance.

Use of the local area also varies with the sphere of activity. In West Philadelphia, McGough found that grocery shopping was more locally based than any other activity investigated. One-half of the respondents shopped for their groceries only in their own areas. The next most widely used "local" service was medical care, with from 40 to 60 percent of the residents going to physicians within their local areas. One-third to one-half of the respondents worshiped only in local churches. Only one-tenth worked locally, however. The author concludes that the use that residents make of local facilities is not related to such characteristics as class, race, or family size; rather, it seems strongly associated with the social mix of the area. In racially mixed areas, for example, she discovered a strong tendency for residents to go outside their areas for the satisfaction of their needs.[2]

The local area is clearly more important for some groups than for others. Just as intensive neighboring is closely correlated with conditions of relative helplessness or need, so the importance of the neighborhood seems to vary according to the resources of the residents. These resources may be economic, psychological, cultural, or ecological. Those immobilized by old age, family responsibilities, ill health, ignorance, or isolation need the neighborhood most, not only for the satisfaction of their tangible wants for goods and services but also for intangibles such as gossip and information. The traditional shops, cafes, and pubs in working class areas are also centers of information for their patrons. Some residents who may be quite isolated from human contact otherwise will, in this way, be kept up to date with local news and events. According to one observer, such individuals would quickly disintegrate if they moved to a new housing estate lacking such "news" centers. The very young or old, the disabled and the overburdened who cannot venture very far from their immediate dwelling, are really no more than "block dwellers," to use Schorr's phrase, in contrast to the young and relatively better off who are city dwellers and city users. The old and poor are "no more citizens of the city than was the kitchen maid of former generations a citizen of her mistress' house."[3] This is further confirmed by Glass and her associates, who found dispersal rather than concentration of activities "the very norm" in the twenty-six areas she studied, leading her to conclude that only a particular combination of negative characteristics, such as geographic isolation, poverty, and social homogeneity, made for any significant concentrated use of local areas.[4] This study also showed that the most prosperous neighborhoods ranked lowest on social integration as indicated by concentrated use of local institutions and services, a finding that perplexed the authors. On the basis of the present analysis of neighboring, we would say that since neighboring in general is directly related to self-sufficiency and fluidity, which are greater in the more prosperous neighborhoods, it follows that such neighborhoods should show the least concentrated use of local services.

NEIGHBORHOOD ATTACHMENT AND SATISFACTION

The three dimensions considered thus far—neighboring in an area, identifying the name or boundaries of an area, and use of area facilities—are not reliable guides to locating the presence of functioning neighborhoods, although each may be associated with this functioning in some manner.

Neighboring in an area cannot generally serve as a yardstick for determining physical boundaries because it is either too diffused and intertwined with many other activities, as in small towns or solidary urban districts, or it is too restricted and sporadic, as in larger urban centers. The extent and type of neighboring activity is mainly a function of the self-sufficiency of individuals and groups as reflected in their established traditions and practices.

Nor is probing for area names or boundaries of much help, since most people either do not have precise notions of such boundaries or they differ on the spatial referents of the names they use.

Even the use of local facilities and services is no sure guide to estimating the existence of coherent neighborhoods because most people do not use local services exclusively. They travel far and wide for work, shopping, and amusement. For example, grocery shops, most consistently preferred close to home, nevertheless show inconsistent use according to the day of the week, economic resources, personal mobility, and availability of alternatives. Some people are, of course, more confined to local areas than others, notably the physically handicapped, culturally isolated, or economically deprived, but even they are not irrevocably committed users of local facilities. The physically handicapped, moreover, are literally no more than house or apartment dwellers, and the culturally isolated will, in fact, travel some distance for their shops and churches if necessary.

There remains, then, a final dimension to be considered—that of attachments to some part of a local area. Even if people have only casual relations with neighbors, even if they do not have a clear sense of the boundaries of an area, nor make concentrated or exclusive use of local facilities and services, they may have a special feeling for a given place, a special sort of pride in living there, a sense of attachment transcending physical inconvenience or social undesirability.

This attachment may be rooted in childhood experiences or family involvement with the area over a long period or in historical events endowing an area with a special meaning. It may also stem from current attractions such as the presence of favored friends, material or cultural advantages, or a particular aesthetic component. Any one or a combination of these may help tie people to a local place. And it is perhaps this feeling, this link, above all, that planners would like to inspire in the neighborhoods that they design.

Investigations of the degree and kinds of satisfactions with and sentiments for a local area are neither as wide-ranging nor as systematic as one would wish. Nevertheless, some suggestive patterns emerge from the existing data. It appears that people are generally more satisfied than dissatisfied with their residential areas, although the precise meaning of satisfaction is difficult to ascertain. It appears, moreover, that this satisfaction is indicative of a general outlook on life and is not substantially affected by specific local characteristics of an area. In certain areas of San Juan, Puerto Rico, for example, whose living conditions might strike outsiders as shockingly inadequate, residential satisfaction was high, seven-tenths of the respondents considering their areas as good places in which to live. Although one-half of the Puerto Rican immigrants in New York City were dissatisfied with their living quarters, only 26 percent were dissatisfied with their neighborhoods. Lest this be considered peculiar to Puerto Ricans, West Enders in Boston also indicated a strong attachment and sense of belonging to their area quite apart from their feelings about their dwellings. Perhaps this illustrates an oft-noted tendency among working class people not to restrict their social lives to their immediate dwellings as middle class people tend to do nor to differentiate quite as sharply between private and public space. Of course, much depends on what is implied by the expressions of approval. That they do not necessarily imply permanent loyalties to an area is suggested by one study. This study showed that while most of those interviewed considered their areas as a "fairly good" place in which to live, fully three-fourths could imagine living elsewhere. One suspects that this would be far less true of residents in villages and small towns, especially in the less industrialized parts of the world.

Some of the studies cited hint at an important question, namely, the scale of place loyalties in the modern urban world. Such loyalties are not absent even in the large metropolis, but they do tend to adhere to fairly small areas adjacent to where one happens to live or work. Sprott suggests that this is implicitly recognized in Chinese villages and in Japanese cities, where neighborhood "cells" are very small, including no more than five neighbors on either side of a given house in the Chinese villages and no more than twenty households in the Japanese cities.

It is difficult to know how to interpret these expressed attachments to local areas, whatever their size. Liking an area, as the following examples suggest, does not necessarily commit an individual to staying in an area or to exclusive or predominant use of its facilities and services. In one racially mixed area of Philadelphia, both white and Negro residents appreciated the area for its cleanliness, quietness, convenient location, well-maintained property, and even the pleasant people. However, the white residents went outside the area for shopping and recreation and refused to participate in the single community organization, thus staying in the area physically but not in spirit. In Mantua, an area of San Juan having many social and economic problems, residents expressed liking for the area but felt no strong attachment to it. Alternatively, people may feel an identification with certain streets, shops, and other inhabitants of an area but fail to transform their individual loyalties into a general community spirit.

The expressed intention or desire to move away from an area has often been used as an index of attachment to it, but this overlooks those people who may stay in an area they dislike because of economic necessity or because they own property there, or those who may move from an area they like for status reasons. Commitment to an area, being a compound of necessity and emotional identification, is not easy to assess and probably requires the use of several subtle techniques. It has been observed that the reasons given for liking a neighborhood tend to be general and abstract, whereas those given for disliking it are more specific and concrete, illustrating the well-known fact that it is easier to know what one does not want than the converse. But it really depends on how carefully one probes into the meaning and intensity of the attitudes expressed. A general question will usually elicit a general, if not also superficial, answer that needs to be supplemented by more specific, detailed probing.

The significance of other residents in determining residential satisfaction emerges whether one asks about reasons for liking or disliking an area. Often, complaints about inadequate dwellings or unsafe streets turn out to be complaints about the habits and standards of neighbors.

In general, then, people are quite favorably disposed toward their residential environments provided these satisfy one or more of their basic value preferences, which vary in content and priority and determine what they are likely to appreciate or criticize most. Surprisingly, perhaps, objective amenities, such as the conditions of dwellings or convenience of transportation, are not of utmost importance to all. The characteristics of other residents, however, seem to be high on everyone's list and contribute to an area's intangible ambiance. These characteristics may determine how people will react to the adequacy of their houses and facilities, whether they intend to stay or move away, and how they cope with noise, overcrowding, and other inconveniences.

In an unusually detailed study of middle class families in two southern cities in the United States, these matters were explored with exceptional skill and care as is evident from the following selective summary of the study's findings. To assess the relative salience of different elements of neighborhood satisfaction, Wilson asked the respondents to choose among alternatives of the following sort: If you could live in "a very good neighborhood but located so that it would be difficult for you to travel to other parts of town or a less desirable neighborhood but located so that it would be easy for you to travel to other parts of town," which would you choose? The respondents favored the good but relatively inaccessible neighborhood 3 to 1. Similarly, a less desirable house in a good neighborhood was preferred 6 to 1 over a good house in a less desirable neighborhood. What did they have in mind when they thought of a "good" neighborhood? The nature of the people living there figured prominently in both sets of responses, followed by the location of stores, schools, churches, and bus lines and a respect for privacy. The relative rank order of the qualities most valued in a neighborhood by one of the samples was: spaciousness (most valued), beauty, good for children, exclusiveness, countrylike, privacy, greenery, homeyness, quietness, cleanliness, newness, friendliness, crowdedness, dirtiness (least valued). The respondents also indicated the following qualities as those that they most missed in their current neighborhoods: beauty, exclusiveness, a countrylike character, and spaciousness. The importance of beauty, privacy, and quiet calls for imaginative design quite as much as for appealing social arrangements.

Finally, individuals were shown a list of seventeen facilities and asked to choose those that they most wanted in their "neighborhood" (this was not specified further) and how many of them that they wanted close to home (within a twenty-minute walk). The seven facilities considered most important by respondents in both cities, though with a slightly different rank order, were: an elementary school, grocery store, shopping center, bus stop, religious building, and drugstore. The five items considered least important in a neighborhood were such recreational facilities as a movie theater and a swimming pool and such educational facilities as nurseries and preschool play space. The pattern discovered for these family- and home-centered individuals may not, of course, apply to other types, who should also be studied in the same intensive manner.

The overall qualities of neighborhood are the most difficult to assess, and yet they often decisively affect people's reactions. Sometimes these qualities have historical significance, as in the Shitamachi and Yamanote districts of modern Tokyo, or they may reflect current status designations such as gold coasts, slums, and bohemias. These overriding qualities are particularly inaccessible to those unfamiliar with an area or district, and they are not always, or even generally, associated with objective adequacies or inadequacies. Planners may be especially interested in the fact that some of the elements they themselves consider to contribute most to an area's desirability may not turn out to do so in fact. Meyerson has written:

There is a city in the United States that violates most of the first principles of sound urban planning. Its land use is chaotic; its streets come in patches of gridiron fitted neither to themselves nor to their topography; its "in-town" houses are usually made of wood frame and are three-or-four story walkups. Yet it is considered here and abroad one of the most attractive cities in the world. It is, of course, San Francisco.

FACTORS ASSOCIATED WITH LIKING AND DISLIKING NEIGHBORHOOD AREAS

Some areas may exhibit less neighborhood satisfaction than others, not because they are objectively less satisfactory but because they have a higher concentration of residents predisposed to being critical and fault-finding—principally as a prelude to their moving away from the area. Such individuals, whom Mogey calls "status-dissenting," constantly try to exercise some personal influence over their environments, and they are thus more likely to be recent migrants in any setting, since the process of moving from a familiar to an unfamiliar environment stimulates one's critical faculties. Thus, reactions to the environment are one aspect of a general outlook on life. And just as people may stay in poor surroundings because they believe that the future will be better, so people may abandon superior environments because these do not meet their tacit status needs.

As the following examples indicate, status aspirations along with family size, age, and other personal characteristics are important correlates of neighborhood statisfaction.

Higher socioeconomic status tends to be associated with neighborhood satisfaction and a disinclination to move out of an area.[5] This reflects both the superiority of facilities and services such areas provide and an actual or imputed likemindedness among their inhabitants. It seems that satisfied residents perceive greater social similarities between themselves and their neighbors than may actually exist. Conversely, dissatisfied residents tend to perceive social differences even where these are minimal. The mechanism of projection that is operative here must thus be taken into account when trying to interpret the reasons for failures and successes in physically planned environments.

In addition to social status factors, neighborhood satisfaction, as revealed in the intention to move, is also closely tied to the phase of a family's life cycle. Young couples with small children are most eager to move in search of more space. Their decision to move is not unreleated to their ambitions, however, for while the lack of space may be the primary determinant, unsatisfied status needs may give an added impetus.

Finally, length of residence and age of resident strengthen attachment to an area. Older, long-term residents express more neighborhood satisfaction than do younger and newer residents. In the uprootings occasioned by urban renewal, it is especially the aged who suffer from the disruption of ties to local churches, doctors, grocery shops, and clubs (though not always to other residents). Of course, this is linked to the availability of actual or perceived alternatives. Where these are few, people may say that they are satisfied in their present surroundings, but they may be among the first to move once a realistic opportunity presents itself. For this reason it is difficult to predict residential turnover solely on the basis of current attitudes.

In view of the importance of the social characteristics of neighbors in the positive assessments of neighborhoods, physical improvements in housing and services may not achieve the effects desired or assumed by those who stress their priority. Even where the dwelling is of first importance, "isolated houses of desirable quality would not in themselves hold and attract" people. The reputation of an area is often determined by its social rather than its physical climate.

In sum, neither subjectively identified boundaries, nor concentrated use of area facilities, nor neighborly relations, nor sentiments permit us to locate and classify distinctive urban neighborhoods. Today, neighborhoods so identified are either so poor or so wealthy as to be relatively isolated from the mainstream of urban life. The lack of overlap between neighboring, use of facilities, and sentimental attachments means that these cannot be used as indexes for consistently subdividing a larger urban area satisfactorily from both the physical and the social points of view.

On the basis of the admittedly sparse data on how people use given local areas, where they draw boundary lines, and whether they are attached to a local area, we can only conclude, while pleading for more and more systematic data, that the local area is no longer of primary importance. With the exception of grocery stores and perhaps of primary schools, there are very few facilities that must be located near homes for everyone. And as for neighborhood attachments, some urban residents are strongly involved, others only minimally. At best, this is a subjective phenomenon greatly dependent on perceived and actual alternatives to friends, facilities, and dependency on a wider urban area. The economically better off are generally more mobile and less tied to their neighborhoods than the poorer urban residents. Expanded or narrow local horizons seem very much dependent on opportunities for mobility and on personal selectivity. Although physical neighborhoods may still be identified, their leading positions as providers of information, identity, and social relations have been displaced by social change in the family, work, and mass entertainment and amusement.

Concentration on the local area, no matter how imprecisely defined, seems to be most strongly correlated with a lack of alternatives. This applies, for example, when town centers are too distant, their facilities too costly, or not appealing due to unfamiliarity or ignorance. It also applies when isolation is due either to local self-sufficiency or to strong ideological and social pressures. That is, where a solidary local network of close economic, cultural, social, and physical ties already exists, there local loyalties and activities will be strong. This does not, however, mean that the provision of local services will by themselves stimulate the desired local loyalties and sentiments in areas lacking the social and historic preconditions for such solidarity.

Today, it seems that local self-sufficiency and self-reliance are diminishing everywhere. Even remote villages are linked to the urban-industrial world via mass transport and mass media of communication, local branches of national associations, and personal use of urban centers for amusement or learning. The utility of the neighborhood conception has in consequence been reexamined by many planners who increasingly find it wanting.

THE USES OF CITY NEIGHBORHOODS

JANE JACOBS

Neighborhood is a word that has come to sound like a Valentine. As a sentimental concept, "neighborhood" is harmful to city planning. It leads to attempts at warping city life into imitations of town or suburban life. Sentimentality plays with sweet intentions in place of good sense.

A successful city neighborhood is a place that keeps sufficiently abreast of its problems so it is not destroyed by them. An unsuccessful neighborhood is a place that is overwhelmed by its defects and problems and is progressively more helpless before them. Our cities contain all degrees of success and failure. But on the whole, we Americans are poor at handling city neighborhoods, as can be seen by the long accumulations of failures in our great gray belts on the one hand, and by the Turfs of re-built city on the other hand.

It is fashionable to suppose that certain touchstones of the good life will create good neighborhoods—schools, parks, clean housing, and the like. How easy life would be if this were so! How charming to control a complicated and ornery society by bestowing upon it rather simple physical goodies. In real life, cause and effect are not so simple. Thus, a Pittsburgh study, undertaken to show the supposed clear correlation between better housing and improved social conditions, compared delinquency records in still uncleared slums to delinquency records in new housing projects, and came to the embarrassing discovery that the delinquency was higher in the improved housing. Does this mean im-

---

proved shelter increases delinquency? Not at all. It means other things may be more important than housing, however, and it means also that there is no direct, simple relationship between good housing and good behavior, a fact which the whole tale of the Western world's history, the whole collection of our literature, and the whole fund of observation open to any of us should long since have made evident. Good shelter is a useful good in itself, as shelter. When we try to justify good shelter instead on the pretentious grounds that it will work social or family miracles, we fool ourselves. Reinhold Niebuhr has called this particular self-deception, "The doctrine of salvation by bricks."

It is even the same with schools. Important as good schools are, they prove totally undependable at rescuing bad neighborhoods and at creating good neighborhoods. Nor does a good school building guarantee a good education. Schools, like parks, are apt to be volatile creatures of their neighborhoods (as well as being creatures of larger policy). In bad neighborhoods, schools are brought to ruination, physically and socially; while successful neighborhoods improve their schools by fighting for them.*

Nor can we conclude, either, that middle-class families or upper-class families build good neighborhoods, and poor families fail to. For example, within the poverty of the North End in Boston, within the poverty of the West Greenwich Village waterfront neighborhoods, within the poverty of the slaughterhouse district in Chicago (three areas, incidentally, that were all written off as hopeless by their cities' planners), good neighborhoods were created: neighborhoods whose internal problems have grown less with time instead of greater. Meantime, within the once upper-class grace and serenity of Baltimore's beautiful Eutaw Place, within the one-time upper-class solidity of Boston's South End, within the culturally privileged purlieus of New York's Morningside Heights, within miles upon miles of dull, respectable, middle-class gray area, bad neighborhoods were created, neighborhoods whose apathy and internal failure grew greater with time instead of less.

---

*In the Upper East Side of Manhattan, a badly failed area where social disintegration has been compounded by ruthless bulldozing, project building, and shoving people around, annual pupil turnover in schools was more than 50 percent in 1959–60. In 16 schools, it reached an average of 92 percent. It is ludicrous to think that with any amount of effort, official or unofficial, even a tolerable school is possible in a neighborhood of such extreme instability. Good schools are impossible in any unstable neighborhoods with high pupil turnover rates, and this includes unstable neighborhoods which *also* have good housing.

To hunt for city neighborhood touchstones of success in high standards of physical facilities, or in supposedly competent and nonproblem populations, or in nostalgic memories of town life, is a waste of time. It evades the meat of the question, which is the problem of what city neighborhoods do, if anything, that may be socially and economically useful in cities themselves, and how they do it.

We shall have something solid to chew on if we think of city neighborhoods as mundane organs of self-government. Our failures with city neighborhoods are, ultimately, failures in localized self-government. And our successes are successes at localized self-government. I am using self-government in its broadest sense, meaning both the informal and formal self-management of society.

Both the demands on self-government and the techniques for it differ in big cities from the demands and techniques in smaller places. For instance, there is the problem of all those strangers. To think of city neighborhoods as organs of city self-government or self-management, we must first jettison some orthodox but irrelevant notions about neighborhoods which may apply to communities in smaller settlements but not in cities. We must first of all drop any ideal of neighborhoods as self-contained or introverted units.

Unfortunately, orthodox planning theory is deeply committed to the ideal of supposedly cozy, inward-turned city neighborhoods. In its pure form, the ideal is a neighborhood composed of about 7,000 persons, a unit supposedly of sufficient size to populate an elementary school and to support convenience shopping and a community center. This unit is then further rationalized into smaller groupings of a size scaled to the play and supposed management of children and the chitchat of housewives. Although the "ideal" is seldom literally reproduced, it is the point of departure for nearly all neighborhood renewal plans, for all project building, for much modern zoning, and also for the practice work done by today's architectural-planning students, who will be inflicting their adaptations of it on cities tomorrow. In New York City alone, by 1959, more than half a million people were already living in adaptations of this vision of planned neighborhoods. This "ideal" of the city neighborhood as an island, turned inward on itself, is an important factor in our lives nowadays.

To see why it is a silly and even harmful "ideal" for cities, we must recognize a basic difference between these concoctions grafted into cities, and town life. In a town of 5,000 or 10,000 population, if you go to Main Street (analogous to the consolidated commercial facilities or community center for a planned neighborhood), you run into people you also know at work, or went to school with, or see at church, or people who are your children's teachers, or who have sold or given you professional or artisan's services, or whom you know to be friends of your casual acquaintances, or whom you know by reputation. Within the limits of a town or village, the connections among its people keep crossing and recrossing, and this can make workable and essentially cohesive communities out of even larger towns than those of 7,000 population, and to some extent out of little cities.

But a population of 5,000 or 10,000 residents in a big city has no such innate degree of natural cross-connections within itself, except under the most extraordinary circumstances. Nor can city neighborhood planning, no matter how cozy in intent, change this fact. If it could, the price would be destruction of a city by converting it into a parcel of towns. As it is, the price of trying and not even succeeding at a misguided aim is conversion of a city into a parcel of mutually suspicious and hostile Turfs. There are many other flaws in this "ideal" of the planned neighborhood and its various adaptations.*

Lately a few planners, notably Reginald Isaacs of Harvard, have daringly begun to question whether the conception of neighborhood in big cities has any meaning at all. Isaacs points out that city people are mobile. They can and do pick and choose from the entire city (and beyond) for everything from a job, a dentist, recreation, or friends, to shops, entertainment, or even in some cases, their children's schools. City people, says Isaacs, are not stuck with the provincialism of a neighborhood, and why should they be? Isn't wide choice and rich opportunity the point of cities?

---

*Even the old reason for settling on an ideal population of about 7,000—sufficient to populate an elementary school—is silly the moment it is applied to big cities, as we discover if we merely ask the question: Which school? In many American cities, parochial-school enrollment rivals or surpasses public-school enrollment. Does this mean there should be two schools as presumed neighborhood glue, and the population should be twice as large? Or is the population right, and should the schools be half as large? And why the elementary school? If school is to be the touchstone of scale, why not the junior high school, an institution typically far more troublesome in our cities than the elementary school? The question "Which school?" is never asked, because this vision is based on no more realism about schools than about anything else. The school is a plausible, and usually abstract, excuse for defining *some* size for a unit that comes out of dreams about imaginary cities. It is necessary as a formal framework, to preserve designers from intellectual chaos, and it has no other reason for being. Ebenezer Howard's model towns are the ancestors of the idea, to be sure, but its durability comes from the need to fill an intellectual vacuum.

This is indeed the point of cities. Furthermore, this very fluidity of use and choice among city people is precisely the foundation underlying most city cultural activities and special enterprises of all kinds. Because these can draw skills, materials, customers, or clienteles from a great pool, they can exist in extraordinary variety, and not only downtown but in other city districts that develop specialties and characters of their own. And in drawing upon the great pool of the city in this way, city enterprises increase, in turn, the choices available to city people for jobs, goods, entertainment, ideas, contacts, services.

Whatever city neighborhoods may be, or may not be, and whatever usefulness they may have, or may be coaxed into having, their qualities cannot work at cross-purposes to thoroughgoing city mobility and fluidity of *use,* without economically weakening the city of which they are a part. The lack of either economic or social self-containment is natural and necessary to city neighborhoods—simply because they are parts of cities. Isaacs is right when he implies that the conception of neighborhood in cities in meaningless—so long as we think of neighborhoods as being self-contained units to any significant degree, modeled upon town neighborhoods.

But for all the innate extroversion of city neighborhoods, it fails to follow that city people can therefore get along magically without neighborhoods. Even the most urbane citizen does care about the atmosphere of the street and district where he lives, no matter how much choice he has of pursuits outside it; and the common run of city people do depend greatly on their neighborhoods for the kind of everyday lives they lead.

Let us assume (as is often the case) that city neighbors have nothing more fundamental in common with each other than that they share a fragment of geography. Even so, if they fail at managing that fragment decently, the fragment will fail. There exists no inconceivably energetic and all-wise "They" to take over and substitute for localized self-management. Neighborhoods in cities need not supply for their people an artificial town or village life, and to aim at this is both silly and destructive. But neighborhoods in cities do need to supply some means for civilized self-government. This is the problem.

Looking at city neighborhoods as organs of self-government, I can see evidence that only three kinds of neighborhoods are useful: (1) the city as a whole; (2) street neighborhoods; and (3) districts of large, subcity size, composed of 100,000 people or more in the case of the largest cities.

Each of these kinds of neighborhoods has different functions, but the three supplement each other in complex fashion. It is impossible to say that one is more important than the others. For success with staying power at any spot, all three are necessary. But I think that other neighborhoods than these three kinds just get in the way, and make successful self-government difficult or impossible.

The most obvious of the three, although it is seldom called a neighborhood, is the city as a whole. We must never forget or minimize this parent community while thinking of a city's smaller parts. This is the source from which most public money flows, even when it comes ultimately from the federal or state coffers. This is where most administrative and policy decisions are made, for good or ill. This is where general welfare often comes into direct conflict, open or hidden, with illegal or other destructive interests.

Moreover, up on this plane we find vital special-interest communities and pressure groups. The neighborhood of the entire city is where people especially interested in the theater or in music or in other arts find one another and get together, no matter where they may live. This is where people immersed in specific professions or businesses or concerned about particular problems exchange ideas and sometimes start action. Professor P. Sargant Florence, a British specialist on urban economics, has written, "My own experience is that, apart from the special habitat of intellectuals like Oxford or Cambridge, a city of a million is required to give me, say, the twenty or thirty congenial friends I require!" This sounds rather snooty, to be sure, but Professor Florence has an important truth here. Presumably he likes his friends to know what he is talking about. When William Kirk of Union Settlement and Helen Hall of Henry Street Settlement, miles apart in New York City, get together with *Consumer's Union,* a magazine located still other miles away, and with researchers from Columbia University, and with the trustees of a foundation, to consider the personal and community ruin wrought by loan shark–installment peddlers in low-income projects, they know what each is talking about and, what is more, can put their peculiar kinds of knowledge together with a special kind of money to learn more about the trouble and find ways to fight it. When my sister, Betty, a housewife, helps devise a scheme in the Manhattan public school which one of her children attends, whereby parents who know English give homework help to the children of parents who do not, and the scheme works, this knowledge filters into a special-interest neighborhood of the city as a whole; as a result, one evening Betty finds herself away over in the Bedford-Stuyvesant section of Brooklyn, telling a district group of ten PTA residents how the scheme works, and learning some new things herself.

A city's very wholeness in bringing together people with communities of interest is one of its greatest assets, possibly the greatest. And, in turn, one of the assets a city district needs is people with access to the political, the administrative, and the special-interest communities of the city as a whole.

In most big cities, we Americans do reasonably well at creating useful neighborhoods belonging to the whole city. People with similar and supplementing interests do find each other fairly well. Indeed, they typically do so most efficiently in the largest cities (except for Los Angeles which does miserably at this, and Boston which is pretty pathetic). Moreover, big-city governments, as Seymour Freedgood of *Fortune* magazine so well documented in *The Exploding Metropolis,* are able and energetic at the top in many instances, more so than one would surmise from looking at social and economic affairs in the endless failed neighborhoods of the same cities. Whatever our disastrous weakness may be, it is hardly sheer incapability for forming neighborhoods at the top, out of cities as a whole.

At the other end of the scale are a city's streets, and the minuscule neighborhoods they form, like our neighborhood of Hudson Street for example.

In the first seven chapters of this book, I have dwelt heavily upon the self-government functions of city streets: to weave webs of public surveillance and thus to protect strangers as well as themselves; to grow networks of small-scale, everyday public life and thus of trust and social control; and to help assimilate children into reasonably responsible and tolerant city life.

The street neighborhoods of a city have still another function in self-government, however, and a vital one: they must draw effectively on help when trouble comes along that is too big for the street to handle. This help must sometimes come from the city as a whole, at the other end of the scale. This is a loose end I shall leave hanging, but ask you to remember.

The self-government functions of streets are all humble, but they are indispensable. In spite of much experiment, planned and unplanned, there exists no substitute for lively streets.

How large is a city street neighborhood that functions capably? If we look at successful street-neighborhood networks in real life, we find this is a meaningless question, because wherever they work best, street neighborhoods have no beginnings and ends setting them apart as distinct units. The size even differs for different people from the same spot, because some people range farther, or hang around more, or extend their street acquaintance farther than others. Indeed, a great part of the success of these neighborhoods of the streets depends on their overlapping and interweaving, turning the corners. This is one means by which they become capable of economic and visual variation for their users. Residential Park Avenue in New York appears to be an extreme example of neighborhood monotony, and so it would be if it were an isolated strip of street neighborhood. But the street neighborhood of a Park Avenue resident only begins on Park, quickly turns a corner off it, and then another corner. It is part of a set of interweaving neighborhoods containing great diversity, not a strip.

Isolated street neighborhoods that do have definite boundaries can be found in plenty, to be sure. They are typically associated with long blocks (and hence with infrequent streets), because long blocks tend almost always to be physically isolating. Distinctly separate street neighborhoods are nothing to aim for; they are generally characteristic of failure. Describing the troubles of an area of long, monotonous, self-isolating blocks on Manhattan's West Side, Dr. Dan W. Dodson of New York University's Center for Human Relations Studies, notes: "Each [street] appears to be a separate world of its own with a separate culture. Many of those interviewed had no conception of the neighborhood other than the street on which they resided."

Summing up the incompetence of the area, Dr. Dodson comments, "The present state of the neighborhood indicates that the people there have lost the capacity for collective action, or else they would long since have pressured the city government and the social agencies into correcting some of the problems of community living." These two observations by Dr. Dodson on street isolation and incompetence are closely related.

Successful street neighborhoods, in short, are not discrete units. They are physical, social, and economic continuities—small scale to be sure, but small scale in the sense that the lengths of fibers making up a rope are small scale.

Where our city streets do have sufficient frequency of commerce, general liveliness, use, and interest, to cultivate continuities of public street life, we Americans do prove fairly capable at street self-government. This capability is most often noticed and commented on in districts of poor, or one-time poor people. But casual street neighborhoods, good at their functions, are also characteristic of high-income areas that maintain a persistent popularity—rather than ephemeral fashion—such as Manhattan's East Side from the Fifties to the Eighties, or the Rittenhouse Square district in Philadelphia, for example.

To be sure, our cities lack sufficient streets equipped for city life.

We have too much area afflicted with the Great Blight of Dullness instead. But many, many city streets perform their humble jobs well and command loyalty, too, unless and until they are destroyed by the impingement of city problems too big for them, or by neglect for too long a time of facilities that can be supplied only from the city as a whole, or by deliberate planning policies that the people of the neighborhood are too weak to defeat.

And here we come to the third kind of city neighborhood that is useful for self-government: the district. This, I think, is where we are typically most weak and fail most disastrously. We have plenty of city districts in name. We have few that function.

The chief function of a successful district is to mediate between the indispensable, but inherently politically powerless, street neighborhoods, and the inherently powerful city as a whole.

Among those responsible for cities, at the top, there is much ignorance. This is inescapable, because big cities are just too big and too complex to be comprehended in detail from any vantage point—even if this vantage point is at the top—or to be comprehended by any human; yet detail is of the essence. A district citizens' group from East Harlem, in anticipation of a meeting it had arranged with the Mayor and his commissioners, prepared a document recounting the devastation wrought in the district by remote decisions (most of them well meant, of course), and they added this comment: "We must state how often we find that those of us who live or work in East Harlem, coming into daily contact with it, see it quite differently from . . . the people who only ride through on their way to work, or read about it in their daily papers, or, too often, we believe, make decisions about it from desks downtown." I have heard almost these same words in Boston, in Chicago, in Cincinnati, in St. Louis. It is a complaint that echoes and re-echoes in all our big cities.

Districts have to help bring the resources of a city down to where they are needed by street neighborhoods, and they have to help translate the experiences of real life, in street neighborhoods, into policies and purposes of their city as a whole. And they have to help maintain an area that is usable, in a civilized way, not only for its own residents but for other users—workers, customers, visitors—from the city as a whole.

To accomplish these functions, an effective district has to be large enough to count as a force in the life of the city as a whole. The "ideal" neighborhood of planning theory is useless for such a role. A district has to be big and powerful enough to fight city hall. Nothing less is to any purpose. To be sure, fighting city hall is not a district's only function, or necessarily the most important. Nevertheless, this is a good definition of size, in functional terms, because sometimes a district has to do exactly this, and also because a district lacking the power and will to fight city hall—and to win—when its people feel deeply threatened, is unlikely to possess the power and the will to contend with other serious problems.

Let us go back to the street neighborhoods for a moment, and pick up a loose end I left dangling: the job, incumbent upon good street neighborhoods, to get help when too big a problem comes along.

Nothing is more helpless than a city street alone, when its problems exceed its powers. Consider, as an illustration, what happened with respect to a case of narcotics pushing on a street in uptown West Side Manhattan in 1955. The street on which this case occurred had residents who worked all over the city and had friends and acquaintances outside the street as well as on it. On the street itself they had a reasonably flourishing public life centered around the stoops, but they had no neighborhood stores and no regular public characters. They also had no connection with a district neighborhood; indeed, their area has no such thing, except in name.

When heroin began to be sold from one of the apartments, a stream of drug addicts filtered into the street—not to live, but to make their connections. They needed money to buy the drugs. An epidemic of hold-ups and robberies on the street was one answer. People became afraid to come home with their pay on Fridays. Sometimes at night terrible screaming terrorized the residents. They were ashamed to have friends visit them. Some of the adolescents on the street were addicts, and more were becoming so.

The residents, most of whom were conscientious and respectable, did what they could. They called the police many times. Some individuals took the initiative of finding that the responsible outfit to talk with was the Narcotics Squad. They told the detectives of the squad where the heroin was being sold, and by whom, and when, and what days supplies seemed to come.

Nothing happened—except that things continued to get worse.

Nothing much ever happens when one helpless little street fights alone some of the most serious problems of a great city.

Had the police been bribed? How is anybody to know?

Lacking a district neighborhood, lacking knowledge of any other persons who cared about this problem in this place and could bring weight to bear on it, the residents had gone as far as they knew how to go. Why didn't they at least call their local assemblyman, or get in touch with the political club? Nobody on the street knew these people (an assemblyman has about 115,000 constituents) or knew anybody who did know them. In short, this street simply had no connections of any kind with a district neighborhood, let alone effective connections with an effective district neighborhood. Those on the street who could possibly manage it moved away when they saw that the street's situation was evidently hopeless. The street plunged into thorough chaos and barbarism.

New York had an able and energetic police commissioner during these events, but he could not be reached by everyone. Without effective intelligence from the streets and pressure from districts, he too must become to a degree helpless. Because of this gap, so much good intent at the top comes to so little purpose at the bottom, and vice-versa.

Sometimes the city is not the potential helper, but the antagonist of a street, and again, unless the street contains extraordinarily influential citizens, it is usually helpless alone. On Hudson Street we recently had this problem. The Manhattan Borough engineers decided to cut ten feet off our sidewalks. This was part of a mindless, routinized city program of vehicular road widening.

We people on the street did what we could. The job printer stopped his press, took off of it work on which he had an urgent deadline, and printed emergency petitions on a Saturday morning so the children, out of school, could help get them around. People from overlapping street neighborhoods took petitions and spread them farther. The two parochial schools, Episcopal and Catholic, sent petitions home with their children. We gathered about a thousand signatures from the street and the tributaries off it; these signatures must have represented most of the adults directly affected. Many businessmen and residents wrote letters, and a representative group formed a delegation to visit the Borough President, the elected official responsible.

But by ourselves, we would still hardly have had a chance. We were up against a sanctified general policy on street treatment, and were opposing a construction job that would mean a lot of money for somebody, on which arrangements were already far advanced. We had learned of the plan in advance of the demolition purely by luck. No public hearing was required, for technically this was merely an adjustment in the curb line.

We were told at first that the plans would not be changed; the sidewalk must go. We needed power to back up our pipsqueak protest. This power came from our district—Greenwich Village. Indeed, a main purpose of our petitions, although not an ostensible purpose, was to dramatize to the district at large that an issue had erupted. The swift resolutions passed by district-wide organizations counted more for us than the street-neighborhood expressions of opinion. The man who got our delegation its appointment, Anthony Dapolito, the president of the citizens' Greenwich Village Association, and the people on our delegation who swung the most weight, were from other streets than ours entirely; some from the other side of the district. They swung weight precisely because they represented opinion and opinion makers, at district scale. With their help, we won.

Without the possibility of such support, most city streets hardly try to fight back—whether their troubles emanate from city hall or from other drawbacks of the human condition. Nobody likes to practice futility.

The help we got put some individuals on our street under obligation, of course, to help other streets or aid more general district causes when help is wanted. If we neglect this, we may not get help next time we need it.

Districts effective at carrying the intelligence from the streets upward sometimes help translate it into city policy. There is no end to such examples, but this will do for illustration: As this is written, New York City is supposedly somewhat reforming its treatment for drug addicts, and simultaneously city hall is pressuring the federal government to expand and reform its treatment work, and to increase its efforts at blocking narcotics smuggling from abroad. The study and agitation that have helped push these moves did not originate with some mysterious "They." The first public agitation for reform and expansion of treatment was stirred not by officials at all, but by district pressure groups from districts like East Harlem and Greenwich Village. The disgraceful way in which arrest rolls are padded with victims while sellers operate openly and untouched is exposed and publicized by just these pressure groups, not by officials and least of all by the police. These pressure groups studied the problem and have pressed for changes and will continue to, precisely because they are in direct touch with experiences in street neighborhoods. The experience of an orphaned street like that on the Upper West Side, on the other hand, never teaches anybody anything—except to get the hell out.

It is tempting to suppose that districts can be formed federally out of distinct separate neighborhoods. The Lower East Side of New York is attempting to form an effective district today, on this pattern, and has received large philanthropic grants for the purpose. The formalized federation system seems to work fairly well for purposes on which virtually everyone is agreed, such as applying pressure for a new hospital. But many vital questions in local city life turn out to be controversial. In the Lower East Side, for example, the federated district organizational structure includes, as this is written, people trying to defend their homes and neighborhoods from obliteration by the bulldozers;

and it also contains the developers of cooperative projects and various other business interests who wish the governmental powers of condemnation to be used to wipe out these residents. These are genuine conflicts of interest—in this case, the ancient conflict between predator and prey. The people trying to save themselves spend much of their effort, futilely, trying to get resolutions adopted and letters approved by boards of directors that contain their chief enemies!

Both sides in hot fights on important local questions need to bring their full, consolidated, district-scale strength (nothing less is effective) to bear on the city policy they want to shape or the decisions they want to influence. They have to fight it out with each other, and with officials, on the plane where the effective decisions are made, because this is what counts in winning. Anything that diverts such contenders into fragmenting their power and watering their efforts by going through "decision-making" motions with hierarchies and boards at ineffectual levels where no responsible government powers of decision reside, vitiates political life, citizen effectiveness, and self-government. This becomes play at self-government, not the real thing.

When Greenwich Village fought to prevent its park, Washington Square, from being bisected by a highway, for example, majority opinion was overwhelmingly against the highway. But not unanimous opinion; among those for the highway were numerous people of prominence, with leadership positions in smaller sections of the district. Naturally they tried to keep the battle on a level of sectional organization, and so did the city government. Majority opinion would have frittered itself away in these tactics, instead of winning. Indeed, it was frittering itself away until this truth was pointed out by Raymond Rubinow, a man who happened to work in the district, but did not live there. Rubinow helped form a *Joint* Emergency Committee, a true district organization cutting through other organizational lines. Effective districts operate as Things in their own right, and most particularly must their citizens who are in agreement with each other on controversial questions act together at district scale, or they get nowhere. Districts are not groups of petty principalities, working in federation. If they work, they work as integral units of power and opinion, large enough to count.

Our cities possess many islandlike neighborhoods too small to work as districts, and these include not only the project neighborhoods inflicted by planning, but also many unplanned neighborhoods. These unplanned, too-small units have grown up historically, and often are enclaves of distinctive ethnic groups. They frequently perform well and strongly in the neighborhood functions of streets and thus keep marvelously in hand the kinds of neighborhood social problems and rot that develop from within. But also, just such too small neighborhoods are helpless, in the same way streets are helpless, against the problems and rot that develop from without. They are shortchanged on public improvements and services because they lack power to get them. They are helpless to reverse the slow-death warrants of area credit-blacklisting by mortgage lenders, a problem terribly difficult to fight even with impressive district power. If they develop conflicts with people in adjoining neighborhoods, both they and the adjoining people are apt to be helpless at improving relationships. Indeed, insularity makes these relationships deteriorate further.

Sometimes, to be sure, a neighborhood too small to function as a district gets the benefit of power through possessing an exceptionally influential citizen or an important institution. But the citizens of such a neighborhood pay for their "free" gift of power when the day comes that their interests run counter to those of Papa Bigwheel or Papa Institution. They are helpless to defeat Papa in the government offices, up where the decisions are made, *and therefore they are helpless also to teach him or influence him.* Citizens of neighborhoods that include a university, for example, are often in this helpless fix.

Whether a district of sufficient potential power does become effective and useful as an organ of democratic self-government depends much on whether the insularity of too-small neighborhoods within it is overcome. This is principally a social and political problem for a district and the contenders within it, but it is also a physical problem. To plan deliberately, and physically, on the premise that separated city neighborhoods of less than district size are a worthy ideal, is to subvert self-government; that the motives are sentimental or paternalistic is no help. When the physical isolation of too-small neighborhoods is abetted by blatant social distinctions, as in projects whose populations are price-tagged, the policy is savagely destructive to effective self-government and self-management in cities.

The value of city districts that swing real power (but in which street neighborhoods are not lost as infinitesimal units) is no discovery of mine. Their value is rediscovered and demonstrated empirically over and over. Nearly every large city has at least one such effective district. Many more areas struggle sporadically to function like districts in time of crisis.

Not surprisingly, a reasonably effective district usually accrues to itself, with time, considerable political power. It eventually generates, too, whole series of individuals able to operate simultaneously at street scale and district scale, and on district scale and in neighborhoods of the city as a whole.

To correct our general disastrous failure to develop functional districts is in great part a problem of city administrative change, which we need not go into at this point. But we also need, among other things, to abandon conventional planning about city neighborhoods. The "ideal" neighborhood of planning and zoning theory, too large in scale to possess any competence or meaning as a street neighborhood, is at the same time too small in scale to operate as a district. It is unfit for anything. It will not serve as even a point of departure. Like the belief in medical bloodletting, it was a wrong turn in the search for understanding.

If the only kinds of city neighborhoods that demonstrate useful functions in real-life self-government are the city as a whole, streets, and districts, then effective neighborhood physical planning for cities should aim at these purposes:

First, to foster lively and interesting streets.

Second, to make the fabric of these streets as continuous a network as possible *throughout* a district of potential subcity size and power.

Third, to use parks and squares and public buildings as part of this street fabric; use them to intensify and knit together the fabric's complexity and multiple use. They should not be used to island off different uses from each other, or to island off subdistrict neighborhoods.

Fourth, to emphasize the functional identity of areas large enough to work as districts.

If the first three aims are well pursued, the fourth will follow. Here is why: Few people, unless they live in a world of paper maps, can identify with an abstraction called a district, or care much about it. Most of us identify with a place in the city because we use it, and get to know it reasonably intimately. We take our two feet and move around in it and come to count on it. The only reason anyone does this much is that useful or interesting or convenient differences fairly nearby exert an attraction.

Almost nobody travels willingly from sameness to sameness and repetition to repetition, even if the physical effort required is trivial.*

---

*Thus it was discovered in Jefferson Houses, in East Harlem, that many people who had lived in the project four years had never laid eyes on the community center. It is at the dead end of the project (dead end, in the sense that no city life, only more park, lies beyond). People from other portions of the project had no normal reason for traveling to it from their portions and every normal reason not to. It looked, over there, like more of the same. A settlement-house director in the Lower East Side, Dora Tannenbaum of Grand Street Settlement, says of people in different

Differences, *not duplications,* make for cross-use and hence for a person's identification with an area greater than his immediate street network. Monotony is the enemy of cross-use and hence of functional unity. As for Turf, planned or unplanned, nobody outside the Turf can possibly feel a natural identity of interest with it or with what it contains.

Centers of use grow up in lively, diverse districts, just as centers of use occur on a smaller scale in parks, and such centers count especially in district identification if they contain also a landmark that comes to stand for the place symbolically and, in a way, for the district. But centers cannot carry the load of district identification by themselves; differing commercial and cultural facilities, and different-looking scenes, must crop up all through. Within this fabric, physical barriers, such as huge traffic arteries, too-large parks, big institutional groupings, are functionally destructive because they block cross-use.

How big, in absolute terms, must an effective district be? I have given a functional definition of size: big enough to fight city hall, but not so big that street neighborhoods are unable to draw district attention and to count.

In absolute terms, this means different sizes in different cities, depending partly on the size of the city as a whole. In Boston, when the North End had a population upward of 30,000 people, it was strong in district power. Now its population is about half that, partly from the salutary process of uncrowding its dwellings as its people have un-slummed, and partly from the unsalutary process of being ruthlessly amputated by a new highway. Cohesive though the North End is, it has lost an important sum of district power. In a city like Boston, Pittsburgh, or possibly even Philadelphia, as few as 30,000 people may be sufficient to form a district. In New York or Chicago, however, a district as small as 30,000 amounts to nothing. Chicago's most effective district, the Back-of-the-Yards, embraces about 100,000 people, according to the director of the district Council, and is building up its population further. In New York, Greenwich Village is on the small side for an effective district, but is viable because it manages to make up for this with other advantages. It contains approximately 80,000 residents, along with a working population (perhaps a sixth of them the same people) of

---

building groupings of an adjacent project: "These people cannot seem to get the idea they have anything in common with one another. They act as if the other parts of the project were on a different planet." Visually, these projects are units. Functionally, they are no such thing. The appearance tells a lie.

approximately 125,000. East Harlem and the Lower East Side of New York, both struggling to create effective districts, each contain about 200,000 residents, and need them.

Of course, other qualities than sheer population size count in effectiveness—especially good communication and good morale. But population size is vital because it represents, if most of the time only by implication, votes. There are only two ultimate public powers in shaping and running American cities: votes and control of the money. To sound nicer, we may call these "public opinion" and "disbursement of funds," but they are still votes and money. An effective district—and through its mediation, the street neighborhoods—possesses one of these powers: the power of votes. Through this, and this alone, can it effectively influence the power brought to bear on it, for good or ill, by public money.

Robert Moses, whose genius at getting things done largely consists in understanding this, has made an art of using control of public money to get his way with those whom the voters elect and depend on to represent their frequently opposing interests. This is, of course, in other guises, an old, sad story of democratic government. The art of negating the power of votes with the power of money can be practiced just as effectively by honest public administrators as by dishonest representatives of purely private interests. Either way, seduction or subversion of the elected is easiest when the electorate is fragmented into ineffectual units of power.

On the maximum side, I know of no district larger than 200,000 which operates like a district. Geographical size imposes empirical population limits, in any case. In real life, the maximum size of naturally evolved, effective districts seems to be roughly about a mile and a half square.* Probably this is because anything larger gets too inconvenient for sufficient local cross-use and for the functional identity that underlies district political identity. In a very big city, populations must therefore be dense to achieve successful districts; otherwise, sufficient political power is never reconciled with viable geographic identity.

This point on geographic size does not mean a city can be mapped out in segments of about a square mile, the segments defined with boundaries,

---

*The Back-of-the-Yards in Chicago is the only significant exception to this rule that I know of. It is an exception with perhaps useful implications in some areas, which need not concern us here but will be dealt with later in this book as an administrative question.

and districts thereby brought to life. It is not boundaries that make a district, but the cross-use and life. The point in considering the physical size and limits of a district is this: the kinds of objects, natural or man-made, that form physical barriers to easy cross-use must be somewhere. It is better that they be at the edges of areas large enough to work as districts than that they cut into the continuity of otherwise feasible districts. The fact of a district lies in what it *is* internally, and in the internal continuity and overlapping with which it is used, not in the way it ends or in how it looks in an air view. Indeed, in many cases very popular city districts spontaneously extend their edges, unless prevented from doing so by physical barriers. A district too thoroughly buffered off also runs the danger of losing economically stimulating visitors from other parts of the city.

Neighborhood planning units that are significantly defined only by their fabric and the life and intricate cross-use they generate, rather than by formalistic boundaries, are of course at odds with orthodox planning conceptions. The difference is the difference between dealing with living, complex organisms, capable of shaping their own destinies, and dealing with fixed and inert settlements, capable merely of custodial care (if that) of what has been bestowed upon them.

In dwelling on the necessity for districts, I do not want to give the impression that an effective city district is self-contained either economically, politically, or socially. Of course, it is not and cannot be, any more than a street can be. Nor can districts be duplicates of one another; they differ immensely, and should. A city is not a collection of repetitious towns. An interesting district has a character of its own and specialties of its own. It draws users from outside (it has little truly urban economic variety unless it does), and its own people go forth.

Nor is there necessity for district self-containment. In Chicago's Back-of-the-Yards, most of the breadwinners used to work, until the 1940s, at the slaughterhouses within the district. This did have a bearing on district formation in this case, because district organization here was a sequel to labor union organization. But as these residents and their children have graduated from the slaughterhouse jobs, they have moved into the working life and public life of the greater city. Most, other than teen-agers with afterschool jobs, now work outside the district. This movement has not weakened the district; coincident with it, the district has grown stronger.

The constructive factor that has been operating here meanwhile is time. Time, in cities, is the substitute for self-containment. Time, in cities, is indispensable.

The cross-links that enable a district to function as a Thing are neither vague nor mysterious. They consist of working relationships among specific people, many of them without much else in common than that they share a fragment of geography.

The first relationships to form in city areas, given any neighborhood stability, are those in street neighborhoods and those among people who do have something else in common and belong to organizations with one another—churches, PTA's, businessmen's associations, political clubs, local civic leagues, fund-raising committees for health campaigns or other public causes, sons of such-and-such a village (common clubs among Puerto Ricans today, as they have been with Italians), property owners' associations, block improvement associations, protesters against injustices, and so on, ad infinitum.

To look into almost any relatively established area of a big city turns up so many organizations, mostly little, as to make one's head swim. Mrs. Goldie Hoffman, one of the commissioners of Philadelphia's redevelopment agency, decided to try the experiment of casing the organizations, if any, and the institutions in a drear little Philadelphia section of about ten thousand people, which was up for renewal. To her astonishment and everyone else's, she found nineteen. Small organizations and special-interest organizations grow in our cities like leaves on the trees, and in their own way are just as awesome a manifestation of the persistence and doggedness of life.

The crucial stage in the formation of an effective district goes much beyond this, however. An interweaving, but different, set of relationships must grow up; these are working relationships among people, usually leaders, who enlarge their local public life beyond the neighborhoods of streets and specific organizations or institutions and form relationships with people whose roots and backgrounds are in entirely different constituencies, so to speak. These hop-and-skip relationships are more fortuitous in cities than are the analogous, almost enforced, hop-and-skip links among people from different small groupings within self-contained settlements. Perhaps because we are typically more advanced at forming whole-city neighborhoods of interest than at forming districts, hop-skip district relationships sometimes originate fortuitously among people from a district who meet in a special-interest neighborhood of the whole city, and then carry over this relationship into their district. Many district networks in New York, for instance, start in this fashion.

It takes surprisingly few hop-skip people, relative to a whole population, to weld a district into a real Thing. A hundred or so people do it in a population a thousand times their size. But these people must have time to find each other, time to try expedient cooperation—as well as time to have rooted themselves, too, in various smaller neighborhoods of place or special interest.

When my sister and I first came to New York from a small city, we used to amuse ourselves with a game we called Messages. I suppose we were trying, in a dim way, to get a grip on the great, bewildering world into which we had come from our cocoon. The idea was to pick two wildly dissimilar individuals—say a headhunter in the Solomon Islands and a cobbler in Rock Island, Illinois—and assume that one had to get a message to the other by word of mouth; then we would each silently figure out a plausible, or at least possible, chain of persons through whom the message could go. The one who could make the shortest plausible chain of messengers won. The headhunter would speak to the headman of his village, who would speak to the trader who came to buy copra, who would speak to the Australian patrol officer when he came through, who would tell the man who was next slated to go to Melbourne on leave, etc. Down at the other end, the cobbler would hear from his priest, who got it from the mayor, who got it from the state senator, who got it from the governor, etc. We soon had these close-to-home messengers down to a routine for almost everybody we could conjure up, but we would get tangled in long chains at the middle until we began employing Mrs. Roosevelt. Mrs. Roosevelt made it suddenly possible to skip whole chains of intermediate connections. She knew the most unlikely people. The world shrank remarkably. It shrank us right out of our game, which became too cut and dried.

A city district requires a small quota of its own Mrs. Roosevelts—people who know unlikely people, and therefore eliminate the necessity for long chains of communication (which in real life would not occur at all).

Settlement house directors are often the ones who begin such systems of district hop-skip links, but they can only begin them and work at opportune ways to extend them; they cannot carry the load. These links require the growth of trust, the growth of cooperation that is, at least at first, apt to be happenstance and tentative; and they require people who have considerable self-confidence, or sufficient concern about local public problems to stand them in the stead of self-confidence. In East Harlem, where, after terrible disruption and population turnover, an effective district is slowly re-forming against great odds, fifty-two organizations participated in a 1960 pressure meeting to tell the Mayor and fourteen of his commissioners what the district wants. The organizations included PTA's, churches, settlements and welfare groups, civic clubs, tenant associations, businessmen's associations, political clubs, and the local congressman, assemblyman, and councilman. Fifty-eight individuals had specific responsibilities in getting up the meeting and setting its policy; they included people of all sorts of talents and occupations, and a great ethnic range—Negroes, Italians, Puerto Ricans, and undefinables. This represents a lot of hop-skip district links. It has taken years and skill on the part of half a dozen people to achieve this amount of network, and the process is only starting to reach the stage of being effective.

Once a good, strong network of these hop-skip links does get going in a city district, the net can enlarge relatively swiftly and weave all kinds of resilient new patterns. One sign that it is doing so, sometimes, is the growth of a new kind of organization, more or less district-wide, but impermanent, formed specifically for *ad hoc* purposes.* But to get going, a district network needs these three requisites: a start of some kind; a physical area with which sufficient people can identify as users; and Time.

The people who form hop-skip links, like the people who form the smaller links in streets and special-interest organizations, are not at all the statistics that are presumed to represent people in planning and housing schemes. Statistical people are a fiction for many reasons, one of which is that they are treated as if infinitely interchangeable. Real people are unique, they invest years of their lives in significant relationships with other unique people, and are not interchangeable in the least. Severed from their relationships, they are destroyed as effective social beings—sometimes for a little while, sometimes forever.†

In city neighborhoods, whether streets or districts, if too many slowly grown public relationships are disrupted at once, all kinds of havoc can occur—so much havoc, instability, and helplessness that it sometimes seems time will never again get in its licks.

---

*In Greenwich Village, these frequently run to long, explicit names: e.g., the Joint Emergency Committee to Close Washington Square Park to All but Emergency Traffic; the Cellar Dwellers' Tenant Emergency Committee; the Committee of Neighbors to Get the Clock on Jefferson Market Courthouse Started; the Joint Village Committee to Defeat the West Village Proposal and Get a Proper One.

†There are people who seemingly can behave like interchangeable statistics and take up in a different place exactly where they left off, but they must belong to one of our fairly homogeneous and ingrown nomad societies, like Beatniks, or Regular Army officers and their families, or the peripatetic junior executive families of suburbia, described by William H. Whyte, Jr., in *The Organization Man*.

Harrison Salisbury, in a series of *New York Times* articles, "The Shook-Up Generation," put well this vital point about city relationships and their disruption.

"Even a ghetto [he quoted a pastor as saying], after it has remained a ghetto for a period of time, builds up its social structure and this makes for more stability, more leadership, more agencies for helping the solution of public problems."

But when slum clearance enters an area [Salisbury went on], it does not merely rip out slatternly houses. It uproots the people. It tears out the churches. It destroys the local business man. It sends the neighborhood lawyer to new offices downtown, and it mangles the tight skein of community friendships and group relationships beyond repair.

It drives the old-timers from their broken-down flats or modest homes and forces them to find new and alien quarters. And it pours into a neighborhood hundreds and thousands of new faces. . . .

Renewal planning, which is largely aimed at saving buildings, and incidentally some of the population, but at strewing the rest of a locality's population, has much the same result. So does too heavily concentrated private building, capitalizing in a rush on the high values created by a stable city neighborhood. From Yorkville, in New York, an estimated 15,000 families have been driven out between 1951 and 1960 by this means; virtually all of them left unwillingly. In Greenwich Village, the same thing is happening. Indeed, it is a miracle that our cities have any functioning districts, not that they have so few. In the first place, there is relatively little city territory at present which is, by luck, well suited physically to forming districts with good cross-use and identity. And within this, incipient or slightly too weak districts are forever being amputated, bisected, and generally shaken up by misguided planning policies. The districts that are effective enough to defend themselves from planned disruption are eventually trampled in an unplanned gold rush by those who aim to get a cut of these rare social treasures.

To be sure, a good city neighborhood can absorb newcomers into itself, both newcomers by choice and immigrants settling by expediency, and it can protect a reasonable amount of transient population, too. But these increments or displacements have to be gradual. If self-government in the place is to work, underlying any float of population must be a continuity of people who have forged neighborhood networks. These networks are a city's irreplaceable social capital. Whenever the capital is lost, from whatever the cause, the income from it disappears, never to return until and unless new capital is slowly and chancily accumulated.

Some observers of city life, noting that strong city neighborhoods are so frequently ethnic communities—especially communities of Italians,

Poles, Jews, or Irish—have speculated that a cohesive ethnic base is required for a city neighborhood that works as a social unit. In effect, this is to say that only hyphenated-Americans are capable of local self-government in big cities. I think this is absurd.

In the first place, these ethnically cohesive communities are not always as naturally cohesive as they may look to outsiders. Again citing the Back-of-the-Yards as an example, its backbone population is mainly Central European, but all kinds of Central European. It has, for example, literally dozens of national churches. The traditional enmities and rivalries among these groups were a most severe handicap. Greenwich Village's three main parts derive from an Italian community, an Irish community, and a Henry Jamesian patrician community. Ethnic cohesiveness may have played a part in the formation of these sections, but it has been no help in welding district cross-links—a job that was begun many years ago by a remarkable settlement-house director, Mary K. Simkhovich. Today many streets in these old ethnic communities have assimilated into their neighborhoods a fantastic ethnic variety from almost the whole world. They have also assimilated a great sprinkling of middle-class professionals and their families, who prove to do very well at city street and district life, in spite of the planning myth that such people need protective islands of pseudosuburban "togetherness." Some of the streets that functioned best in the Lower East Side (before they were wiped out) were loosely called "Jewish," but contained, as people actually involved in the street neighborhoods, individuals of more than forty differing ethnic origins. One of New York's most effective neighborhoods, with an internal communication that is a marvel, is the midtown East Side of predominately high-income people, utterly undefinable except as Americans.

In the second place, wherever ethnically cohesive neighborhoods develop and are stable, they possess another quality besides ethnic identity. They contain many individuals who stay put. This, I think, more than sheer ethnic identity, is the significant factor. It typically takes many years after such groups have settled in for time to work and for the inhabitants to attain stable, effective neighborhoods.

Here is a seeming paradox: To maintain in a neighborhood sufficient people who stay put, a city must have the very fluidity and mobility of use that Reginald Isaacs noted, as mentioned early in this chapter, when he speculated whether neighborhoods can therefore mean anything very significant to cities.

Over intervals of time, many people change their jobs and the locations of their jobs, shift or enlarge their outside friendships and interests, change their family sizes, change their incomes up or down, even change many of their tastes. In short, they live, rather than just exist. If they live in diversified, rather than monotonous, districts—in districts, particularly, where many details of physical change can constantly be accommodated—and if they like the place, they can stay put despite changes in the locales or natures of their other pursuits or interests. Unlike the people who must move from a lower-middle to a middle-middle to an upper-middle suburb as their incomes and leisure activities change (or be very outré indeed), or the people of a little town who must move to another town or to a city to find different opportunities, city people need not pull up stakes for such reasons.

A city's collection of opportunities of all kinds, and the fluidity with which these opportunities and choices can be used, is an asset—not a detriment—for encouraging city–neighborhood stability.

However, this asset has to be capitalized upon. It is thrown away where districts are handicapped by sameness and are suitable, therefore, to only a narrow range of incomes, tastes, and family circumstances. Neighborhood accommodations for fixed, bodiless, statistical people are accommodations for instability. The people in them, as statistics, may stay the same. But the people in them, as people, do not. Such places are forever way stations.

In the first section of this book, of which this is the close, I have been emphasizing assets and strengths peculiar to big cities, and weaknesses peculiar to them also. Cities, like anything else, succeed only by making the most of their assets. I have tried to point out the kinds of places in cities that do this, and the way they work. My idea, however, is not that we should therefore try to reproduce, routinely and in a surface way, the streets and districts that do display strength and success as fragments of city life. This would be impossible, and sometimes would be an exercise in architectural antiquarianism. Moreover, even the best streets and districts can stand improvement, especially amenity.

But, if we understand the principles behind the behavior of cities, we can build on potential assets and strengths, instead of acting at cross-purposes to them. First we have to know the general results we want—and know because of knowing how life in cities works. We have to know, for instance, that we want lively, well-used streets and other public spaces, and why we want them. But knowing what to want, although it is a first step, is far from enough. The next step is to examine some of the workings of cities at another level: the economic workings that produce those lively streets and districts for city users.

BUFFALO'S BLACK ROCK
A Neighborhood and the City
MARK GOLDMAN

Throughout much of the nineteenth century many American cities were highly fragmented. Divided into pockets of virtually separate settlements, the typical American city was a loosely knit collection of distinct neighborhood communities. With only tentative connection to each other and to the main body of settlement downtown, these communities developed as geographically contained, economically independent, and institutionally cohesive neighborhoods, within but not really a part of the larger metropolitan whole. As a result of a variety of historical patterns and processes, these local neighborhood communities tended to function actually and conceptually as the primary reference point of urban life. During the second half of the nineteenth century, however, this multi-nucleated urban structure began to change. The rise of the streetcar suburb as the most desirable urban residential section, in addition to the emergence of downtown as the dominant geographical, economic, and political center of the metropolis, sapped the vitality of the local neighborhood communities. These changes had a dramatic impact on all aspects of urban life—on the actual structure and institutions of the city as well as on the way people lived in and thought about their neighborhood and their city. How these changes occurred and the impact that they had on one neighborhood community—Black Rock in Buffalo, New York—is the subject of this article.

The original version of this article appeared under the title, "Buffalo's Black Rock: A Neighborhood and the City," by Mark Goldman, published in *Journal of Urban History,* vol. 5, no. 4 (August 1979), pp. 447–468 and is reprinted herewith by permission of the publisher, Sage Publications, Inc.

Black Rock, one of the oldest neighborhoods in Buffalo, developed around a lock in the Erie Canal, about two and a half miles up the Niagara River from the Canal's terminal point in South Buffalo. Because a canal lock is a break-point in traffic as well as a source of water power, it is an inevitable generator of urban growth. By 1850, twenty-five years after the completion of the Black Rock lock, a politically independent and economically self-sufficient community had developed, based on the wheat and lumber mills, starch factories, and iron foundries on the Canal towpath. At this time there were close to 2,000 people living within walking distance of the lock.

Although Black Rock's separate community structure was not directly threatened by the growth of Buffalo, its political independence was. The rapid growth of the city from under 10,000 in 1830 to close to 42,000 in 1850 created tremendous pressure for expansion; and in 1854 Buffalo annexed the Village of Black Rock and another adjacent territory, thereby doubling the city's land area.

Even had it been so inclined, there was little that Black Rock could have done to prevent annexation. After all, by the middle of the nineteenth century, Buffalo had become the preeminent inland port in the United States, the center of an international commercial network that extended from the American Midwest to the cities of western Europe. Sitting at the juncture of the Erie Canal and Lake Erie, Buffalo guarded this most important crossroads of American commerce like Cerebus at the gates of Hades.

Annexation had little direct impact on the structure of local life. Black Rock remained geographically isolated from the rest of the metropolis for most of the remainder of the century. There was no streetcar line connecting it with downtown until the 1890s, and while there was a rail-road—the Buffalo and Niagara Falls Railroad had passed through Black Rock since the 1830s—it made no tangible dent in the structure of neighborhood life. Thus, Black Rock remained largely separate and distinct: It had its own marketplace, its own locally owned small-store economy, a reliable source of jobs within walking distance on the banks of the Erie Canal, its own church, and an elaborate and intricate gemeinschaft social structure with a highly developed sense of neighboring.[1] In addition, Black Rock retained, despite annexation, its own political identity. Political power in most nineteenth-century American cities was apportioned to the wards, to places not to people, and Black Rock had never been gerrymandered. When it was annexed, Black Rock was designated a ward unto itself, and like other wards, was given two aldermen to represent it in city government. Thus, from the very beginning, Black

Rock was able to take its place as a political equal with older, larger, and more economically important subsections of the city.

Black Rock's tradition of localism was reinforced by a mythic factor which had come to play an equally important role in the development of the area: consciousness as a neighborhood. Before the construction of the Erie Canal and the lock which fostered the initial growth of Black Rock, there had been another village immediately adjacent to Buffalo's northern boundary. Equal in size to Buffalo (approximately one thousand people in 1820) and just as eager to grow, the village, known as Upper Black Rock, had sought to convince the New York State Canal Commissioners that their town and not Buffalo was best suited to be the terminal point of the soon-to-be completed Erie Canal. Buffalo, of course, had other ideas, and between 1820 and 1823 a bitter rivalry between these two frontier towns ensued. Buffalo's eventual selection and the sudden growth of that city led to the absorption of Upper Black Rock. Well before its legal annexation in 1854, the village of Upper Black Rock had lost its separate identity. Meanwhile, the new settlement of Black Rock had sprung up at the canal lock. It was in this new settlement that the memory of the older village's struggle with Buffalo lingered. Passed on as part of the neighborhood's folklore, the story of the village of Upper Black Rock and its rivalry with Buffalo became a constant source of pride and point of reference to the residents of the neighborhood of Black Rock as they struggled to cope with the often overwhelming forces of urbanization that began to engulf them at the end of the nineteenth century.

What Buffalo's decentralized political structure did for the perpetuation of Black Rock's political cohesiveness, the accident of the city's location did for the neighborhood's economy. By the 1870s Buffalo had become, after Chicago, the leading railroad center in the nation with more than a dozen railroad lines radiating out from the several railroad terminals south of the central business district. Because of Buffalo's location on the eastern banks of Lake Erie, all but one of these lines entered the city from the east and south. Thus, Black Rock, located on a north-south axis, was spared the heavy industrialization that followed the railroads into other neighborhoods in the city. As late as 1880 only one railroad, the Buffalo and Niagara Falls, passed through the neighborhood. And this road, built in 1834, represented continuity more than change. The neighborhood thus remained outside the industrializing process somewhat longer than neighborhoods on the direct route of the railroad. As a result, Black Rock's primarily locally owned, pre-industrial entrepot-oriented economy remained intact into the late nineteenth century.[2]

By the 1870s this situation began to change. In 1873 a Canadian railroad company constructed a railroad bridge connecting the United States and Canada at the narrowest point in the Niagara River, which, on the American side, was at Black Rock. By thus joining the United States and Canada, the International Bridge, as it was called, put Black Rock in the middle of the first direct railroad link between the East Coast and such inland cities as Detroit and Chicago.

Black Rock's integration into the rapidly expanding national industrial network was further accelerated by completion of the Belt Line Railroad in 1883. By circling the city, the Belt Line ended Buffalo's dependence on a longitudinal railroad system and permitted the decentralization of industry in a city whose industrial infrastructure, built around the old midcentury railroad terminals, was already overbuilt. The Belt Line, owned and operated by the New York Central, was a powerful inducement for industrial decentralization. It offered cheap, transportation-serviced land for expansion, direct rail access to all of the city's trunk lines, and, because it was a commuter as well as a freight line, it created opportunities for residential settlement too. A supply of industrial laborers was thereby guaranteed. Thus, by bringing hitherto distant areas of the city into the increasingly integrated urban-industrial economy, the Belt Line radically altered Buffalo's social geography.

Yet, this development, critical to the process of the city's industrialization, had little direct impact on the internal structure of Black Rock itself. Because of Black Rock's sharply defined physical boundaries—the Niagara River in the west, the Scajaquada Creek in the south, and grade-level railroad lines in the east and north—virtually all of the available land area in Black Rock had been built up well before the completion of the Belt Line.[3] Thus, with little room left for either new construction or for future expansion, companies that were attracted to the area as a result of the Belt Line had to look elsewhere. They did not have to look far, however, for just east of Black Rock, at the junction of the Buffalo–Niagara Falls line and the Belt Line, there was a practically unsettled area that afforded limitless room for industrial growth. In the years following the completion of the Belt Line, this adjacent yet separate area developed into one of the largest working-class industrial communities in the city.[4]

Despite the fact that industrialization had little direct impact on Black Rock itself, the people in the neighborhood were not immune to the changes that were occurring everywhere around them. In fact, it was because of this awareness that a group of businessmen—some storeowners, other small local manufacturers—formed, in 1886, the Black Rock Businessmen's Association. Perhaps realizing that Black Rock's gemeinschaft village days were numbered the association's first action was the publication of a neighborhood newspaper. The minutes of the Black Rock Businessmen's Association, often printed in the newspaper, along with the back editions of this neighborhood newspaper, are invaluable sources if we are to understand how neighborhood leaders, not only in Black Rock, but throughout urban America, perceived urbanization and the impact that it was having on their neighborhoods.

The newspaper was called the *International Gazette,* a name which reveals both the ambitions of the neighborhood leaders as well as their parochial naiveté. Much of what was written in it was little more than traditional boosterism on a neighborhood level. For example, this excerpt from the first edition: "The first robin was here and went away again, for so many changes have taken place in Black Rock he thought he made a mistake." This was followed with a primer on "How to Build Up Black Rock: Talk about it. Write about it. Help to improve it. Beautify the streets. Patronize the merchants, advertise in the newspaper, elect good men to all offices, remember that every dollar that you invest in a permanent improvement is that much more money to your interest."

Notwithstanding the boosterish rhetoric of its founding editor, Alfred Tovey, the paper reflected the concerns of a neighborhood which, because of its location and its history, sensed that it was discriminated against by the downtown political establishment. The sense of ill treatment—particularly the belief that Black Rock was not getting its fair share of urban improvements—was reinforced by the attitude of downtown-oriented political leaders, who did, in fact, tend to forget the concerns of areas beyond the fringe of the central business district. The new group of leaders in Black Rock were not content, however, to suffer these indignities silently, and shortly after the group's formation—in fact it was the probable reason for the decision to form it in the first place—the leaders dedicated themselves to somehow guaranteeing that Black Rock was accorded equal treatment with any and all parts of the city. In their efforts to win these improvements—particularly electric lights, asphalt streets, and sewer lines—a serious controversy developed between neighborhood leaders and the mayor of Buffalo—a conflict which, as we will see, raises critical questions about the perceptions different interest groups within the city had about Buffalo and casts light on important structural changes that were occurring in the city.

By the middle of the 1890s, electric lights had replaced gas lamps on more than half of the city's streets, almost all of them in the central business district. The board of aldermen, as representatives of the city's wards, were eager to spread the improvements to their neighborhoods. In November, 1887, they passed a resolution stating that it was their intention to install electric lights on every street in Buffalo. Jumping at the opportunity to "bring Black Rock into the Age of Electricity," as the editor of the *Gazette* put it, one of Black Rock's aldermen secured the passage of a measure calling for the construction of electric lights on three streets in Black Rock. The mayor vetoed it. Similarly, two months later, the mayor vetoed a bill calling for the paving of Niagara Street, a north-south thoroughfare and the only road that linked Black Rock to Buffalo. Then, in August, 1888, Mayor Becker vetoed still another one of the Black Rock aldermen's bills, which would have built a trunk line sewer in the neighborhood. Thus, within less than one year, the mayor vetoed three bills which the leadership of Black Rock considered essential to the well-being of the neighborhood.

Each veto provoked bitter anger and a barrage of blustery rhetoric. The veto of the electric street lights bill led the editor of the *Gazette* to charge that "Mayor Becker Don't Want Black Rock to Boom" and to accuse him of having "unrealistic, unfair attitudes" towards the growing section of Black Rock. When the Mayor shattered the businessmen's hopes of having Niagara Street macadamized and a trunk line sewer built, the president of the association complained about the neighborhood's shabby treatment. In a letter to the *Gazette* that was both rhetorical and genuine in its sentiments, he concluded: "Why was Black Rock ever annexed to the city if her interests were not to be looked after? Better a thousand times it had remained a town by itself and have been able to appoint men to look after its welfare than to be compelled to pay out money year after year and get so little in return."

It is quite possible that the conflict between Black Rock and Mayor Becker was partisan. After all, the neighborhood was consistently Republican while the Mayor was a Democrat. However, as Seymour Mandelbaum suggested in his provocative book on *Boss Tweed's New York,* behind the opposition to the improvement of outlying neighborhoods (in New York City, at least) was the fear that the growth of these fringe areas constituted a political and economic threat to the central business district. The Black Rock–Buffalo story tends to substantiate this idea. Indeed, it goes further by pointing to the conclusion that in addition to the traditional party allegiances and class lines that divided political opinion, there was emerging in the late nineteenth-century city a new and different kind of battle, a conflict that pitted the central business district against the city's neighborhoods. There was, on the one hand, the view of the Mayor who, as one of the few officials in the city elected at large, assigned a low priority to the development of any area not directly within the sphere of the central business district. Using the veto of the Black Rock lighting bill as an opportunity to articulate a more general downtown-oriented conception of the city, Mayor Becker said: "I object as always to the extension of electricity at present rates to the outlying districts of the city." On the other hand, there was the view of the neighborhood leaders who, like those in Black Rock, were outraged by the Mayor's veto. To these men, Becker's views were obsolescent, no longer suited to a city that had long ago expanded beyond the limited borders of the preindustrial walking city. Accusing the Mayor of downtown chauvinism, Tovey wrote that, if permitted, he would "erect a Chinese Wall around Main Street, Delaware Avenue, and North Streets (the de facto and practically the legal boundaries of the city in 1850) beyond which no improvements would be made." If this notion of urban growth and development prevailed, Tovey wrote, Black Rock, and other places like it, would "wither and die."

Because of the fractional character of urban life throughout most of the century, these particular issues had never emerged before. But now, under the pressure of the highly centralizing forces of urbanization, the conflict between downtown and neighborhood began to play an increasingly important role in the political debates of the day. It became most obvious in the struggles that developed between Black Rock and City Hall over the issue of the Hertel Avenue sewer and the conflict between the neighborhood and the city and within the neighborhood itself over the issue of electric streetcars.

From the point of view of Black Rock's leaders, the vision of a modern, barrier-free, integrated metropolis, was not incompatible with a continued commitment to localism and a strong sense of neighborhood identity. In fact, the former was impossible without the latter. Some sense of the coexistence of these two seemingly contradictory notions about the neighborhood and its place within the metropolis can be seen in Tovey's reaction to the passage, over the Mayor's veto by the New York State Legislature, of the Hertel Avenue Sewer Bill: "The people of Black Rock have won a major struggle. The new sewer line is a feather in the cap of the Rock. Wear it proudly. The average Black Rockite [notice the identification with the neighborhood and not with the city] now feels his oats and can carry his head just as high as the full-fledged bison [reference to a common nickname for a resident of Buffalo]." The new sewer line was just the type of improvement that Black Rock's leaders coveted. Not only would it have effected a measurable improvement on the quality of life within the neighborhood itself, but, because a trunk line sewer is an integrating technological improvement, it would link Black Rock actually as well as symbolically to the rest of the city.

What was emerging then from these struggles with Mayor Becker was a two-tiered definition of the metropolis which, on the one hand, required greater integration with the rest of the city and, on the other, a heightened understanding of the importance of the neighborhood community and rootedness on a local level. The trouble with this double vision was that it was tenuous and fraught with contradictions.

This juxtaposition of contradictory notions of metropolitan order was too sophisticated to survive for long, and the fragile consensus within Black Rock that had been built around it soon began to crumble. What finally smashed it was the argument over the electric streetcar. More than anything, the electric streetcar offered the people of Black Rock the most effective opportunity they had ever had to end their isolation and become a more integral part of the metropolitan community. Obviously, the self-appointed neighborhood leaders were thrilled with the announcement in July 1889 that an electric streetcar would soon be built on Niagara Street, the north-south artery linking Black Rock with the rest of the city. The letter written by the president of the Black Rock Businessmen's Association offers a great deal of insight into how people in this neighborhood were responding to the changing structure of the late nineteenth-century city.

The people of Black Rock in the northwest section of Buffalo are entitled to quick and rapid service equally with the people of downtown and of the East Side. It should be possible for the people of our section of the City to cross over to the East Side and to go downtown. There must be no sectionalism is our city. We must use the street-car line to knit the various vicinities of the city closer together rather than keep them distinctly apart.

The development of the electric streetcar presaged a new urban age; an end to the isolation that had for so long characterized communities like Black Rock, and the beginning of an integrated and unified metropolitan community. Black Rock, at least the men in the association, wanted their neighborhood to be a part of that community.

The impact of the electric streetcar on the structure of the American city was dynamic, approaching that of the automobile in terms of its revolutionary implications. For one, as Warner pointed out years ago, the rapid extension of a well-integrated streetcar system opened new suburban areas that had long been beyond the pale of urban settlement. To this extent, the streetcar had a decentralizing impact on metropolitan structure. Yet, on the other hand, the streetcar had a centralizing impact, too, for more than any other development of the late nineteenth century, the streetcar created the modern central business district as the true focal point of the newly emergent metropolitan area. As a result of Warner's brilliant and persuasive study of streetcar suburbs in Boston, scholars of urbanization have long ignored the critical relationship that exists between the electric streetcar and the growth of the modern central business district. For if what happened in Buffalo is any indication of what happened elsewhere, the introduction of the electric streetcar as the dominant form of urban transportation in the 1890s resulted in an upheaval in downtown land use that was unparalleled in the history of the American city. Virtually overnight, large office buildings replaced four- and five-story business blocks, dry-goods stores were quickly expanded into regional department stores, and churches were quickly converted into regional entertainment centers. Clearly, other factors were involved, among them the development of structural steel as a primary building material and vertical changes in American corporate structure. Yet, without the electric streetcar to bring the people into the downtown core, none of the above would have occurred.

The electric streetcar, while creating both the modern suburb and the modern central business district, had a devastating impact on the cities' neighborhoods. Caught in the middle of a squeeze that drained them outward to new residential areas in the suburbs and inward to the new commercial, social, and recreational center downtown, the neighborhoods were hard pressed. Perhaps because he sensed the inherent threat to the neighborhood presented by the streetcar, Alfred Tovey, immediately upon completion of the Niagara Street line, began a weekly column entitled "Trolley Tricks," a blow-by-blow accounting of the hazards of the Niagara Street car line: run-over dogs, electrocuted horses, and countless injuries to pedestrians. Tovey's snide and sometimes bitter taunts soon evolved into more coherent critique, not only of the streetcar line and the company that owned it, but more importantly, of the kind of community that Black Rock would become if more streetcar lines were to be constructed in the neighborhood. While there was opposition to streetcars in many other cities, expressed particularly in efforts to keep them off of residential streets, the response in Black Rock was different in that it involved an argument about the whole shape and structure of the community. What prompted his concern was the sudden announcement in December, 1890, that a streetcar line was planned for Hertel Avenue, one of the primary west-east arteries in the neighborhood.

Tovey was not alone in his growing doubts about the streetcar and Black Rock's inclusion in a system of rapid transit. Indeed, within a week of the December announcement, a group of Hertel Avenue residents had gathered enough signatures to legally prevent construction. Although they couched their petition in the language of the law, according to which construction could not proceed until the owners of abutting property had been fairly compensated, the fact of the matter was that they objected to the streetcar on grounds of principle. When the Buffalo Street Car Company modified its compensation plan and did secure final approval from the Board of Aldermen (over the objections of Black Rock's representatives) to proceed with the construction of the Hertel Avenue line, many residents of the avenue took to the streets in opposition. On March 18, 1891, the day that construction was scheduled to begin, a group of over fifty people lined the street in protest. In an effort to avoid violence, the mayor issued a temporary cease and desist order.

Within a month, construction crews were back at work. While the active opposition to the new line may have faded, its cause, the fears of a changing neighborhood, remained. Alfred Tovey had become an ardent opponent of the streetcar on the grounds that it could, by so eroding the basis of community life, clearly ruin the neighborhood. Sensing that many businesses, his own newspaper included, were very much threatened by the greater integration, Tovey was deeply concerned about Black Rock's ability to survive the streetcar. "Can you not realize the results of a street-car on Hertel Avenue?" he implored. "When combined with the Niagara Street line, the effect will be to drain completely the life-blood of Black Rock." Indicating that the Niagara Street line which linked Black Rock directly with downtown Buffalo would have a negative impact on the neighborhood business, Tovey asked: "How long do you think the people of the Rock will continue to patronize their local merchants?" Following this with a suggestion that the Hertel Avenue line would open up new areas of settlement east of Black Rock, he again appealed to the self-interest of the members of the association: "How long before the hard-working families of Black Rock who have made the Rock their home for so many years will begin to ride the Hertel Avenue street-car away from this place?"

Yet, the Black Rock Businessmen's Association, comprised of businessmen whose local self-interest was every bit as real as Tovey's, had a different view of the streetcar. They believed that the streetcar would have a beneficial impact on the economic life of the neighborhood. Citing the effect of the streetcar on the city's East Side, the president of the association, in a letter to the *Gazette,* urged that the people of Black Rock rally around the inevitable: "The coming of the street-car to Broadway [the main arterial on the East Side] has more than tripled that section's commercial activity, doubled the value of their real estate and done much to make it one of the most rapidly advancing and desirable sections of the city. All of this and more will be ours when the street-car comes to Hertel Avenue. Should not Black Rock be so blessed?"[5]

His analysis, however, and the example that he used to sustain it, was faulty. Because the east end of Broadway was largely unsettled territory when the streetcar line was built there, with no established community structure to speak of, the coming of the streetcar line could only lead to the growth of that community. In a long, self-contained and largely independent area like Black Rock, the stakes were different, and Tovey, a vigilant watch-dog of community affairs, sensed it.

What is particularly interesting about the streetcar controversy is that for the first time the people of Black Rock were forced by the phenomenon of urbanization to think and debate about what kind of community they wanted Black Rock to be. Until now, there had been little question about it. The absence of an integrating technology, in addition to more than a half-century legacy of separate development, had left moot the question of community definition. However, the introduction of the electric streetcar had changed all that, and conflicts about "community," now removed from the theoretical and abstract level, had become an important part of neighborhood dialogue. As people in the community debated among themselves the relative virtues and disadvantages of metropolitan integration, the neighborhood stood on the threshold of major structural changes.

The rise of the central business district as the economic focal point of the metropolis threatened to sap the economic vitality of the city's neighborhoods. The concurrent emergence of a downtown-oriented reform movement whose goal was the centralization of many of the city's long decentralized governmental functions now threatened the neighborhood's political strength. Since the middle of the 1870s, the ward system had been under attack in cities across the United States as an outmoded, cumbersome, and inefficient means of executing the city's business. For not only was political power rooted in the neighborhood in nineteenth-century Buffalo, but also the whole decision-making process tended to favor the neighborhoods. This is well-illustrated in the way monies were levied for intrastructural improvements. According to New York State law, which determined these matters for the municipalities, street-pavings, sewer projects, and the like were to be funded not out of a general citywide fund but rather to be paid for by those people who, based on proximity, were deemed to be the direct beneficiaries of the improvements. If those people chose, for whatever reason, not to fund a project, it was not built. It was consequently possible for individual property owners living in the city's separate neighborhoods to impede the progress of city building whenever it suited them. Thus, given the extent to which political power was locally based, it was extremely difficult to develop not only a commonly arrived-at image of the whole city but a citywide public policy as well. Indeed, James Parton's reaction to the "anatomy of fragmentation" that characterized New York City in 1886 might well have been applied to Buffalo: "Was there ever such a hodge-podge of government before in the world?" As much as any area in Buffalo, Black Rock benefited from the decentralized political structure prevalent in the middle of the nineteenth century.

Indeed, it was just this kind of situation that by the middle of the 1880s made the elimination of the ward system the central goal of the city's reform groups. Under the aegis of the citizen's association, a bipartisan gathering of reformers, most of whom fit Sprout's description of progressive reformers as among the city's "Best Men," launched a campaign to pass a new city charter which would, along with other centralizing devices, eliminate the ward system of representation. The association's drive for charter reform was popular, and soon a broad spectrum of opinion—most of the city's newspapers, the central labor union, plus a large number of civic associations—teamed with the citizen's association in its effort to centralize the city's government. While most of the organized and articulate groups in the city favored a general tightening up of the city's loose and fragmented governmental infrastructure, this mixed coalition of reformers had difficulty agreeing on all of the details. While most agreed that the public works functions of the city should be centralized into one department, they could not, for example, agree on just how much centralization should occur in the board of education.[6] Most controversial of all and the issue on which the large, broadly-based procharter coalition came apart, was the civic association's demand that the unicameral, ward-based board of aldermen be replaced with a single system of councilmen elected by the city at large.

Partisanship had little to do with one's position on this subject. Affirmative and oppositional positions could be found among all of the city's diversified interest groups. The majority, however, opposed it. At the turn of the century, both Democratic and Republican newspapers, small business groups, the central labor union, in addition to strongly entrenched local political leaders, all opposed this drastic and radical proposal for a unicameral system of at-large representation. So great, in fact, was the opposition that the civic association, fearing for its whole reform package, dropped its demand and instead endorsed a compromise bicameral system. In the final version of the new charter of 1892, there was a twenty-five member board of aldermen elected by the wards and a separate council elected at large. Under this arrangement, legislation still originated in the board of aldermen, but the council now acted as a check upon it, providing time and scrutiny before a measure could become law.

The final version of the charter of 1892 with its provisions for a strengthened mayor, an appointed commissioner of public works, and its bicameral legislature, was greeted by practically everyone as a reform that was long overdue. Most everybody agreed with the sentiments of the Buffalo *Evening News:*

There has long been a widespread and growing dissatisfaction with the complexity and cumbrousness of our unwieldy city government. The aldermanic system has long been adjudged a failure. Graft and corruption have been repeatedly charged and not infrequently exposed. The organization of our municipal government has been such as to encourage inefficiency and corruption—decentralized, irresponsible, with divided powers and responsibility, innumerable elected officials with the dissipation of elective control, its factional jealousies and its invitation to corporate interference and control—all have been characteristics which have resulted from the ward system.

Even John Sheehan, the prototypical Irish ward boss, a powerful influence both in Buffalo and Albany, supported the compromise charter and in the spring of 1892, it was passed and signed into law.

The citywide, procharter consensus was not duplicated in Black Rock, where opinion was sharply divided. On the one hand, there was the businessmen's association which joined the procharter bandwagon and sent a representative with the rest of the city's delegation that was traveling to Albany to witness the governor sign the bill into law. Flouting the dictates of neighborhood self-interest, the members of the association—perhaps because they wanted to avoid Black Rock's historical stigma as a place distant and therefore different from the metropolitan mainstream, or perhaps because as businessmen they genuinely believed the rhetoric of business and efficiency bandied about by the reformers, or perhaps because they genuinely believed, like the great majority of the citizenry, that at-large representation was good for the city—once again broke with Tovey.

Tovey obviously had different ideas, and while he most certainly had objections to the whole drift of the charter, he saved his most vituperative comments for the provision for councilmen-at-large. He could not in good faith support any tampering with the system of ward representation. It was, he said, "an offense to good government and to all that intelligent people in Black Rock hold sacred." The charter was, he wrote, an "unjustified and ominous infringement on the home rule privileges of both the City of Buffalo and Black Rock." He was polemical on the erosion of ward-based political power: "Finally and most strenuously we oppose the Charter because of the provision for councilmen-at-large. This constitutes a direct attack on the principles of local government. It is a serious infringement and a dangerous assault on the system of popular government and an injury to all representative institutions."

Tovey in his opposition objected to political centralization for basically the same reason that he had earlier objected to the centralizing tendencies that resulted from the construction of the streetcar. As his reference to "home rule" for Black Rock indicates, Tovey had come to view the neighborhood, his neighborhood at least, and perhaps even neighborhoods in general, as more than a simple gemeinschaft community but rather as a political entity capable of and entitled to substantial political power.

The struggle over the charter of 1892, which, as it would subsequently develop, was merely a dry-run of the far more bitter battle that would be fought over the commission charter in 1914, reflected many of the processes of change that were at work in the late nineteenth-century city. In her thoughtful and extensively researched book on turn-of-the-century Buffalo, Brenda Shelton, like many contemporary social historians working in other cities, has argued that the reformers' efforts to centralize the city's political structure was simply another round in the continued class war between working-class immigrants and a politically and socially embattled Anglo-Saxon aristocracy. While there may well have been elements of this, the breadth of the procharter consensus suggests that other factors were equally if not more important in the struggles over governmental reform. The fact of the matter, and something that should not be forgotten when we think about the nineteenth-century reform efforts to centralize city governments, is that since the middle of the nineteenth century there have been virtually no change in the city's political system despite the enormity of the changes wrought by urbanization. Thus, despite the emergence of downtown as the focal point of a steadily expanding metropolitan order, the city's neighborhoods, like urban rotten boroughs, had managed to cling to their antiquated political power. And while class interests and conflicts may well have motivated some of the more aristocratic reformers in their efforts to snatch power away from the predominantly working-class neighborhoods and wards, it must be noted that these reformers, who were not an elite but rather a broad and diversified coalition, were more probably united by a desire to create a political system that reflected the centralizing economic and structural developments that had reshaped the metropolis by the end of the nineteenth century. The emergence of downtown, then, and the rise of newer outlying residential neighborhoods made possible by the rapid spread of the electric streetcar, had begun to produce a tilt in metropolitan life away from the neighborhoods. A political change, like the one proposed in the charter of 1892 which, on the one hand, centralized political power while, on the other, dispersing it throughout the city, was a natural and inevitable development given the changes that had occurred in the rest of the fabric of urban life.

Despite the fact that Tovey's views were out of step and directly at odds with what was considered to be progressive thinking in turn-of-the-century Buffalo, the fact of the matter is that his views of neighborhood political power and of neighborhood life in general were more in tune with the realities of life in Black Rock. Notwithstanding the accelerating forces of urbanization and industrialization, the structure of community life in Black Rock remained essentially preindustrial. The population of the community had increased—1,400 in 1855, 1,750 in 1866, 2,200 in 1875, 3,170 in 1892, 3,620 in 1905—but there had been no demographic upheavals within the neighborhood.[7] There had been a huge influx of Poles into the industrial community east of Black Rock, but it was well-contained on the other side of the grade-level railroad tracks and therefore remained separate and apart from Black Rock. These same grade-level railroads tended to protect Black Rock from the disorienting impact of industrialization. Secure behind its borders, Black Rock enjoyed the advantages of industrialization, such as jobs within walking distance, but suffered few of its disruptions.

Similarly, the cohesiveness of Black Rock's spatial structure reinforced the localistic vision that continued to prevail here into the twentieth century. As a result of the constriction of neighborhood space—remember, Black Rock was sandwiched in between the Niagara River in the west, the Scajaquada Creek in the south and grade-level railroads in both east and north—there was an intense competition for land use, which produced an overlap and interaction of neighborhood activities that makes contemporary urbanites envious.

Within this narrow neighborhood space, local social life blossomed despite the lures of a modern entertainment center downtown. Every tavern continued to serve as the headquarters for at least one social group, and everybody seemed to belong to several. The obituary of one Black Rock storeowner reveals membership in the Black Rock Cycle Club, the Occidental Lodge of the Free Masons, the Black Rock Lodge of the International Order of Foresters, the Rock Circle of the Protected

Home Circle, the Black Rock Lodge of the Deutscher Harugari, and the St. Francis Xavier Catholic Mutual Benefit Association. In addition to these groups, the Black Rock Savings and Loan Association had been formed in 1892 by a group of local businessmen and skilled laborers who felt the need, despite the sudden availability of downtown banking facilities, for a neighborhood-owned and -operated bank.

While in many ways, then, Black Rock remained remarkably unaffected by the advent of metropolitanization, the events of the 1890s made it clear that it was just a question of time before the neighborhood would be engulfed by the metropolitan age. The impact of the electric street-car, the rise of new outlying residential areas, and the creation of a compelling downtown central business district began a drain on the older neighborhoods that has only accelerated in our own day. Similarly, the gradual erosion of the ward system of government beginning with the charter of 1892 and ending with the establishment of commission government in 1916, denied the separate neighborhood communities the political power that had, for so long, been essential to their strength and stability.

These technological, economic, and political developments affected not only the structure of the city, but also its image. For a long time, the fractionalized, multinucleated structure of that city had made impossible the creation of a common image of the city. The vision of the pre-metropolitan American city, like its structure, was oriented toward the separate neighborhood communities and not toward the city as a whole. This, too, had begun to change at the turn of the century as a growing number of people, both downtown and within the neighborhoods, began to conceive of the city as a linked, integral, and unified entity.

These changes in the structure as well as the image of the city were not taken for granted by the city's residents but were rather, as the struggles between Black Rock and Mayor Becker suggest, hotly debated. Politicians, journalists, and common citizens discussed this issue among themselves, clearly and consciously trying to come to terms with the forces that were changing the structure of their city. By the early twentieth century, the question had become increasingly theoretical. For by then, the patterns had been set and the future was clear. The neighborhood as it had existed throughout most of the nineteenth century was dying.

2

NEIGHBORHOOD GROUPS

Ethnic neighborhoods have appeared throughout urban America. Developing during the immigration period, they persist in today's cities in varying degrees.

Often located in slum areas during the early period of migration, the ethnic neighborhood or ghetto did not always furnish decent housing, sanitation, or other amenities. Native contemporaries of the immigrants could not understand the attraction of the ethnic neighborhoods and often asked why their residents did not move into rural areas of America rather than crowd into certain parts of the city. However, the ghettos offered much to their inhabitants. They provided a way of adjusting to the New World while remaining somewhat within the Old World culture. These neighborhoods were places where the native language, whether it was German, Italian, or Yiddish, could be heard, the familiar foods of the old country could be bought, and the group's cultural and religious life could flourish. It was also a place where employment could be found. Since few neighborhoods contained only one group, these areas also became places to meet and interact with people of other cultural backgrounds—an interaction that sometimes led to conflict.

In the two selections in this chapter, the establishment of and migration patterns within the ethnic neighborhoods are discussed.

Concentrating on Philadelphia's Polish community, Caroline Golab examines the formation and location of their ethnic enclaves, stressing economic, demographic, and cultural factors. It was place of work which determined where in the city the Poles would settle, for they wanted to be within walking distance of their jobs. The clustering within these settlements and their persistence over time were the result of cultural needs—the desire of these network people to live within a social-emotional community. Golab makes an important distinction between community and neighborhood. Philadelphia's neighborhoods, as in other cities, were rarely ethnically homogeneous areas; rather, they contained many groups, including Jews, Irish, Germans, Italians, blacks, and others. How these groups interacted within the same neighborhood is another aspect of Golab's essay. That many ethnic communities could live within the same neighborhood, often having little to do with each other, explains to some extent the ability of diverse peoples to coexist. Yet conflict did sometimes occur, mainly between already established neighborhood groups and those migrating into the area.

Neighborhood invasion and succession are discussed in the second selection. Ronald H. Bayor examines three New York City neighborhoods (West and East Harlem, Washington Heights) during periods of in-migration and notes the reaction among the area's Jews, Italians, blacks, Irish, and Puerto Ricans. Looking at these three ethnic neighborhoods as case studies with which to test earlier neighborhood succession theories, Bayor presents a more complex model. The movement of an ethnic group into an area inhabited by others did not always produce a simple invasion–conflict–recession–reorganization pattern. For example, recession or out-migration of the original group could take place either many years after the invasion–conflict stage, as occurred in Italian East Harlem, or not at all, as in Washington Heights. The variables that slowed or changed the pattern are discussed.

THE GEOGRAPHY OF NEIGHBORHOOD
CAROLINE GOLAB

One of the notably outstanding features is that in the Port Richmond section we have people of many different old world extractions, truly typical of cosmopolitan America. They live quietly, peacefully and happily with each other.

One fact that has often been commented upon is the location of the Polish-American, Irish-American and German-American Roman Catholic churches on one of the main thoroughfares, East Allegheny Avenue—all within a distance of three blocks.

Philadelphia *Bulletin*

The same combination of economic, demographic, and cultural factors that influenced immigrant distribution across North America also determined the geographic arrangement of immigrant peoples within specific areas and cities. The forces that drew the immigrants out of their home areas in Europe—making them migrant-workers of the Atlantic Economy, attracting many of them across the ocean to the United States, and sending those directly to the industrial core—also affected their settlement in the places where they finally found work.

Avoiding the West and South, immigrant groups chose different destinations in the large industrial centers of the North and Midwest. As we have noted, the Poles went to Chicago, Cleveland, Milwaukee, Buffalo, Detroit,

Reprinted by permission of the publishers from *Immigrant Destinations,* pp. 111–13, 116–20, 122–23, 129–33, 156, by Caroline Golab, Philadelphia: Temple University Press. Copyright © 1977 by Temple University.

and the parts of Pennsylvania outside Philadelphia. Eastern European Jews stayed in the older seaport cities of New York, Philadelphia, Boston, and Baltimore; less than 10% of them ventured inland. The Italians also chose the large eastern seaport cities as well as smaller ones in New Jersey, New York, central and northeastern Pennsylvania. Once in a city, immigrants did not scatter randomly around the urban landscape. Their ultimate destination was (or became) a particular ethnic neighborhood.

Thus, the final result of immigrant distribution was the ethnic neighborhood or, as Anglo-Americans called it, "the ethnic ghetto." The formation and location of the ethnic neighborhood followed certain laws. Rather than being the forced creation of a racist or nativist society, the immigrant ghetto grew logically out of the special cultural needs of southern and eastern European peoples and the particular economic structure that they encountered in America. Furthermore, the immigrant neighborhood showed patterns and characteristics that belied the traditional image of the stagnant, homogeneous ghetto. The immigrant neighborhood was never that.

PATTERNS OF DISTRIBUTION

Polish settlement in Philadelphia showed the following patterns and characteristics, which also illuminate the experience of other groups.

1. Polish settlement in Philadelphia was highly decentralized; Poles did not confine themselves to one or even to two sections of the city but settled in at least twelve distinct areas. Their dispersion, however, was a group rather than an individual matter; only 65 of 4,464 Polish persons listed in the 1915 *City Directory* could not be placed in one of these twelve enclaves.

2. Although their settlement was decentralized, their concentration within each neighborhood was intense. The Poles formed twelve highly compact clusters, settling as close to each other as possible in each location. If Poles were the dominant or largest group in the area, they often occupied most of the houses on a street, block after block. Larger clusters tended to have a definite center, a point where concentration was greatest.

3. Although they may have been the dominant group in an area (as in Port Richmond or Bridesburg), at no time did the Poles monopolize the entire physical area of a neighborhood. The relative smallness of the Polish population may have accounted for this lack of monopoly, but closer examination reveals that the same pattern held for the city's

Jews and Italians, groups that, by any standard, were very large. No immigrant group in the city ever totally monopolized a particular neighborhood to the extent that it achieved isolation from members of other groups.

4. The urban *neighborhood,* defined here as a physical or geographical entity with specific (subjective) boundaries, was always shared by two or more groups; or, to be more accurate, by three or four or more groups. Each group constituted its own *community* or network of social-emotional relationships. The urban neighborhoods we are examining always housed, or were composed of, several ethnic communities or social-emotional networks. *Neighborhood* and *community* were never synonymous. Diverse peoples shared the same city-space, but proximity did not lead them as a matter of course to interact with one another at the social or emotional level; rather, each group kept to its own network of affective structures. The distinction between neighborhood and community is critical, for it explains how neighborhoods could physically integrate diverse cultures and yet be "provincial" and "isolated" places. The provinciality and isolation of the immigrant resulted not from physical or spatial segregation but from the effectiveness of the many separate community networks, none of which needed or wanted to interact at the social or emotional level.

5. Unlike the bulk of Jewish or Italian settlements, most Polish settlements were not located in the oldest sections of the city, the slum areas traditionally associated with immigrants as their port-of-entry. Poles in Philadelphia tended to settle in newer or frontier sections characterized by open spaces and fluidity and newness of physical structures.

6. Each Polish settlement directly reflected the industrial structure of the neighborhood or area in which it was located. It was the availability of work that determined the location of the Polish colony, for the Poles were invariably employed in the neighborhoods where they resided.

7. Each Polish settlement had a great amount of population turnover. It was not unusual for a settlement to experience a turnover of 75% to 80% of its inhabitants in the course of a single year. This extreme mobility was most characteristic of the unskilled.

8. In light of such high population turnover, the formation and persistence of Polish communities within neighborhoods depended on (a) the establishment of an infrastructure of specifically Polish institutions such as parish, church, school, newspaper, beneficial and fraternal associations; and (b) enough occupational stratification so that a cadre of professional and self-employed persons were permanently present to provide structure and leadership for the transient members of the group.

9. For the Poles, marriage, the presence of women and children, and the ability to own a house were the most effective brakes on population turnover and were also the greatest incentives to create permanent community institutions such as church, school, newspapers, associations, and so on.

10. From the Poles' perspective, the neighborhood was a self-contained entity able to satisfy all the community's needs, physical, spiritual, social, economic and emotional; its members walked to work, to church, to school, to shops and services; they were born at home, and in some neighborhoods they were even carried to the cemetery. Poles had no reason to venture beyond the neighborhood, and in this sense they were indeed very provincial persons. To them, the neighborhood was the reality and the city an abstraction. If anything, the city was a confederation of many neighborhoods—how many they couldn't be sure—each of which, just like their own, sheltered many communities. Even when they traveled from Polish neighborhood to Polish neighborhood across the American continent in search of work, they remained provincial people, for their needs were taken care of by the new neighborhood and the Polish community within that neighborhood.

THE LOCATION OF IMMIGRANT NEIGHBORHOODS

Decentralized but highly clustered patterns of urban settlement were characteristic not only of the Poles but of all the newer immigrant peoples who settled in Philadelphia between 1880 and 1920. The three largest eastern European Jewish settlements, for example, were in South Philadelphia, the Northern Liberties and Port Richmond, but there were others of substantial size in Frankford, Nicetown, Southwest and West Philadelphia. The Ukrainians had settlements in South Philadelphia, the Northern Liberties, Port Richmond, Fairmount, Nicetown and Frankford. The Slovaks had colonies in South Philadelphia, the Northern Liberties, Nicetown, Kensington and Port Richmond.

Although the vast majority of Philadelphia's Italians lived in that part of South Philadelphia directly adjacent to Center City, it is unfair to speak of South Philadelphia as if it held only Italians or only one Italian colony. Rather, South Philadelphia housed innumerable Italian colonies, each separated by seas and bands of Irish, Germans, Jews, blacks, British and Anglo-Americans. Oftentimes, these colonies had very specific origins: a man was not just from Italy, but from Sicily, or Calabria, or Abruzzi or Campania. Althouth most Italian colonies, like most Jewish colonies, were located in the central city, there were also smaller Italian settlements in Frankford, Port Richmond. Manayunk, Nicetown, Germantown, Chestnut Hill, Southwest Philadelphia, Greys Ferry, the Northern Liberties and West Philadelphia.

The factor most responsible for the location of immigrant settlements was work. Work brought the immigrant and the neighborhood together because it was an essential part of both experiences. The immigrant was defined by the work he performed: he came to America in search of work and livelihood but with definite preferences for certain types of work and aversions to others, as the discussion of Poles, Italians, and Jews has already shown. Work was also important in structuring the city. Most of Philadelphia's factories and industries were located where they were because of their age and type of activity. Philadelphia, it must be remembered, established its industrial structure as early as the eighteenth century, before the coming of full scale industrialization. By 1880 the city's urban core had experienced great concentration of streets, buildings and general land use as well as a general escalation in land values. Newer industries employing the latest technology and mechanization, requiring enormous transportation facilities and seeking to achieve economies of scale through bigness of operations were forced to locate on the urban frontier. Steel plants such as Midvale or Disston's, with Bessemer converters, open hearth furnaces, and coking ovens requiring tons of coal and iron ore and hence miles of railroad trackage, had to locate away from congested areas of the central city; they located in Nicetown and Port Richmond. The same was true of new oil refineries, slaughterhouses, chemical plants, and tanneries that needed large amounts of land on the riverfront (water was a cleanser, coolant, and conduit for industrial waste), and access to railroad facilities in order to bring in raw materials and send out finished products.

Certain industries and factories epitomized the work of a particular area and thus the type of labor that would be attracted by its presence. For the Poles, these industries and factories were usually primary and basic ones. In Bridesburg/Frankford their chief employers were metal, chemical, glass, rubber, and leather factories: Henry Disston and Sons, the famous saw and file maker who also manufactured its own steel; William and Harvey Rowland, manufacturers of carriage springs; American Fork and Hoe Company, manufacturers of farm tools; Miller Lock Company; Carver File Company; Fayette R. Plumb, a major tool works; Charles Lennig and Company, which became Rohm and Haas Chemical Company in 1920; Barrett Manufacturing Company, makers of coal tar products and roofing materials; Gillender and Sons, glass manufacturers; Quaker City Rubber Company; Robert H. Foerderer, leather and glue makers;

and the Edwin H. Fitler Rope Company. All these establishments had large plants, labor requirements, transportation needs, and capital. All used the latest technologies or machinery; all employed substantial numbers of unskilled male laborers.

In Port Richmond there was a similar diversity of industries—metals, chemicals, glass, lumber, leather, and textiles as well as railroads and shipping on a massive scale. Among the more popular employers of Poles were David Lupton Sons, manufacturers of metal cornices and sheet metal products; Williamson and Bros., engine builders and machinists; Hero Manufacturing Company, makers of aluminum, brass and bronze products; William Cramp and Sons, ship and engine building company; H. W. Butterworth and Sons, manufacturers of textile machinery; Baeder, Adamson and Company, glue and gelatin makers; Berg Company, manufacturers of fertilizers, grease and tallow; John T. Lewis and Bros., manufacturers of lead, linseed oil, paints and varnishes; M. L. Shoemaker and Company, makers of fertilizers; Gill and Company, makers of glass and lamps; Atlantic Oil Refining Company; Dill and Collins Company, paper mill; McNeely, Price, and Brooks, glazed kid manufacturers; Schlicter Jute and Cordage Company; the Philadelphia and Reading and Pennsylvania Railroads, complete with coal yards and terminals.

Nicetown owed its existence to the Midvale Steel Company, manufacturers of automobile and battleship steel and military ordnance. Edwin G. Budd Manufacturing Company, auto manufacturers; Link Belt Company, machinery and parts manufacturers; Niles, Bemont, Pond Company, crane manufacturers; Davis Spike Works; American Pulley Company; Blabon Oil Cloth and Linoleum Works. Felin Slaughterhouse; Emil Wahl Button Manufacturers and several railroad and coal companies were also large establishments employing unskilled Polish laborers.

In Manayunk, also, metal manufacture was primarily responsible for the Polish presence. Here it was the incomparable Pencoyd Iron Works, bridge makers to the world.

In Southwest Philadelphia and Greys Ferry, an abundance of chemical refineries and abattoirs hugging the Schuylkill River and the nation's major streetcar builder, J. B. Brill, were the chief employers of Polish labor. The Greys Ferry area was also a large river entrepôt for supplies of coal, lumber, iron, and steel coming from upstate Pennsylvania; there Poles often served as stevedores and traffic handlers.

In South Philadelphia the major industries employing Poles were sugar and oil refining, and shipping; in the latter industry Poles were stevedores and longshoremen.

In Fairmount and the Northern Liberties the chief employer was overwhelmingly the enormous Baldwin Locomotive Works, but there were also bakeries, breweries and miscellaneous leather and metal manufacturers. In Kensington textile companies predominated—John B. Stetson Company, the famous hat maker and John Bromley and Sons, rug makers—but various leather and metal manufacturers also employed Polish labor.

The factories that were the main employers of Poles tended to be the newest and largest ones in Philadelphia, utilizing the latest in industrialized technologies and requiring ample room for plant and transportation facilities. They were usually located in the newer or less settled areas of the city—Nicetown, Port Richmond, Bridesburg, Southwest Philadelphia, and Northwest Philadelphia (Manayunk). If the Pole was not employed by a factory-type industry, he was employed by another that had just as precise a location—the shipping industry of South Philadelphia, Port Richmond, and Greys Ferry.

In the early industrial city, it was imperative that workers reside as close as possible to their place of work. Walking was more than accepted; often it was the only way to get to work. While taking the trolley was technically possible, commuting to work cost both time and money. This was especially important to the unskilled workers, who, it appears, worked longer hours per day (twelve or more) and also earned less. For the unskilled Polish worker, living in America temporarily and for the express purpose of earning as much as possible, spending money to commute was never given a first, let alone a second, thought. The time required by commuting could be spent in more profitable ways, including sleeping. The need and the desire was to work as many hours as possible and to save as much money as possible. The intense spatial agglomeration or clustering of immigrant workers was very much a result of their need to live within walking distance of their places of work. As Edward E. Pratt observed in 1911, "the problem of congestion of population . . . seems to be closely linked with that of congestion of industries."

Not all of Philadelphia's work, however, had a precise place of performance. Where the location of work was ubiquitous or constantly changing or where its sources of supply were significantly diffused, there was a greater need for laborers to settle in central locations. Italian workers, for example, were most often employed in public works construction, street paving, street cleaning, street railway construction and maintenance, or as independent artisans and truck farm laborers. Any of these activities could take them anywhere in the city and possibly beyond. Italians consequently were more likely to settle in the central city than along its fringes. Indeed, this appears to have been the preferred pattern for Italian settlement in any large northern city during this period. Here it is helpful to think of the city as an enclosed circle. The worker who lives close to the center can reach all areas of the circle, including its periphery, with equal ease. Someone who lives on the circumference of the circle, however, can reach only points in his own quarter with such ease. Central location meant access to a wider work area.

There were other activities that, because they served a scattered or decentralized market, also required a central location—meat and produce marketing; wholesaling and retailing of furniture, clothing, and so on. Once again, it is no coincidence that Philadelphia's Jews and Italians settled in central parts of the city next to the major wholesale and retail markets that employed them in large numbers. For the Jews in particular, the availability of store lofts and warehouse space, sufficiently concentrated for easy distribution of tons of textile materials and the subsequent retrieval of finished products, contributed to the existence of a vast garment industry in the central part of the city.

The rule, then, is that if work had to be performed in specific locations, immigrants formed their colonies near to their work. If work to be performed was ubiquitous or served diffused markets and suppliers, immigrants formed colonies in central locations of the city. Thus, Philadelphia's Poles had no need to seek central locations as did the Italians and Jews. Rather, they settled in newer, outlying areas of the city where specific work opportunities existed for them: factory labor employing large numbers of unskilled men. In fact, all Polish settlements were in areas annexed to the city after 1850, and only three were in areas directly adjacent to the central or original city.

THE CULTURAL IMPERATIVES OF CLUSTERING

The need to reside as close as possible to their places of work may have been the chief factor determining the location of immigrant settlements within the city, but it does not fully explain the intense clustering within each settlement.

In clustering tightly together in America's cities, the immigrants of southern and eastern Europe were doing what came naturally. It could even be argued that had America in 1900 been a blank slate, devoid of all physical as well as social and economic structures, southern and eastern Europeans would still have chosen to cluster tightly because of the social imperatives of their cultural systems. The peoples of southern and eastern Europe had a very different sense of society and personal identity from those of northern and western Europe—and hence from the bulk of Americans. Southern and eastern Europeans were "network" peoples. Their identity, security, self-control, and stimulation derived not just from their membership in a group but in a group that they could see, hear, touch, and smell at all times. They could not function without the constant presence of the group because a person became an individual only by belonging to and interacting within a group. The group provided mechanisms for social control and determined codes of personal behavior. For the Poles, who placed great importance on personal status within the group, status could be defined only by interacting with other Poles. Interacting with Italians, Irish, Jews, or Anglo-Americans had no meaning; it was irrelevant. Agglomerated and highly clustered settlement, therefore, was essential. Indeed, in an age before telephones, automobiles, radio, and television, such settlement was automatic: the world of network people, whether in the village of the Old Country or in the neighborhood of the New, was a walking world, highly dependent on oral, visual, and personal interaction.

Southern and eastern Europeans had been close-knit villagers for more than a millenium. Their agglomerated village system embodied the unseen social and emotional networks of the culture. Unlike their northern European and American counterparts, they had never lived on isolated or separately enclosed farms, a concept which had no meaning in their social systems. Lacking the internal capacity for identity, self-control, and stimulation that characterized their Scandinavian and British predecessors, Poles and Italians were not cut out to be lone pioneers on the Great Plains; never could they exist on isolated farms far from others. Poles and Italians succeeded as farmers in America only when they were able to settle on the land *en masse,* bringing their networks with them. Poles moved into farms of the Connecticut Valley and Italians established vineyards and truck farms in California, but only because they settled as groups. In thus forming clusters, "ghettoes" or ethnic neighborhoods, southern and eastern Europeans were attempting to recreate the network pattern of the village, something that, ironic as it may seem, was easy to do on the streets of urban America but hard to do on America's farms and open spaces.

THE NEIGHBORHOOD'S COMMUNITIES

The capacity for community, for forming social and emotional networks, was ingrained in the peoples of southern and eastern Europe. They carried this compulsion for creating community with them wherever they settled in America. It was only a matter of time before they gave more formal and visual expression to their communities by establishing parishes, churches, synagogues, schools, newspapers, fraternal and beneficial associations. The visible setting for those institutions was, of course, the neighborhood. As we have observed, neighborhood, at least in Philadelphia, never became coterminous with a single community. Philadelphia's neighborhoods contained a multiplicity of communities or social-emotional networks. One immigrant group sometimes dominated an area, that is, was the largest single group present, but no group ever monopolized an area or lived totally apart from members of other groups.

Port Richmond—or Bridesburg, Fairmount, Southwark, Greys Ferry, Nicetown (it doesn't matter which Philadelphia neighborhood is examined)—was recognized as a neighborhood with definable boundaries by all the area's inhabitants, but these inhabitants made up at least ten separate communities, each with its effective and acknowledged social-emotional boundaries, and each with its institutions of churches, schools, newspapers, and associational or recreational patterns. These communities were defined by ethnicity, race, religion, and social status. Port Richmond supported five Roman Catholic churches and parishes, four of which were organized along "nationality" lines—Polish, Lithuanian, German and Italian—and one that was the territorial or "Irish" church. There was also a Jewish synagogue and at least a half-dozen churches representing Episcopalians, Presbyterians, Methodists, and Baptists, both black and white. As illustrated by the accompanying maps, these religious institutions were often very close to one another—across the street, next door, or down the block. This pattern, observable in any neighborhood in Philadelphia during the period, persisted until at least the Second World War. The only variations were in the number and variety of community networks contained within each neighborhood.

Given the way neighborhoods were settled—in waves and layers—cultural and structural homogeneity was virtually impossible. When Poles, Italians, and eastern European Jews arrived in the late nineteenth and early twentieth centuries, they found a typical Philadelphia neighborhood inhabited by some combination of Anglo-Americans, Irish and German Catholics, German Jews, German Lutherans, Welshmen, Englishmen, and, in many instances, a few blacks. Each of these groups formed its own network or community. They all coexisted, though with very little interaction at the social and emotional levels—between Irish Catholics and American Protestants for example; or German Jews and American Protestants; or American Baptists and American Episcopalians; or white American Baptists and black American Baptists.

When Poles, Italians and Jews moved in, each carrying with them their implicit sense of community, they merely added to the number of structures and networks already present. They did not enter into or identify with any of the structures or networks already established. Poles, Italians, Jews, Irish, Germans, Anglo-Americans, and blacks shared the same space and identified with the same neighborhood, but they did not, as a result, feel impelled to interact socially or emotionally. Indeed, the separate cultural or ethnic networks, each with intangible boundaries eventually embodied in formal institutions, were what enabled such diverse peoples to live together as successfully as they did—for conflict was always possible.

Neighborhood conflict invariably occurred between old-established groups and newer ones moving in on top of them—the sort of successive arrival best illustrated by Irish and German opposition to Poles, Italians, and Jews, or German Jewish opposition to their "poor cousins" from eastern Europe. Conflict rarely occurred among groups that came to an area simultaneously, as illustrated by the lack of conflict among Italians, Jews, and Poles who happened to enter a neighborhood approximately at the same time.

When new groups with latent networks and institutions moved into an area already inhabited by groups with matured institutions and networks, it appears that conflict between newcomers and older residents was normal until a new balance was worked out. It was always more difficult for a new group to move into areas with established structures and values, especially if that group's values and structures differed greatly from existing ones. Groups arriving simultaneously engaged in little or no conflict at the neighborhood level because each faced the same problems and confronted the same existing structures and institutions. Each intent on making the new neighborhood meet its implicit requirements, the new groups found themselves in confrontation with previously established groups rather than with each other. To the "insiders," there was little difference between Poles and Jews and Italians; they were all "outsiders" trying to get in. The outsiders, consequently, had little time to compete with one another, as their chief preoccupation was with the insiders—the Irish, Germans, and Anglo-Americans who had preceded them in the neighborhood.

The Poles shared specific relationships with the other groups in their neighborhood, with those who were there before them, primarily the Irish and Germans, and those who arrived with them, Jews, other Slavs, and Italians. In 1870 the Germans were one of Philadelphia's largest immigrant groups, second in number only to the Irish. Because of the Germans, Poles from Poznań, Silesia, and West Prussia were able to make inroads within the city and form the kernel of future Polish settlements. German language skills and contacts enabled them to find housing with German landlords and to secure jobs with German employers, especially in sugar and oil refineries and chemical and textile plants. The first Polish colonies in Philadelphia put down roots among the Germans of Southwark, the Northern Liberties, Bridesburg, and Manayunk. These first Poles attended local German Catholic churches until they were ready to form parishes of their own; this was the case in South Philadelphia, Port Richmond, Bridesburg, Kensington, and the Northern Liberties.

Relations between Poles and Germans, however, were usually neither cordial nor even peaceful. Conflict within the neighborhood over housing and church use was common. Encouraged to emigrate because of Bismarck's *Kulturkampf,* Prussian Poles were not well disposed toward their German neighbors. Discrimination against them by German landlords and employers appeared as the American version of the *Kulturkampf.* Because of such discrimination, Philadelphia's Poles were often compelled to pass themselves off as Germans (as they had done in Germany) in order to find jobs, to secure lodgings or to buy land to build a church. The record of Polish-German interaction in Buffalo, Milwaukee, and Chicago reveals the same kind of tensions.

In varying degrees, the Irish were present in every neighborhood where the Poles settled. In fact, the Poles often associated the Irish and Irish ways with being American—a perfect illustration of the efforts of successive v. simultaneous arrival in a neighborhood, for never did the Poles mistake Italians or Jews for "Americans." Although they shared the same neighborhoods and often worked in the same factories or industries (where the Irishman frequently was the Pole's "boss"), it was the Church that remained the greatest scene of Polish-Irish interaction and conflict; the official territorial parish of each neighborhood was invariably controlled by the Irish.

While Roman Catholicism may have appeared monolithic to other religious bodies, the immigrants realized only too well that each group had its unique historical relationship to the Church as well as its own cultural style. As in Ireland, the Church in Poland was responsible for holding together a besieged and divided nation and preserving its language, literature and culture. The Poles, consequently, identified strongly with their Church and could not conceive of letting a foreign element represent them in it or exercise control over it. A local parish without a Polish priest, or a church hierarchy containing only Irishmen, was an abomination.

This clash of cultural needs and preconceptions was not fully appreciated nor articulated as such at the time. The Irish version of Roman Catholicism was permeated with puritanical Jansenism while the Polish form was not. The Irish God was a God of unremitting justice and eternal punishment; God the Almighty Father was the archetypal representative. The Polish God was a God of forgiveness and mercy; and the Blessed Virgin Mary softened the sternness of the Father. Failure to perceive these differences as historical and cultural resulted in virtual battles between the Irish hierarchy and the Polish faithful. An Irish bishop remarked in 1903 that "it is well known that the Poles have a deep religious sense; that they are attached to their faith; that they are industrious, generous and courageous. But it is also evident that they are hot-tempered, as a rule, and their lack of familiarity with the ways of Americans renders them often suspicious, where there is otherwise no reason for distrust."

Although they were also Roman Catholic in faith, the Italians' attitude toward religion, especially that of the men, was extremely nonchalant, even indifferent. No bulwark of the Italian peasant, the Church in Italy had been a chief antagonist. The Irish established church schools to protect their children from the American or Protestant schools; the Poles established church schools to protect their children from both the Protestants and the Irish; the Italians, during their early years in Philadelphia, were content to send their children to the local public school. Only after the Second World War did "Americanized" or "Hibernicized" Italian-American Catholics begin to patronize parochial schools in increasing numbers.

Thus, although they often shared the same neighborhoods in the city, Italians and Poles largely avoided conflict because their social networks and institutions, established simultaneously, kept them sufficiently segregated. In the workplace there was also little cause for conflict because these two groups usually performed different types of work in different industries. Even in the same factory Polish and Italian workers had different jobs; at the gigantic Midvale Steel complex in North Philadelphia, for example, Poles were employed as furnace tenders, smelters, steel rollers, and general metalworkers, and Italians worked with railway cars, railway beds, coal, and slag.

Wherever Poles were found in the city, so were Ukrainians, Lithuanians, Russians, Slovaks, Croatians, Serbs, Slovenes, and Hungarians. Slavic peoples always settled near each other, often on the same streets or even in the same buildings, because they were drawn to the area by the same types of work and were employed in the same industries. The larger American world had great difficulty in differentiating the various Slavic peoples and tended to lump them together under a common name of "Slav," "Hunky," or "Polack." This was not entirely unjustified, at least from the outsider's point of view, since languages, although distinct, were not always mutually incomprehensible, and customs, manners, values, and religion were often the same.

In many instances, the proximity of Slavic settlements represented Old World relationships transplanted to the New. In Galicia and Russian Poland, Poles, Ukrainians, Lithuanians, Russians, Jews, and even Moslems and Tartars shared the same villages in much the same way that a myriad of peoples shared the same neighborhood in the American city. Through the course of centuries, these peoples had worked out a way of life in which they coexisted in a common space or village but yet went their separate ways; each, in other words, adhered to its own social network. The practice of sharing territory with a diversity of peoples followed the Poles to America. Coexistence was possible in both places precisely because unseen networks were recognized and respected.

The Poles' settlement patterns in relation to their Jewish contemporaries is the most interesting and lucid example of Old World traits transplanted; it is also a vivid illustration of adaptation to new circumstances by duplication of previous experience. Eastern European Jews had always lived in the midst of or adjacent to the Poles. In America, Galician Jews tended to settle near Poles from Galicia, Jews from Suwalki and Plock near Poles from Suwalki and Plock, Jews from Lublin near Poles from Lublin, and so on. This arrangement was not coincidental, for it occurred in every Polish settlement in Philadelphia and in every major city of the nation where Poles and Jews were found.

Although each group may have harbored misgivings about the other, there were positive elements which prompted them to become next-door neighbors. Louis Wirth in his classic study of Chicago Jewry noted of the Jews and Poles who lived together on Chicago's Northwest Side: "These two immigrant groups, having lived side by side in Poland and Galicia, are used to each other's business methods. They have accommodated themselves one to another, and this accommodation persists in America." The Chicago Jews opened shops on Milwaukee Avenue and Division Street "because they know that the Poles are the predominant population in these neighborhoods." In addition, "Poles come from all over the city to trade on Maxwell Street because they know that they can find the familiar stands owned by Jews." These same conditions prevailed in Philadelphia. Accustomed to Old World trade patterns, Jews and Poles soon reestablished them in every Polish neighborhood. Jewish settlements in Slavic areas were invariably linear and always extended along major arteries of commerce and transit. In Port Richmond Jewish merchants settled along Richmond Street; in Manayunk, along Cresson and Main Streets; in Fairmount, along Ridge Avenue; in Bridesburg and Frankford, along Frankford Avenue; in Nicetown, along Germantown and Hunting Park Avenues.

This tacit alliance between the two groups, however, was based on more than mutual toleration for the sake of commerce: language was important, and so were common experiences. "The Jews are versatile; they speak Yiddish among themselves, and Polish, Russian, Lithuanian, Hungarian, Bohemian and what not, to their customers." The Poles and Jews also shared a common country and could not help exchanging information concerning methods, routes and ultimate destinations. In most Polish provinces, especially those of Galicia and Russia, the Jews were the first to emigrate, often with government approval or encouragement. As forerunners, they paved the way for others, Jews and Gentiles alike. In later years, Jews and Poles sailed for America on the same ships.

Jews and Poles settled next to each other in the New World because the presence of the other was one of the few Old World realities that continued to make sense: Jews and Poles simply duplicated their age-old roles. By maintaining separate social networks and institutions, Poles and Jews were able to share the same neighborhoods quite peacefully; in these early years structural collision between the two groups was slight, if it occurred at all.

* * * * *

SUMMARY

The immigrant neighborhood was an institutionally complete and self-contained entity. The presence of congenial work was the impetus for its creation and location, for it was the need to reside as close as possible to the place of work that brought the immigrants to the neighborhood. If the work had precise locations, they settled next to it. If the work was ubiquitous, they settled in neighborhoods in central portions of the city; centrality of location gave them the greatest accessibility to jobs.

The creation of an institutional infrastructure in the form of churches, schools, newspapers and associations; the development of a cadre of professionals and self-employed persons to staff these institutions; the location of shops and services within the neighborhood; the development of a hierarchical relationship among the many immigrant neighborhoods in shops and services; and the "network" culture of the eastern and southern European immigrants themselves—all contributed to the self-sufficiency and provinciality of the neighborhood.

This self-sufficiency and provinciality extended beyond economic and commercial needs and encompassed social and emotional ones as well. Because the neighborhood was the physical locus for their system of social and emotional networks, immigrant workers identified with the neighborhood rather than with the city as a whole. The city remained an abstraction, the neighborhood was a reality. It was the neighborhood, not the city, which provided immigrants with their identity, security, and stimulation. Philadelphia, one of the nation's largest cities, was for them a very provincial place—not because of any geographic or physical isolation, but because of the networks that the immigrants themselves created.

THE NEIGHBORHOOD INVASION PATTERN
RONALD H. BAYOR

Urban neighborhoods in the United States, particularly in cities which were immigrant centers, have undergone periodic transformations of their populations. A number of social scientists have investigated population succession as it involves ethnic groups and ethnic neighborhoods in these cities and offered theories on the process involved. For example, Paul Frederick Cressey, writing about the ethnic residential shifts in Chicago during the 1898 to 1930 period, detailed a pattern of neighborhood succession which included invasion, conflict, recession, and reorganization. Invasion, according to Cressey's definition, involved the penetration by a new ethnic group into an area considered the domain of another. The result of invasion might be a gradual ethnic transition, or it could cause rapid abandonment of an area. Conflict could follow invasion, its intensity depending on the

cultural differences and prejudices of the groups involved. Where the groups are of a similar social and economic level with no particular dislike for each other, the supplanting of one group by another usually involves only a minimum of friction. But where marked prejudices exist and there is fear that the invading group will cause a serious loss in real estate values, violent opposition may develop.

The recession stage, which occurs because of the entrance of the unwanted new group, is the result of a decrease in the desirability of the

An original essay written for this volume. Please consult the bibliographic essay, part 1, for the sources used in this article.

area in the eyes of the older residents, and they begin to move out. The final stage is reorganization, in which the culture and institutions of the invading group become dominant in the new area. This is an ongoing process, and the invaders may someday face a challenge to their own dominance in the new neighborhood.

Cressey's conclusions have been supported by Richard Ford, who brought the Chicago study up to 1940, and by William F. Whyte, who investigated the Italian invasion of the Irish North End in Boston and noted widespread hostility between the two groups, particularly "along the advancing frontier of the Italian settlement, where sovereignty was still undecided." The struggle eventually came to an end with the recession stage when the Irish moved out. Humbert Nelli, however, in a book on the Italians in Chicago, questioned whether the succession process was as orderly and logical as previously stated. He found, for example, many individuals of the older group remaining in neighborhoods which had been taken over by a new group. "Ethnic colonies did not quickly, readily or willingly disintegrate." However, he agreed that the large scale invasion of a "new, different and unacceptable group . . . could eliminate the hard core of earlier inhabitants." The population succession pattern according to Nelli depended more on the groups involved than on the basic act of invasion. Besides these works, which center on the white ethnics, there is a large body of literature which concentrates on racial groups in an effort to understand white out-migration from areas experiencing black invasion.

The effort of this study will be to investigate the theory of neighborhood succession, as stated by Cressey and others, for New York City during the 1900 to 1940 period. In the process two questions will be considered. First, what happens when ethnic boundaries are crossed, and second, whether invasion is the only cause of neighborhood transition. The neighborhoods discussed include two which were dominated by a single ethnic group (West and East Harlem), and one which was mixed (Washington Heights). All reacted to the invasion sequence in some way. These were not the only communities which experienced invasion, but in terms of numbers and groups involved, the most notable.

At various times in New York's history, massive intracity migrations have occurred. Such a period were the decades of 1910 to 1930. On a borough-wide basis New York experienced great shifts in its population during these years. Manhattan, reaching a peak population of 2,331,500 in 1910, after years of steady growth, declined to 2,284,100 in 1920 and 1,867,300 in 1930 (a 19.1 percent decline from 1910 to 1930). The boroughs which seemed to attract this population were the Bronx, expanding from 431,000 in 1910 to 732,000 in 1920 and

1,265,300 in 1930 (a 193 percent increase from 1910 to 1930), Brooklyn, which went from 1,634,400 in 1910 to 2,018,400 in 1920 and 2,560,400 in 1930 (a 56.6 percent increase from 1910 to 1930), and Queens, expanding from 284,000 in 1910 to 469,000 in 1920 and 1,079,000 in 1930 (a 279.9 percent increase from 1910 to 1930). Within the general picture are more important trends. In Manhattan, although the general population declined 18.2 percent in the decade 1920–1930, the black population increased 105.9 percent (from 109,100 in 1920 to 224,700 in 1930). This increase was particularly important in relation to the expansion of the black area in Harlem.

Manhattan was also losing its foreign-born population. In the 1920–1930 decade a decrease of 279,700 foreign-born was noted (921,300 to 641,600, a 30.3 percent decline) while the Bronx, Brooklyn, and Queens registered large gains. By 1930, for the first time in the city's history, a majority of the foreign-born and second generation were living outside of Manhattan. The Bronx, for example, showed an increase in its Jewish population from 211,000 in 1918 to 420,000 in 1927 (a 99 percent increase). Brooklyn also noted a large Jewish influx which sent the Jewish population from 568,000 in 1918 to 732,000 in 1927 (a 28.9 percent increase). Manhattan's Jewish population meanwhile decreased by 33.2 percent in the same period (696,000 in 1918 to 465,000 in 1927). The Italians (foreign stock) also saw large increases in their numbers in the Bronx and Brooklyn as their Manhattan population decreased: in Manhattan they decreased from 356,100 in 1920 to 260,700 in 1930 (a 26.8 percent decrease). The Bronx Italian population increased from 83,600 in 1920 to 165,000 in 1930 (a 97.4 percent increase); Brooklyn's Italians jumped in number from 299,800 in 1920 to 487,300 in 1930 (a 62.5 percent increase). Queens and Richmond also showed increases. The same process could be observed in the older groups as the Irish and Germans also left Manhattan (the Irish showing a 36.2 percent decrease from 1920 to 1930, and the Germans decreasing 21.3 percent for the same period). For both groups the largest increases were in Queens. Borough-wide totals, however, are not really effective in relating the true shifts occurring. For this, the neighborhoods must be considered.

West Harlem and some parts of East Harlem (see map) represent communities which fit clearly into the invasion–succession process, as Cressey and others have stated. (West Harlem's boundaries are 159th Street on the north, 110th Street on the south, and 5th to 8th avenues. East Harlem takes in the area from East 99th Street and 3rd Avenue on the south, traveling west to 5th Avenue at 105th Street and running north to the Harlem River. The East River is the eastern boundary.) Here within the Jewish area there is invasion, conflict, and recession within a short

NEW YORK CITY, BOROUGH OF MANHATTAN
CENSUS TRACTS

space of time. Both areas have housed some of New York's largest ethnic groups. The expansion of the black and Puerto Rican communities into Jewish and Italian sections illustrates the variables involved in the response to invasion and the factors to be considered when studying neighborhood transition.

The population of West and East Harlem at the turn of the century was predominantly of German, Irish, and English ancestry and for the most part middle class. The southern portion of West Harlem and part of East Harlem, particularly the area from East 99th to 125th Street, Park to 8th Avenue, housed a large and growing Jewish community which had come to the area in the 1880 to 1920 period. The Jews, mainly of eastern European background, had moved up from the Lower East Side. By 1923 the Jews in West Harlem numbered 75,500 and were approximately 41.2 percent of the population in the area. Coming to Harlem at about the same time as the Jews were the blacks and the Italians.

The blacks had secured a foothold in the section surrounding 135th Street and 7th Avenue (tract 228) in an area with many luxury apartment houses. However, within this section overbuilding had occurred. Subway lines had not been completed on time, and apartment houses were left standing empty. Rather than have vacancies, some landlords began renting to blacks, who were anxious for decent housing. Whites in the neighborhood attempted to limit the black invasion through restrictive covenants, with the center of resistance coming from associations of landlords, representing either single blocks or entire neighborhoods, who agreed not to rent to blacks. This battle went on mainly between 1910 and 1915, a few years before the black community would expand into the Jewish and Italian sections. The covenants failed because of the inability of the whites to get total cooperation from all property owners in the area. Within a short time, after the blacks had made further gains, the white community reluctantly gave up and fled. However, there were hopes as late as 1931 that central West Harlem would become white again. *Harlem Magazine,* a publication of the all-white Harlem Board of Commerce, contained the statement that perhaps the opening of the Triborough Bridge and the new 8th Avenue subway line would make Harlem so attractive as a residential area that rents would go up and blacks would be forced to move away.

The black community in the central part of West Harlem continued to expand. Tract 228 was 77.2 percent black by 1920; tracts 214, 212, and 230 were all over 85 percent black by 1920. According to a 1934 Home Relief survey, the black population which moved into the outer zones of the black community was not the poorest of this group. The furthest point of expansion south for the blacks by 1920 was tract

208 (44 percent black). West 126th Street was the boundary line, although there was some penetration as far as 122nd Street with tract 222, 12.8 percent black. In the next southward tract, part of the Jewish section, tract 200, there was only a 1.2 percent black population. In tract 220 the blacks were only 1.3 percent of the population. Apparently, there were agreements among property owners to hold the line at this point. For example, in 1922 a protest was lodged against the landlord of a building at St. Nicholas Avenue and West 118th Street (tract 218) by the West Harlem Property Owners Association for opening the building to blacks. The landlord did so because he was able to get $100 rents for $40 apartments. This tract was 1 percent black in 1920; by 1930, after the failure of this type of pressure to keep the neighborhood white, the tract registered 40.9 percent black. Restrictive covenants among landlords and anti-black neighborhood protests had been tried in the wealthier section of central West Harlem, but they failed there and also failed in the poorer Jewish sections to the south.

Out-migration of the Jews, which had already begun before invasion, now proceeded at a very rapid pace. In 1923 the Jewish population of West Harlem was 75,500; by 1930 it was 2,518, and in 1940 the Jews numbered 883 (a 96.6 percent decline between 1923 and 1930). However, migration out of the Jewish area occurred at different times for each street or house. Information based on voter registration lists indicates that 105 West 120th Street, between Lenox and 7th avenues, in tract 220, listed 20 registered voters in 1920, 16 of whom had identifiable Jewish names. In 1925 there were 8 registered voters at this address; 7 were Jewish. By 1926 there were 8 registered voters, but only 2 were Jewish. In 1930, out of 16 registered voters, none was Jewish. For this house, the out-migration of Jews began between November, 1925, and November, 1926. At 2010 7th Avenue (121st Street) in tract 220 there were 19 Jews out of 28 registered voters in 1920. By 1924 there were only 2 Jews out of 11 registered voters. In 1930 there were no Jews, according to the registration lists, left in this building. Out-migration of most Jewish residents of this apartment house had begun before 1924. Tract 220, in which both these houses were located, went from 1.3 percent black in 1920 to 71.7 percent black in 1930. However, out-migration occurred much later at 2, 3, 5, and 7 West 120th Street, which still had 25 Jews out of 55 registered voters in 1930. By 1935 there were 4 Jewish residents listed out of 27 registered voters. These houses were in tract 200, which was only 6.9 percent black in 1930. Different parts of the neighborhood had different out-migration rates, depending upon such factors as landlord resistance, condition of dwellings, and ability and desire of individuals to leave the area. The last group of houses on 120th Street, which were well-built brownstones, bordered on fashionable Mount Morris Park and were the last houses in the neighborhood to see the racial shift. People who lived in these buildings were reluctant to give them up.

Within the neighborhood indications of change were evident everywhere. Temple Israel of Harlem at 201 Lenox Avenue became Mount Olivet Baptist Church. The Hotel Grampion at St. Nicholas Avenue and 119th Street, after having served a white only clientele for 27 years, was turned over for the exclusive use of blacks in 1927. By 1930 the black community had reached as far south as 110th Street, where they met not only a retreating Jewish population but also an expanding Hispanic one. Public School 170 in tract 186 was described in a 1931 survey as being in a neighborhood which had changed from predominantly Jewish in 1926 to Puerto Rican and black in 1930.

Puerto Ricans, South Americans, Cubans and others of Hispanic background entered the area in the 1920s. Although it was not possible to get a census count on the extent of their invasion, it was possible through neighborhood surveys, newspapers, and interviews to note the streets where the penetration occurred and the reaction to it. The Hispanic invasion was smaller than the black one and therefore more strenuously resisted in the hope of driving the newcomers out of the neighborhood. The main Hispanic penetration was in the Madison Avenue to 7th Avenue area, from 102nd to 119th streets, with inroads being made as far east as 3rd Avenue. This was basically the Jewish West Harlem section but also contained part of East Harlem. The Jewish population of East Harlem in 1923 was 101,300, approximately 45.3 percent of the population of the area. In 1919 the Jews were over 50 percent of the population in tracts 164, 174, 182, and 184. During the 1920s this neighborhood became mixed Hispanic, black, and Jewish, but with a fast disappearing Jewish population. As in West Harlem, East Harlem Jewish out-migration began in 1919, before the invasion, and was due to a desire to improve social status by moving to new dwellings recently built in the Bronx. The invasion of blacks and Puerto Ricans and the expansion of the Italian area in East Harlem turned a small out-migration of Jews into a stampede. From 101,300 in 1923, the Jewish population decreased to 2,900 by 1930 (a 97.1 percent decline). Another indication of Jewish out-migration was the decreasing Jewish student population in the schools. For example, Public School 57 at 176 East 115th Street in tract 182 had 2,046 Jewish students out of 3,331 in 1923. By 1930 there were only 567 Jews out of 3,017 students and in 1935, 245 Jewish students out of 3,211. There was a steady influx of blacks and

Puerto Ricans into the area where the school was located. All the other public schools in the neighborhood exhibited a similar Jewish decline.

Further illustrations of the shift can be drawn from the voter registration lists. For example, an apartment house at 73 East 116th Street (tract 184) indicated in 1920 10 registered voters, 7 Jews, 2 Italians, and 1 unidentified. In 1930, with 13 people recorded, there were 12 Hispanic names and 1 unidentified. By 1940, out of 20 names 18 were Hispanic and none Jews. From 54 to 93 East 116th Street in 1920 there were 150 Jews out of 168 registered voters. By 1930, out of 96 names, 86 were Hispanic and 10 were Jewish. By 1940 there were 200 registered voters, with no Jews, mainly Hispanic and, judging from census material, blacks who had entered this block after the Hispanics.

As in West Harlem, different houses in the neighborhood changed at different times. For example, at 112 East 111th Street between Lexington and 3rd avenues in tract 172 (45.1 percent Jewish in 1919) there were 9 Jews and 1 Hispanic out of 11 registered voters in 1930. In 1933, out of 19 registered voters there were 15 Hispanics and no Jews. However, the house next door at 108 East 111th Street still had Jews living in it until 1935. The Hispanics first began to move into this building in 1934. By 1935 there were 8 Hispanics and 6 Jews out of 17 registered voters.

A 1931 Jewish Welfare Board survey explains in part why neighboring houses experienced transition at different times. The report notes a Jewish family on Madison Avenue between 112th and 113th streets which moved from a house that became entirely Puerto Rican to one next door which was wholly Jewish. This family could not leave the neighborhood, because of business interests. Other Jewish families who were financially able and who did not have restricting ties to the community moved to the Bronx, mainly because of the Puerto Rican influx and a fear of crime increase. Some families who did not have enough money to move were aided by Jewish communal agencies in abandoning the area. Although the Jewish sections of East Harlem were rapidly changing, this process could be quickened or slowed by personal concerns.

Another survey provides insights into the reasons that conflict emerged in this neighborhood. Once the middle class Jews had left, the poorer ones had to contend with an increased Hispanic influx. Resentments grew because of a clash of cultures and the fact that the Hispanic residents were poorer and had to take in boarders to pay the rent. This the Jews interpreted as a deterioration of the neighborhood, which was accentuated by the fact that landlords, with the out-migration of the wealthier residents, allowed the buildings to fall into disrepair. The Jews who were not able to move became increasingly angry at what they felt was their bad luck. Violent conflict soon emerged as the Jews tried to protect what was left of their area. Conflict took the form of Jewish youths attacking Hispanic intruders, particularly in the section between 110th and 116th streets. Reports of beatings and street fights were frequent. The Hispanic community at first retaliated with violence. At the end of July, 1926, after an intense week of street fights and arguments between the two groups, a large number of Hispanic youths marched on 115th Street and Lenox Avenue to settle the feud. They were stopped by the police. When the neighborhood attacks against the Hispanics continued, other methods to deal with the problem were sought. For a long time the Spanish-speaking people of Harlem had not been able to respond as an organized group because of frictions within their own community. However, they did finally submerge their differences and form a temporary alliance to push their demands. First, there were complaints to the Puerto Rican resident commissioner, who brought pressure on the Police Department to increase their presence in the community. Second, there was the creation of a defense league of people of Hispanic background designed to prevent assaults and promote the welfare of the Hispanic community. Sporadic violence continued during the transition period but did not in any way stop the invasion. Conflict and recession took place at the same time. Invasion, however, merely quickened the pace of out-migration; the desire to move was already there.

In the Italian parts of East Harlem a different out-migration pattern emerged. The Italians had come to East Harlem in the late 1890s and by 1910 dominated large sections of the community, with the nucleus of the group along 2nd Avenue from 102nd to 116th streets and around Thomas Jefferson Park at Pleasant Avenue and 115th Street. By 1920 tracts 170, 178, 180, 188, 192, and 194 were predominantly Italian. The Italian community was being pressed by the Hispanics from the south and west and the blacks from the north. However, the blacks apparently were less of a problem since their migration was southwest rather than southeast. For example, while tract 204 indicated 33.2 percent black in 1930, tract 202 was only 14.6 percent black and tract 194 only .4 percent black. Rather, the blacks came into Italian East Harlem on the heels of the Hispanic invasion.

The Italian and Jewish reaction to the initial Hispanic penetration was similar in that conflict developed. Apparently both groups perceived the newcomers as a cultural and economic threat to their neighborhoods. However, disintegration of the Italian community was extremely slow; although it had begun before the invasion, apparently in the case of those who could afford to move to the Bronx or Queens and who wished to leave the congestion of East Harlem. Conflict emerged in the form of fights, killings, restrictions on rentals, and refusal to work with the newcomers in community activities. Recession did not follow conflict. While some Italian tracts show a decrease in the total Italian population, there is an increase in their proportion in these tracts. Tract 180, which had approximately 14,000 Italians (foreign stock) in 1920, found 12,400 in 1930. But as a percent of the tract population, the Italians increased from 64.3 percent to 79.1 percent because of a decline in the total tract population. Tracts 162 and 170, which had an Italian population of about 21,000 in 1920 (81 percent) indicated 15,400 by 1930 (84.3 percent). Other tracts show the same mobility pattern.

Rather than many Italians leaving the neighborhood during invasion, the evidence points to an expansion of the Italian community. Tracts 172 and 174 in the Jewish section had an estimated Italian population of 3,565 in 1920, only 9.9 percent in these tracts. By 1930 the Jews and others had left, but the Italians now made up 21.4 percent of the tract population and had increased to 5,691. Public School 83, which served the people of a neighboring tract, was described in 1931 as being in an area that recently had been Irish but was now populated by Italians. Congestion in the Italian section resulted in an attempt to secure the apartments of those people who were departing for other neighborhoods. The main population group, therefore, moving out of East Harlem were the Jews, not the Italians. For example, the south side of 103rd Street between 2nd and 3rd avenues in tract 164 had 86 Italians, 111 Russians (Jews), 23 Poles, and 15 Puerto Ricans in 1925. By 1930 the Russian population had decreased to 18 and the Poles had moved out entirely. The Italian population had increased to 87 and the Puerto Ricans to 44.

Voter registration figures reveal the same pattern. In the houses from 300 to 340 East 112th Street (tract 180) in 1920 there were 50 Italians out of 53 registered voters. In 1935 there were 161 Italians out of 166 registered voters. At 2169, 2171, and 2173 1st Avenue at 113th Street (tract 180) in 1920 there were 15 registered voters, all Italian. In 1935 there were now 38 registered voters, 37 of whom were Italian. Public schools in the area which showed large decreases in their Jewish student population continued to have many Italian students. In 1933, after the initial Hispanic penetration had already occurred, Public School 102 at 315 East 113th Street (tract 180) had 1,090 Italian students out of a total school population of 1,416. Other schools such as Public School 168 on East 105th Street (tract 170), Public School 83 on East 110th

Street (tract 180), and Public School 78 on Pleasant Avenue and 119th Street (tract 192), were over 75 percent Italian in 1933.

The Hispanics during this period were not able to penetrate the core area of the Italian section. The battles went on in the peripheral Italian sections where both groups were moving. One street that did become mixed Italian-Puerto Rican by 1932, 109th Street between Park and 3rd avenues, was in this periphery. At 169 East 109th Street between Lexington and 3rd avenues, there were 12 registered voters in 1930, of whom 8 were Italians, 1 was Jewish, and none Hispanic. By 1935, out of 16 registered voters, the Italians still dominated with 9 names; there were no Jews in this building now, but there were 4 Hispanic residents. This house was in tract 172, which had been only 19.1 percent Italian in 1920 but over 40 percent Jewish. The Jews were moving out, and the Hispanics and Italians competed for the vacated apartments.

The invasion into the main Italian area was stopped for a time in the 1930s. The depression temporarily halted Puerto Rican immigration into the United States and actually forced many to return to their homeland. East Harlem, therefore, was able to remain substantially Italian for many years. Puerto Rican immigration did not appreciably increase again until after World War 2, at which time East Harlem once again began to experience change. Also, the building of low income projects in the area, mainly in the 1950s, helped push the Italians out. The projects housed the blacks and Hispanics since most of the Italians were too wealthy to secure apartments there. Jefferson Houses, a project built at 114th Street between 2nd and 3rd avenues (tracts 180 and 188) in the 1950s, illustrates this point. Before the project was built, the site was 64 percent white; after, it was only 28 percent white. The Italians, unable to get middle instead of low income housing built in the area, moved out or were displaced. By the 1950s many Italians expressed a desire to remain in the neighborhood where their community had existed for many years. However, by this time the Puerto Rican tide could not be stopped. Today the area is basically Puerto Rican and black, with small enclaves of Italians along East 116th Street from 2nd Avenue to the East River (tracts 178 and 188) and along Pleasant Avenue near Thomas Jefferson Park (tract 178). A recent study by the East Harlem Committee on Aging stated that the neighborhood was 14 percent Italian, 65 percent Puerto Rican and the rest black and other groups. The remaining Italian population is made up mostly of older people, the young having moved to the Bronx, Queens, or the suburbs. Here the invasion was followed by conflict, but recession took many years.

Although some writers have assumed that Italians moved less frequently than other groups, because of an ethnic factor—the desire to retain
a village existence in their neighborhood—this contention is not supported
by the evidence. Two other studies of New York Italians (Caroline Ware's
book on Greenwich Village and Leo Grebler's work on the Lower East
Side) note that the reasons this group moved during non-invasion periods
were similar to those for other ethnics, mainly a desire to secure better
housing or a better environment for their children. In East Harlem the
majority of dwelling units in the Italian and Jewish sections were built
before 1899. Both Italians and Jews moved out in an effort to secure
newer housing in other boroughs, but only the Jewish area disappeared
because of this factor combined with the invasion process. The slower
disintegration of the Italian enclave was not related to lack of desire,
at least in the 1930s but mainly to an economic variable. According
to an economic survey of New York City, which contained data from
the 1930 census, the neighborhoods of the city were analyzed on the
basis of annual family expenditure for each census tract. The Jewish
areas of West Harlem were rated lower middle to middle class. The
Jewish section of East Harlem was lower middle class. In contrast, the
predominant areas of Italian concentration, with few exceptions, were
in the lowest income levels. The Jews on the whole were richer than their
neighbors and were better able financially to move to newer areas than the
Italians. Also, Jewish families that could not bear the financial burden
of migration could possibly receive help from Jewish communal
agencies. This was not the case with the Italians, who had to stay and
fight for their neighborhoods. The main Hispanic and black penetration,
therefore, moved into the area of least resistance, the Jewish section.
The newcomers were not able to make inroads into the Italian community until years later. By the 1950s the Italians, as a group, were
better off financially than before, were richer than their black and
Puerto Rican neighbors, and were faced with a new invasion as a result
of the building of the projects. This time the Italian community began
to disappear.

Invasion did not take place only in areas with well-established and
dominant ethnic populations as in the Harlems. Neighborhoods with
mixed ethnic populations, with no one group predominating, also
experienced this process and reacted to it. Ethnic shifting, to a significant
degree, occurred.

While Manhattan was losing its population, Washington Heights (see
map 1) represented the only district showing a marked increase in both
population and density in the 1920–1930 period. (Washington Height's

boundaries are West 158th and 159th streets on the south, Manhattan's borough limits on the north, the Harlem River on the east, and the Hudson River on the west.) Washington Heights saw a continued growth from 70,500 in 1915 to 100,000 in 1920 and 169,300 by 1930 (a 140 percent increase). The area's first inhabitants, before the turn of the century, were upper class Protestants of mixed national backgrounds who settled in a number of large estates. However, the first major ethnic colony was that of the Irish, who came to the Heights in the 1900–1910 period and moved mainly to the section east of Broadway. These people were middle class, having migrated up Amsterdam Avenue from an earlier enclave around the City College area (Amsterdam and 140th). They were later followed by other classes of their group. Also moving into the Heights were German and English Protestants. Although no single group was ever a majority of the neighborhood, the Protestants had the smallest population. The reaction of the Irish to Jewish invasion will be the subject of the next part of the study.

The Jewish penetration of this area began slowly between 1910 and 1915 with middle to upper class Jews of German background. This migration flowed from the Jewish colony in the Morningside Heights section. Jewish settlement was first made on the western side of Broadway, but then soon moved over to the Irish, German, English area of concentration on the east. Beginning about 1917 and extending into the 1920s, a much larger Jewish migration took place, made up primarily of poorer eastern European Jews moving from their colony in lower Harlem (the same group which was fleeing from black and Spanish invasion). In anticipation of the completion of the IND subway through Washington Heights, the western section particularly experienced an apartment house building boom. The Jewish migration went primarily to this section, but again spilled over into the eastern area. An indication of the extent of the Jewish invasion is found in the following figures. In 1923 4.5 percent of the Jewish population of Manhattan lived in the Heights; by 1930, 22 percent were in the area. In other terms, the Jewish population of the Heights went from 31,500 in 1923 (27.3 percent of the Heights population) to 65,300 in 1930 (38.6 percent) and 73,100 in 1940 (35.8 percent). By 1920 all census tracts east and west of Broadway had a substantial and increasing Russian (Jewish) population.

During this early period there was some antagonism toward the Jews because of residential competition. Although relations between the Irish and Jews were particularly strained, conflict did not develop. This heritage of hostility, however, was clearly evident by the late 1930s and early 1940s, when the neighborhood experienced an outburst of anti-

Semitic activity. The main conflict organization was the largely Irish Christian Front. There was also widespread anti-Jewish vandalism in the area at that time.

The Irish as a group showed no inclination to abandon the neighborhood at any time during this period. In fact, census figures indicate that the Irish increased from approximately 6.5 percent (6,589) of the community in 1920 to an estimated 11.7 percent (23,900) in 1940. Percentages for the total Washington Heights area would give the erroneous impression that the Irish and Jews did not move in response to each other. The shift was subtle, extending over a long period of time. Tract statistics only partially indicate what was happening. The percentage and number of Irish increased in the tracts east of and surrounding Broadway. For example, in 1920 the only tracts with an Irish population of more than 10 percent were tract 243 (14.8 percent), tracts 249 and 259 (15.8 percent), tract 251 (15.5 percent), and tracts 297 and 299 (30 percent). By 1940 a number of eastern and northern tracts indicated an estimated Irish presence of over 15 percent, including tract 243 (21.4 percent), 245 (16.6 percent), 251 (17 percent), 253 (17.6 percent), 261 (21.9 percent), 291 (16.1 percent), 293 (16.4 percent), and 297 (22 percent). Irish presence in the Jewish tracts west of Broadway remained minimal; tract 247 was only 3.4 percent (168) Irish in 1920 and 2.2 percent (169) Irish in 1940. The Irish percentage increases were not statistically the result of a total population decrease in these tracts.

Although the number of Jews decreased in tracts 243, 249, and 261, they increased in tracts 245, 251, 253, and 269, indicating that this group continued to move east of Broadway and were a significant part of the population in the tracts where the Irish lived. The area west of Broadway remained heavily Jewish, and there was some Jewish migration north. Tract 247 was 11.1 percent Russian in 1920 (620), and 20.5 percent Russian in 1940 (1,570). Tracts 255 and 257, which were only 6 percent Russian in 1920 (123) increased to 14.2 percent by 1940 (1,010). On a census tract basis, there continued to be much mixing. The Index of Dissimilarity, based on tract statistics, showed a low segregation index between the Irish and Jews in 1920 (26) and 1940 (35.5), although it was higher by the later date. However, voter registration lists reveal that segregation and shifting between the groups existed within the tracts.

Essentially, the Irish and Jews began to regroup along certain streets or in certain houses. For example, in 1910 the Irish were scattered along St. Nicholas Avenue, Broadway, and Amsterdam Avenue and between 160th and 170th streets. By 1920 many of the houses had begun to have their first Jewish residents. At 2153 Amsterdam Avenue (tract 249) there were 12 registered voters in 1910, 7 of whom were identified as Irish and none as Jewish. By 1920, out of 35 registered voters 10 were Irish and 12 Jewish. The neighborhood experienced its greatest degree of ethnic mixing by houses and streets in 1920. However, during the decade of the 1920s, when most of the eastern European Jews came into the area, the Irish began to shift and regroup along their own streets. The houses from 1984 to 2306 Amsterdam Avenue (159th to 174th streets) had a 23.2 percent Irish population in 1910. By 1930 the Irish made up 32.7 percent of the population of these houses, and by 1940 they were 34.2 percent. The Jewish population was minimal along these streets. Tract 243, which included Amsterdam Avenue up to 165th Street, was 14.8 percent Irish (797) in 1920 and 21.4 percent Irish (1,290) in 1940. The Russian (Jewish) population of the tract decreased from 5.5 percent (325) in 1920 to 1.3 percent (81) in 1940. Voter registration in this section of the Heights indicated a significant degree of ethnic shifting. At 434 West 164th Street (tract 243) there were 45 registered voters in 1920, 26 Irish and 9 Jews. By 1930 the same building had 18 Irish out of 26 registered voters, and no Jews. Substantial numerical or percentage increases in either Irish or Jewish residents in a building often resulted in the other group leaving. There was some Irish-Jewish mixing in new and large apartment houses, although one group usually dominated. At 2201 Amsterdam Avenue (tract 253), an apartment house built between 1920 and 1930, there were 51 registered voters in 1930, 32 of whom could be identified as Jewish and only 5 as Irish, although Amsterdam Avenue was essentially an Irish street. Also common was the situation in which one house was predominantly Irish and the one next door predominantly Jewish. At 552, 554, and 556 West 162nd Street (tract 245), there were 4 Irish residents out of 4 registered voters in 1910. By 1930 there were 6 Irish out of 7 registered voters in these buildings. The house next door, 560 and 562 West 162nd Street, which was totally Irish in 1910, had 5 Jews out of 6 registered voters by 1930.

In the western section of the Heights, the Jews had little competition for housing. Voter registration lists for the area bounded by Broadway, Fort Washington Avenue, Riverside Drive, and 161st Street (mainly in tract 247) indicate that the Jews comprised 56 percent of the inhabitants of this area in 1920 and 68 percent by 1930. Few Irish lived in this section.

In the recently developed sections of northern Washington Heights or Inwood, as the eastern zone, various streets and houses became either predominantly Irish or Jewish as both groups migrated to the area during the 1920-1940 period. At 204 and 207 Dyckman Street (tract 291) there were only 26 Irish and 14 Jews who were identifiable out of 95 registered voters in 1920. By 1940 the Irish made up 44 of the 100 registered voters; few Jews were now indicated by the voter registration lists as living at this address. However, at 570 West 204th Street (tract 291) there were 58 Jews and only 12 Irish identifiable out of 120 registered voters in 1940, although at the neighboring building, 590 West 204th Street, there were 34 Irish and 12 Jews out of 75 registered voters. The voter registration data suggest that in Washington Heights streets and houses became either predominantly Irish or Jewish as both groups shifted.

Irish and Jewish migration patterns in this neighborhood can be explained by three factors. First, Washington Heights was a new and growing residential area, a desirable place to live in terms of transportation, park facilities, and new housing. The Irish as a group showed no desire to abandon this area; instead they shifted and regrouped along certain streets and thus continued to enjoy the amenities of the community. Second, an economic factor was involved. Although many poor Jews lived in the neighborhood, this ethnic group on the whole was in a superior economic position, particularly as noted by their presence in the western section, where rents were higher and where the newest housing was located. A 1946 neighborhood survey revealed that approximately 14 percent of the Jews were classified as being in the high income group, compared with only 3 percent of the non-Jewish whites. One economic analysis of the neighborhood indicated in 1930 that the western Jewish area was upper middle to upper class. The eastern section, containing both Jews and Irish, was classified as middle middle class, with a small portion along Amsterdam Avenue, where many Irish lived, as lower middle. By 1940 a similar analysis described the western part as mainly middle middle class and the eastern area as lower middle. In regard to housing, one-fourth of all Washington Heights Catholics were living in dilapidated housing, "where no Jews lived." Even poorer Jews were willing to limit other expenses in order to secure a decent residence. Only 2 percent of the Jews were in low rent apartments, compared with 25 percent of the Catholics. Although the majority of the Catholics did live in decent housing and presumably paid rents similar to those paid by the Jews (at least in the eastern and northern sections), the greater ability and desire of Jews to live in better housing surely contributed to the two groups' living in different houses and on different streets. It also contributed to the third factor, that of hostility between the two. Ethnic friction, although remaining non-violent during the migration years, did seem to play a role in splitting the two communities and setting the stage for conflict later on. However, abandonment and recession were not responses to invasion in this case.

The three neighborhoods described in this study indicate that there are many variables within the general invasion-succession sequence. The Harlem experience reveals that conflict is more likely to develop when the invading group is judged unacceptable by the established resident population. Although this has often signified a racial clash, it has also occurred between white groups, as in Boston's North End, which experienced a signficant outburst of conflict between the Irish and Italians when the Irish perceived the Italians to be culturally inferior and of a lower economic status. Jewish movement into mixed Irish areas, although resented, did not during the invasion period produce the same degree of hostility. Perhaps this was due to the fact that the Jews were not thought of as a lower status group, although there is no evidence to support or refute this point. To understand the manifestation of conflict in a community, the physical neighborhood also must be considered. In Washington Heights, a relatively undeveloped section, territory did not have to be fought for since there were other parts of the same area available for Irish or Jewish housing. In Harlem it was either fight for your territory and win, or leave the area.

Out-migration or recession from a neighborhood also is a product of the evaluation of the newcomers, the physical amenities of the area, and the ability and desire of the residents to move. Invasion did not cause transition but merely accelerated an already present trend, as indicated in the Harlem situation concerning the Jews. The Italians illustrate the economic variable, for this ethnic community remained until invasion coincided with their financial ability to move. By the 1950s they were too rich for the low income projects being built in the neighborhood, were faced with a new invasion, and now had the resources to leave. After so many years of thinking of East Harlem as their community, some left reluctantly and were actually forced out, but the desire to move was evident in the Italian community as early as the 1920s. In Washington Heights the Irish showed no desire to abandon the area, even if another group was dominant. However, if there was no wish to move there was a propensity toward securing control over selected streets and houses.

While Cressey and the other social scientists were correct in their general outline of the invasion-succession process, the cases presented here indicate that there are variations on this basic outline.

3

GOVERNMENT AND NEIGHBORHOOD

The growing political power and activism of neighborhoods are prime forces for change in cities today. The rationale for this neighborhood movement is that city governments have grown distant from the people they represent and do not provide basic services. Some cities, for example New York, have already moved toward decentralization with such features as local community boards which monitor city services on a neighborhood level and serve as an advisory unit on local land use and planning. The desire to give the neighborhood and average citizen more control over government stems from a number of factors: the effort to secure local control over urban renewal beginning in the 1950s, the civil rights movement and war on poverty of the 1960s with its attempt to provide more representation for the urban poor, and the breakdown of city services and growing negative attitudes toward the efficiency of centralized city government evident throughout this period. Also, there is a nostalgic feeling that in the city of the past the government was more responsive to the needs of the local community.

The four selections in this chapter range from the city of the nineteenth century to that of today and discuss various aspects of decentralization.

William Riordan's *Plunkitt of Tammany Hall* is the classic look at the workings of the Tammany Hall political machine in New York City. In this excerpt the daily routine of district leader George Washington Plunkitt is detailed. It is the close attention to the problems of his constituents, although always with votes in mind, for which Plunkitt and the machine were noted. The image of the concerned, always available district leader is one that has great appeal in an era when citizens feel their governments no longer care.

Marsha Hurst's study of nineteenth-century Brooklyn reveals an aspect of early decentralization often neglected. In a discussion of school integration and the elimination of black schools, Hurst examines the local committee system of Brooklyn's educational structure. Before Progressives pushed for centralized municipal government, including that of the school system, Brooklyn's board of education functioned within a workable decentralized format designed to be responsive to community needs. By focusing on black community concerns during this period, Hurst provides the historical background to the school decentralization battles of the late 1960s. Centralization of the school system in the late nineteenth century eliminated local black community input into the schools until the controversies of the late 1960s erupted.

Douglas Yates's essay introduces us to the twentieth-century decentralization issue. He suggests that neighborhood government is a relatively new concept and questions those who see aspects of it in an earlier period, as during the era of political machines. Yates then goes on to define decentralization, noting why it is supported and opposed, and offers his views on its possibility of success. The obstacles are great, as he contends, but more important is that so little is known about the effects of a complete neighborhood government system that it is difficult to say whether it is even desirable.

The last selection in this chapter deals with some of Yates's points by detailing the decentralization structure in New York City as it evolved out of the Great Society programs and by evaluating its impact on one New York community and minority group. Chia-ling Kuo's study of Chinatown reveals the problems associated with the creation and operation of decentralized government. The racial and ethnic cleavages, the factional strife, the increase in powerlessness for some groups, and the lack of funds are all evident in this community. Yet also indicated is the establishment of new channels of communication between city hall and the neighborhoods.

Decentralization today remains an experiment which is developing, with many of the difficulties of any new program.

STRENUOUS LIFE
OF THE TAMMANY DISTRICT LEADER
Recorded by WILLIAM L. RIORDAN

NOTE: This chapter is based on extracts from Plunkitt's Diary and on my daily observation of the work of the district leader.—W.L.R.

The life of the Tammany district leader is strenuous. To his work is due the wonderful recuperative power of the organization.

One year it goes down in defeat and the prediction is made that it will never again raise its head. The district leader, undaunted by defeat, collects his scattered forces, organizes them as only Tammany knows how to organize, and in a little while the organization is as strong as ever.

No other politician in New York or elsewhere is exactly like the Tammany district leader or works as he does. As a rule, he has no business or occupation other than politics. He plays politics every day and night in the year, and his headquarters bears the inscription, "Never closed."

Everybody in the district knows him. Everybody knows where to find him, and nearly everybody goes to him for assistance of one sort or another, especially the poor of the tenements.

He is always obliging. He will go to the police courts to put in a good word for the "drunks and disorderlies" or pay their fines, if a good word is not effective. He will attend christenings, weddings, and funerals. He will feed the hungry and help bury the dead.

A philanthropist? Not at all. He is playing politics all the time.

From *Plunkitt of Tammany Hall,* recorded by William L. Riordan, 1905.

Brought up in Tammany Hall, he has learned how to reach the hearts of the great mass of voters. He does not bother about reaching their heads. It is his belief that arguments and campaign literature have never gained votes.

He seeks direct contact with the people, does them good turns when he can, and relies on their not forgetting him on election day. His heart is always in his work, too, for his subsistence depends on its results.

If he holds his district and Tammany is in power, he is amply rewarded by a good office and the opportunities that go with it. What these opportunities are has been shown by the quick rise to wealth of so many Tammany district leaders. With the examples before him of Richard Croker, once leader of the Twentieth District; John F. Carroll, formerly leader of the Twenty-ninth; Timothy ("Dry Dollar") Sullivan, late leader of the Sixth, and many others, he can always look forward to riches and ease while he is going through the drudgery of his daily routine.

This is a record of a day's work by Plunkitt:

2 A.M.: Aroused from sleep by the ringing of his doorbell; went to the door and found a bartender, who asked him to go to the police station and bail out a saloon-keeper who had been arrested for violating the excise law. Furnished bail and returned to bed at three o'clock.

6 A.M.: Awakened by fire engines passing his house. Hastened to the scene of the fire, according to the custom of the Tammany district leaders, to give assistance to the fire sufferers, if needed. Met several of his election district captains who are always under orders to look out for fires, which are considered great vote-getters. Found several tenants who had been burned out, took them to a hotel, supplied them with clothes, fed them, and arranged temporary quarters for them until they could rent and furnish new apartments.

8:30 A.M.: Went to the police court to look after his constituents. Found six "drunks." Secured the discharge of four by a timely word with the judge, and paid the fines of two.

9 A.M.: Appeared in the Municipal District Court. Directed one of his district captains to act as counsel for a widow against whom dispossess proceedings had been instituted and obtained an extension of time. Paid the rent of a poor family about to be dispossessed and gave them a dollar for food.

11 A.M.: At home again. Found four men waiting for him. One had been discharged by the Metropolitan Railway Company for neglect of duty, and wanted the district leader to fix things. Another wanted a job on the road. The third sought a place on the Subway, and the fourth, a plumber, was looking for work with the Consolidated Gas Company.

The district leader spent nearly three hours fixing things for the four men, and succeeded in each case.

3 P.M.: Attended the funeral of an Italian as far as the ferry. Hurried back to make his appearance at the funeral of a Hebrew constituent. Went conspicuously to the front both in the Catholic church and the synagogue, and later attended the Hebrew confirmation ceremonies in the synagogue.

7 P.M.: Went to district headquarters and presided over a meeting of election district captains. Each captain submitted a list of all the voters in his district, reported on their attitude toward Tammany, suggested who might be won over and how they could be won, told who were in need, and who were in trouble of any kind and the best way to reach them. District leader took notes and gave orders.

8 P.M.: Went to a church fair. Took chances on everything, bought ice cream for the young girls and the children. Kissed the little ones, flattered their mothers and took their fathers out for something down at the corner.

9 P.M.: At the clubhouse again. Spent $10 on tickets for a church excursion and promised a subscription for a new church bell. Bought tickets for a baseball game to be played by two nines from his district. Listened to the complaints of a dozen pushcart peddlers who said they were persecuted by the police and assured them he would go to Police Headquarters in the morning and see about it.

10:30 P.M.: Attended a Hebrew wedding reception and dance. Had previously sent a handsome wedding present to the bride.

12 P.M.: In bed.

That is the actual record of one day in the life of Plunkitt. He does some of the same things every day, but his life is not so monotonous as to be wearisome.

Sometimes the work of a district leader is exciting, especially if he happens to have a rival who intends to make a contest for the leadership at the primaries. In that case, he is even more alert, tries to reach the fires before his rival, sends out runners to look for "drunks and disorderlies" at the police stations, and keeps a very close watch on the obituary columns of the newspapers.

A few years ago there was a bitter contest for the Tammany leadership of the Ninth District between John C. Sheehan and Frank J. Goodwin. Both had had long experience in Tammany politics and both understood every move of the game.

Every morning their agents went to their respective headquarters before seven o'clock and read through the death notices in all the morning papers. If they found that anybody in the district had died, they rushed to the homes of their principals with the information and then there was a race to the house of the deceased to offer condolences, and, if the family were poor, something more substantial.

On the day of the funeral there was another contest. Each faction tried to surpass the other in the number and appearance of the carriages it sent to the funeral, and more than once they almost came to blows at the church or in the cemetery.

On one occasion the Goodwinites played a trick on their adversaries which has since been imitated in other districts. A well-known liquor dealer who had a considerable following died, and both Sheehan and Goodwin were eager to become his political heir by making a big showing at the funeral.

Goodwin managed to catch the enemy napping. He went to all the livery stables in the district, hired all the carriages for the day, and gave orders to two hundred of his men to be on hand as mourners.

Sheehan had never had any trouble about getting all the carriages that he wanted, so he let the matter go until the night before the funeral. Then he found that he could not hire a carriage in the district.

He called his district committee together in a hurry and explained the situation to them. He could get all the vehicles he needed in the adjoining district, he said, but if he did that, Goodwin would rouse the voters of the Ninth by declaring that he (Sheehan) had patronized foreign industries.

Finally, it was decided that there was nothing to do but to go over to Sixth Avenue and Broadway for carriages. Sheehan made a fine turnout at the funeral, but the deceased was hardly in his grave before Goodwin raised the cry of "Protection to home industries," and denounced his rival for patronizing livery-stable keepers outside of his district. The cry had its effect in the primary campaign. At all events, Goodwin was elected leader.

A recent contest for the leadership of the Second District illustrated further the strenuous work of the Tammany district leaders. The contestants were Patrick Divver, who had managed the district for years, and Thomas F. Foley.

Both were particularly anxious to secure the large Italian vote. They not only attended all the Italian christenings and funerals, but also kept a close lookout for the marriages in order to be on hand with wedding presents.

At first, each had his own reporter in the Italian quarter to keep track of the marriages. Later, Foley conceived a better plan. He hired a man to stay all day at the City Hall marriage bureau, where most Italian couples go through the civil ceremony, and telephone to him at his saloon when anything was doing at the bureau.

Foley had a number of presents ready for use and, whenever he received a telephone message from his man, he hastened to the City Hall with a ring or a watch or a piece of silver and handed it to the bride with his congratulations. As a consequence, when Divver got the news and went to the home of the couple with his present, he always found that Foley had been ahead of him. Toward the end of the campaign, Divver also stationed a man at the marriage bureau, and then there were daily foot races and fights between the two heelers.

Sometimes the rivals came into conflict at the deathbed. One night a poor Italian peddler died in Roosevelt Street. The news reached Divver and Foley about the same time, and as they knew the family of the man was destitute, each went to an undertaker and brought him to the Roosevelt Street tenement.

The rivals and the undertakers met at the house, and an altercation ensued. After much discussion the Divver undertaker was selected. Foley had more carriages at the funeral, however, and he further impressed the Italian voters by paying the widow's rent for a month, and sending her half a ton of coal and a barrel of flour.

The rivals were put on their mettle toward the end of the campaign by the wedding of a daughter of one of the original Cohens of the Baxter Street region. The Hebrew vote in the district is nearly as large as the Italian vote, and Divver and Foley set out to capture the Cohens and their friends.

They stayed up nights thinking what they would give the bride. Neither knew how much the other was prepared to spend on a wedding present, or what form it would take; so spies were employed by both sides to keep watch on the jewelry stores, and the jewelers of the district were bribed by each side to impart the desired information.

At last Foley heard that Divver had purchased a set of silver knives, forks, and spoons. He at once bought a duplicate set and added a silver tea service. When the presents were displayed at the home of the bride, Divver was not in a pleasant mood and he charged his jeweler with treachery. It may be added that Foley won at the primaries.

One of the fixed duties of a Tammany district leader is to give two outings every summer, one for the men of his district and the other for the women and children, and a beefsteak dinner and a ball every winter. The scene of the outings is, usually, one of the groves along the Sound.

The ambition of the district leader on these occasions is to demonstrate that his men have broken all records in the matter of eating and drinking.

He gives out the exact number of pounds of beef, poultry, butter, etc., that they have consumed and professes to know how many potatoes and ears of corn have been served.

According to his figures, the average eating record of each man at the outing is about ten pounds of beef, two or three chickens, a pound of butter, a half peck of potatoes, and two dozen ears of corn. The drinking records, as given out, are still more phenomenal. For some reason, not yet explained, the district leader thinks that his popularity will be greatly increased if he can show that his followers can eat and drink more than the followers of any other district leader.

The same idea governs the beefsteak dinners in the winter. It matters not what sort of steak is served or how it is cooked; the district leader considers only the question of quantity, and when he excels all others in this particular, he feels, somehow, that he is a bigger man and deserves more patronage than his associates in the Tammany Executive Committee.

As to the balls, they are the events of the winter in the extreme East Side and West Side society. Mamie and Maggie and Jennie prepare for them months in advance, and their young men save up for the occasion just as they save for the summer trips to Coney Island.

The district leader is in his glory at the opening of the ball. He leads the cotillion with the prettiest woman present—his wife, if he has one, permitting—and spends almost the whole night shaking hands with his constituents. The ball costs him a pretty penny, but he has found that the investment pays.

By these means the Tammany district leader reaches out into the homes of his district, keeps watch not only on the men, but also on the women and children; knows their needs, their likes and dislikes, their troubles and their hopes, and places himself in a position to use his knowledge for the benefit of his organization and himself. Is it any wonder that scandals do not permanently disable Tammany and that it speedily recovers from what seems to be crushing defeat?

INTEGRATION, FREEDOM OF CHOICE, AND COMMUNITY CONTROL IN NINETEENTH-CENTURY BROOKLYN

MARSHA HURST

Conflict over the best means of achieving equal educational opportunity is not new; nor are power struggles over centralized versus decentralized, bureaucratic versus community control of the schools. Although the concepts of integration, decentralization and community control have particular contemporary meanings acquired through recent court decisions and current urban controversies, these same concepts were meaningful and important to Blacks in Brooklyn almost 100 years ago.

In the last decades of the 19th century, in the City of Brooklyn, the politics of education attracted the attention of many. Educational professionals under the banner of progressivism, and political progressives under the banner of professionalism exerted pressure on the decentralized Brooklyn Board of Education to eliminate its local committee system, to centralize its decision-making procedures, to reduce financial waste, and to decrease its membership. Neighboring New York City was in the process of centralizing its municipal services, including education. As part of the movement toward consolidation of these two distinct cities, Brooklyn's school board came under increasing attack. The major controversy centered around Brooklyn's local committee system. Brooklyn Board members defended the concept of local school committees on the grounds that they were more responsive

"Integration, Freedom of Choice and Community Control in Nineteenth Century Brooklyn," *Journal of Ethnic Studies* 3 (fall, 1975): 33–55. Reprinted by permission of *Journal of Ethnic Studies*.

to community and educational needs, and in closer contact with the parents, teachers, and school principals. But progressive critics were more concerned with the committees' influence on school staffing decisions. They argued that staffing should be based on uniform, centrally determined, professional standards, and viewed decision-making at the local level as an extension of the spoils system into the field of education.

This drive to reform the Brooklyn Board of Education through centralization washed away in its wake the last separate Black schools in the City. Until the 1890's these segregated "Colored Schools" were supported not only by the Brooklyn Board of Education, but by Black, as well as White residents of the City. Although the Black schools were not neighborhood based (the three Colored schools drew students from all over the City), they were a focus of community organization and activity for Blacks living in scattered pockets throughout Brooklyn, and provided an avenue of mobility for Black teachers and educational administrators. After the first Black man was appointed to the Board of Education in 1882, and was placed on the local committee for the Colored Schools, Blacks had a chain of access, and often influence, through the segregated schools to the Black local committee member, the Board of Education, the Superintendent of Public Instruction, and occasionally to the Mayor. Segregated schools, like segregated party clubs in Brooklyn, served as a popular political base for leaders of the Black community, providing them with a Black constituency that could be readily mobilized, and a link to White decision-makers in the political parties and city government.

Over the course of the last twenty years of the 19th century, Brooklyn Blacks became more supportive of proposals made by some Black leaders to integrate the Brooklyn school system and eliminate the Colored Schools. Although many Blacks felt that their children should be educated in Black schools by Black educators, a growing number of Black parents chose to take advantage of the freedom of choice plan and send their children to the neighborhood White school. The elimination of the first Colored School, however, still involved years of conflict on the Board and in the affected Black and White communities. Once this first school was discontinued, both racial groups became more tolerant of the plan to totally eliminate the separate Black school system. But Blacks recognized that integration could be used by White authorities as a means of denying them community influence and access to educational positions.

After integration the Black member on the Board of Education was assigned to local committees for schools with a substantial proportion of Black students. The Black seat was essential if the Black Brooklyn community was to have any input into decisions affecting the education of its children. The final victory of the progressives, however, not only consolidated the school boards of Brooklyn and New York, but drastically cut the number of Brooklyn board members, abolished the local committee system, and eliminated the Black seat on the Board of Education.

Educational "progressives" in New York favored integration because of their interest in uniform administration, financial efficiency, and centralized nonpartisan decision-making. Opponents of "progressivism" valued a more community-oriented decentralized approach to educational decision-making which implicitly recognized the legitimate role of racial groups, community concerns, and local partisan politics. They thus tended to view segregated schools, staffed by racial group members, as a legitimate response to group demands. Segregation or integration was of secondary concern to the White authorities in their battle over the future form of educational administration. Blacks, however, were deeply concerned about their position and the position of their children in the public schools, and were faced with two unsatisfactory choices: integration with no group input in decision-making, or segregation with token community recognition and little real influence. Although Blacks maintained their vigilance and activity, in the final analysis there was little meaningful choice at all.

Before Blacks began moving uptown to settle in Harlem around 1905, Brooklyn was the center of Black bourgeois activity in the New York area. Most of the middle-class Blacks who were active in race affairs lived and worked in Brooklyn where they had comfortable private homes, reasonably good schools and numerous respectable Black churches. Temporarily at least, these Blacks in Brooklyn faced few of the tensions produced by the new White immigrants and recent Black migrants competing for squalid housing and a meager subsistence in the overcrowded neighborhoods of San Juan Hill and Hell's Kitchen in New York.

The Black population of Brooklyn during these years was spread out over the Borough and did not form a numerically significant bloc in any one district. In 1890, of 26 wards in Brooklyn, only one ward had no Black population, one ward had 9% Black population, one ward 6%, six wards had between 2–4% Black population, and the rest had 1% or less. In 1900 the ward with the most highly concentrated Black population (Ward 11, which today is the Fort Greene neighborhood) had 16% Blacks, but the racial proportion in most other wards remained about the same. The overall population ratio in the City of Brooklyn remained fairly constant between 1870 and 1900. Blacks were about 1% of the population at the time of the 1870 census, rose to almost 2% in 1880, but fell back down to 1% in 1890 and 1900.[1]

The Black bourgeoisie of Brooklyn established political relationships with Brooklyn party organizations and with the municipal government which in many ways were the prototypes for later race relationships in New York. They belonged to segregated political party clubs, were given token patronage positions by the White organizations, and generally practiced an elite-level politics with little relevance to most Blacks in Brooklyn except to confer on the race periodic symbolic recognition. In fact, many of the positions awarded Brooklyn Blacks were as "spokesmen" for their race, and were not held by Blacks in New York City until almost twenty years later. Although a token Black sat on the Brooklyn Board of Education each year from 1882 until full consolidation of the New York City Board in 1902, in Manhattan no Black was appointed to the Board until 1917. A Brooklyn Black Republican was awarded an assembly nomination in 1900, but the Republican party waited until 1917 before nominating a Black in Harlem.

Similarly, Blacks in Brooklyn raised broad race issues which would be of paramount importance to Blacks in New York and throughout the nation for decades afterwards. The debate over whether Blacks should break their Republican ties and vote independent of party reached its peak in Brooklyn in the 1890's, but Black independent voting did not become a political reality in New York until the mid-1910's. The debates in Brooklyn over integration versus segregation were repeated many times by Black politicians in Manhattan, especially by those who tried to destroy political party structures based on separate racial organizations. Discussions and arguments in Brooklyn over these issues, however, usually developed as a result of specific and immediate concerns. For the most part, relationships between the races during the 1880's and 1890's were characterized by comfortable though distinct social and political boundaries, with Blacks occasionally crossing to the White side for purposes of asking for or receiving political favors.

Late nineteenth-century Brooklyn was the social center for a small self-conscious upper-middle class of Negroes, most of whom derived their prestige from being on top of the Black status hierarchy. The vast majority of Blacks at the end of the century were laborers or menials. The middle class, consisting mainly of clerks, teachers, and some small businessmen, was very small. The highest socio-economic class was a tiny group of professionals, doctors, lawyers, writers, and clergymen, and of businessmen or particularly prestigious household servants whose incomes allowed them to live in an upper-middle class life-style. Although there were few professionals among the members of this social elite, it was generally from among these few professionals that Blacks in upper level party or municipal positions were chosen.[2] Blacks in good service positions were respected in the community,[3] but those Blacks with independent businesses or independent professions were looked to more often by both Blacks and Whites as community leaders.

Relative to the declining conditions of Black life in neighboring New York City during the last half of the 19th century,[4] the Black bourgeois community in Brooklyn maintained its employment and status, and, in fact, became more snobbish and ingrown as the fortunes of the rest of the Blacks, especially those recently arrived from the South, declined.[5] After the turn of the century, the *New York Age,* edited and published by T. Thomas Fortune, a prominent member of the Brooklyn Black elite, took every opportunity to reminisce nostalgically about the years when life was comfortable, quiet, cultured and exclusive among the old Black families of Brooklyn: "the Rays, the Downings, the Petersons, the Bowerses, the Guignons, the Whites, the Days, the Marses and others of the old families [who] for . . . years furnished the brains and the public spirit of the Afro-American people of Greater New York." In 1906, Samuel Scottron, prominent speaker and journalist, and the last Black member of the Brooklyn Board of Education, wrote a series of articles on "Old New York and Old New Yorkers" for the *Age.* Scottron wrote extensively about the "sense of refinement" which permeated Colored society. "Notwithstanding [that Blacks] were socially as far apart from the Whites as they are today, they were nevertheless respected. The general atmosphere called for men of refinement in manners, educated men, proud, ambitious, punctilious, . . ." Scottron attributed the decline of "refinement" in New York to the influx of foreign immigrants. He also noted the decline of Negro business in the City. "Years ago it was a common thing for our people to engage in business. There existed no feeling in the community averse to trading with us, nor did anyone seem to be intimidated or have any reason to suspect that the general public would pass him in preference for another."

By 1890, however, the remaining center of Black bourgeois life was in Brooklyn where old Black families could still maintain their businesses and their private homes. The competitiveness which had taken over race relationships in New York City had not yet crossed the river to Brooklyn, and the spirit of paternalistic separatism characteristic of the 1840's and 1850's still prevailed.[6]

Brooklyn race politics during the last decade before consolidation was shaped by the dominance of the social elite described above. The Brooklyn "400" were not only the economic and social leaders of the Brooklyn Black community, but were also the political leaders of the segregated Black Brooklyn Democratic and Republican clubs. Although the structure of Black party politics was somewhat fluid—men occasionally changed parties, new clubs formed, politicians split off into multiple factions, and so forth—the same list of notables constantly reappeared.

The most important problem faced by Blacks in all northern cities during this period was the retreat from a post–Civil War integrationist posture on the part of northern White liberals. Having accepted the principle of equal rights for Black men, the White leaders were anxious to contain this equality within separate institutions. The distinction between this Jim Crow philosophy and that of the South was that in the northern cities it was not considered acceptable to regulate Jim Crow through formal or overt procedures. It was felt, rather, that now that the Black man had attained equality, both races could maintain their separate social, economic, and political spheres, and these spheres need only overlap to settle an issue of mutual concern. A *Brooklyn Eagle* (White) editorial of August 1891 commenting on the resignation of Frederick Douglass from his post as United States Minister Resident and Consul General to Haiti concluded with a telling comment on the state of racial attitudes at that time. After praising Douglass for a long record of brilliance and achievement, the *Eagle* continued:

The distinction of race which is so marked in his case is all the more notable since many esteemed Republicans are at last admitting a truth which their Democratic brethren found out long ago. While the Constitution of the land forbids state legislation which draws the "color line," those who most ardently championed the amendment incorporating that prohibition are gradually coming to the conclusion that so-called Southern "prejudice" against the blacks is more reasonable than it appeared to them "befo do wah," . . . So, in spite of all that has gone before the drawing of the "color line" goes on without relaxing the disposition to secure to the colored man every right which he can reasonably claim and with every desire to promote his happiness and prosperity by giving him the advantages of education and by opening to him every avenue of industry to which he is fitted to enter.

White leaders in Brooklyn structured their relationships with Black spokesmen in such a way as to implement their desire for separatism between the races without appearing overtly racist. Insofar as was possible, each racial population took care of its own affairs, keeping contact between the groups at a minimum. On the surface it appeared that each racial group operated within its own social, economic, and political organizations. Blacks were left alone to manage the Black party organization, Black literary, social or business clubs, the Black press and the Black churches, but political decisions affecting both racial groups were made by White authorities in power.

One example of the operation of paternalistic but separatist relationships is that of the Colored seat on the Brooklyn Board of Education. Brooklyn still had three Colored Schools in 1882 when Philip White, the first Black member of the Board was appointed. These Colored Schools existed as segregated institutions with no clearly defined district boundaries despite the fact that no neighborhood Brooklyn public school denied admission to Black pupils and many Black students took advantage of this "freedom of choice" plan. The Black member of the school board was appointed to deal with Colored School issues. On the Brooklyn Board most decisions related to each public school were made by the local committee of the respective schools. Although the by-laws of the Board did not give formal authority to the committees to rule on teacher appointments, promotions, transfers and so forth, "by the 1880's the local committees became extremely powerful and almost independent of the standing committees."[7] These three-member local committees were intended to provide an opportunity for the development of expertise on local school conditions on the part of certain Board members, and to facilitate communication between the Board, the school staff and the parent community. Appointing two Blacks to the local committees for Colored Schools would have given Blacks majority control of these important decision-making bodies. But token Black representation to the Board gave the Black Brooklyn community symbolic recognition and some access to educational decision-making without granting them any real control over the Board's policies. Appointing one Black man to the Board to serve on local committees for the three Colored Schools, and the Colored orphanage, reinforced the paternalistic Jim Crow philosophy and strengthened the rationale for maintaining the segregated schools.

The struggle over integration in the Brooklyn public schools was carried out not only between the Blacks and Whites in that City, but within the Black community. In the 1870's, a movement led by T. Thomas Fortune sought to completely integrate the Brooklyn schools. Until that time public schools for Blacks were separate from the White schools with a separate identification system, Colored School ('C.S.') 1, 2, 3, and so forth. Black teachers and principals were placed in the Black public schools as a form of patronage for the Black educators. The anti-integration faction in the Black community claimed that the integrationists were ashamed of being known as Blacks. The all-White school board opposed integration, and the Black integrationists themselves were not able to organize any effective protest. The Board stuck with its freedom of choice plan, promising only to abolish the remaining Colored Schools as they became outmoded.

In 1882, Seth Low, the Reform Mayor of Brooklyn, appointed Philip White, a prominent Black Brooklyn pharmacist, to the Board of Education. White was made chairman of the local committee in charge of the Colored Schools. His appointment was not a concession to the integrationists, but rather a reinforcement of the boundaries between the White and Black communities through the extension of these boundaries to the Board of Education itself. White's position on the issue of the Colored Schools was basically to continue the freedom of choice policy of the Board. By appointing a Black man to the Board who agreed with the freedom of choice arrangement, the Board could make a gesture toward integration while forestalling pressure to abolish segregated schools. White introduced a proposal to formalize the freedom of choice policy. It required that all school principals be compelled by law to accept Black children, while separate Colored Schools would continue to exist for children who preferred them. The Colored Schools, said White, were necessary to instill race pride in the Negro children of Brooklyn. Even Fortune admitted that the Black parents were "satisfied with their present educational status." In December 1883 the Board formally accepted this policy. A simultaneous proposal to abolish the Colored Schools entirely was defeated. Four years later the three remaining Colored Schools were changed from the blatantly segregationist C.S. 1, 2, 3 numbering system to the regular numbering system of the Brooklyn public schools, thus becoming P.S. 67, 68 and 69.

During the same year, 1883, the New York City Board of Education decided to eliminate the last three Colored Schools in Manhattan. Discussion about this issue had been going on since 1880 when the Annual Report for that year recommended "gradual absorption" of Black school children by the public schools. An 1873 law had opened all public schools to children in New York regardless of race or color, and since that time attendance in the separate Colored Schools had been declining. One Colored School was eliminated as of September 1883, but Black parents appealed to the City not to discontinue the other two schools, P.S. 80 and 81. Accordingly a new law was passed in 1894 providing for the continuation of these last two Colored Schools, but turning over their control to the wards in which they were located, and opening their admission to any pupil regardless of race. The 1884 Annual Report strongly urged the Black Community to consent to integration of these two schools with the rest of the City system as soon as possible.[8]

In Brooklyn, however, Philip White's appointment to the Board functioned to provide token integration of an important decision-making body, while reinforcing the segregationist position of the Board. Further legitimacy was given to continued segregation by having White himself responsible for formalizing the freedom of choice policy of the Board, which served, as it did in the South after the *Brown v. Board of Education* decision, to give *de jure* recognition to integrate, and the appearance of movement toward that goal, while maintaining a basically segregated school system.[9]

Those members of the Brooklyn Black community who were committed to accelerating the elimination of the Black public schools maintained a watchful eye on the Board of Education, monitoring any legislation that gave unequal treatment to Black and White schools. But vigilance was not enough. Prominent Brooklynites led by Fortune unsuccessfully protested a Board move to amend its by-laws so as to exempt from its standing rules all schools with a "colored" attendance. Philip White had requested that the Board raise the salary of Black assistant principal, Georgiana Putnam (who had been the first Black in Brooklyn to be appointed assistant principal). The Board, however, claimed that only by exempting Colored Schools from the standing rules could Putnam's salary be raised without raising the salaries of all assistant principals, and relied on a letter of support from a number of Black Brooklyn clergymen to justify the amendment. White joined the Fortune group in opposing this measure, and when the Board passed the amendment, White resigned in protest; but his resignation was not accepted, and he remained a member until his death a year later.

A few months before White's death the school integration issue surfaced again. The Board of Education passed a resolution to build a new school building for P.S. 68 (formerly Colored School 2). A number of White citizens of the district sent a petition to the Board objecting to this proposal and claiming that it would mean a depreciation of property in the neighborhood, a now well-worn argument. Faced with the opposition of the White community, the Black Brooklynites dropped their own internal conflict over the value of separate Black schools and united to oppose the White petitioners. Black residents of Brooklyn held a mass meeting at the Bridge Street A.M.E. Church and successfully pressured the Board into altering its decision. Instead of building a school of only ten rooms exclusively for the Black children of P.S. 68, the Board decided to build a school of twenty rooms which would also house a White neighborhood school (P.S. 83). The two schools would be integrated as P.S. 68. The implementation of this decision was contingent on completion of the new school building. The ensuing delay during the construction of the school kept the issue alive for another two-and-a-half years.

In March of 1891 Philip White died, and the President of the Board of Education directed the Black community to choose a successor to be chairman of the Colored Schools committee on the Board. The Black candidate chosen by the community had to be approved by the Mayor of Brooklyn and the full Board of Education. Black political leaders who assumed control of the nomination process divided along party lines in their choice of a successor to White. Democrats and more independent Republicans (like Fortune) favored popular attorney T. McCants Stewart, and most Republicans supported writer and inventor Samuel Scottron.[10] Following his party line on appointments, Democratic Mayor Chapin not surprisingly presented the name of T. McCants Stewart for approval to the Board.[11] Later that year Stewart was reappointed to a full term and placed on committees dealing with Black school children, including the Committee of Free Scholarships, the local committee of schools P.S. 67, 68 and 69, and of the Howard Colored Orphan Asylum (of which Committee he was made chairman).

The Black member of the Board was still clearly expected to deal only with race related institutions and issues,[12] and the Board's earlier decision to integrate P.S. 68 was the first such issue facing Stewart. The number 'P.S. 83' had been put up on the new school house indicating a possible reversal of the Board's decision to combine 68 and 83 into an enlarged, integrated P.S. 68. Stewart introduced a resolution reaffirming the Board's original decision, and requesting the Board to change the number of the school house to P.S. 68.[13] Although Stewart's resolution was adopted, the Board continued to argue over whether the student body would be segregated or integrated within the school building and finally decided to reconsider its previous decision.

Decisions of the full Board of Education almost always followed the majority recommendations of the local committees. On the local committee for P.S. 68 were Stewart and two Whites. One of the two Whites, C. Simis, openly opposed integration of P.S. 68. Eben Miller, an outspoken opponent of the integrationist proposition who was appointed to fill a vacancy on the local committee just prior to the issuance of the committee's report, cast the crucial third vote. In opposing the segregationist majority report of his committee, Stewart argued that the committee had been intentionally weighted with segregationists. Their report therefore recommended continuing the segregation of Black children in the old P.S. 68, and building a new White school in the neighborhood.

The Black community held protest meetings and petitioned the Board, but these protests and Stewart's minority report had no influence. In May 1892, a year-and-a-half after the Board's initial decision to eliminate P.S. 68 as a Colored School, a segregationist policy was again upheld.[14]

The issue lay dormant until the new P.S. 83 was completed, and Black parents began demonstrating outside of the new building. The Board, forever vacillating, acquiesced to the parents' demands and agreed to house Black pupils from P.S. 68 in the new school house until a new Colored School was built. The notion that the Board, by excluding Black school children from P.S. 68, could preserve P.S. 83 as a haven for White children was absurd since other Black children already attended P.S. 83 through the freedom of choice plan. The entire student body of P.S. 68 was moved to the first floor of the new building without incident.

In October, a prominent Black Brooklyn attorney reopened the controversy by petitioning the Board to abolish P.S. 68 and integrate it with P.S. 83. By this time, however, local committee member Simis had been converted to the integrationist position, thus creating, with Stewart, a majority on the local committee for combining the two schools. In order to avert a strong local committee integrationist stand, and subsequent adoption by the full Board of that position, White segregationists on the Board asked for immediate action to build a new school for P.S. 68 and to remove the Black children from P.S. 83. They argued that P.S. 83 was conveniently located and would deny White pupils its facilities if integrated, that social prejudices of Whites would not allow the consolidated school to operate smoothly, and that mixed schools never work.

The weight of Simis's conversion, the strong precedent for adopting a local committee's report, the cost of building a second new school when the first was constructed to amply house the combined student body, and the fact that both schools were at that time operating smoothly in a single building convinced a majority of the Board members to oppose the segregationists' proposal. The Board passed a resolution providing that P.S. 68 be discontinued, and its teachers and students transfered to the new P.S. 83.[15] The consolidation compromise included a provision for a White principal and a Black Head of Department, with both Black and White teachers.[16]

The decision of the Board of Education in 1883 to continue the freedom of choice plan in Brooklyn was accompanied by a commitment to abolish the segregated Colored Schools as they became outmoded. When the Board agreed in 1891 to build a new school for P.S. 68, it created a contradiction in its own politics. According to the 1883 resolution, if P.S. 68 was outmoded, it should be abolished as a Colored School, and its students integrated into other public schools. But most Board members were not ready to proceed with the elimination of the dual school system.

Given the conflict within the Board between its own 1883 policy decision and the continued segregationist slant of its membership, pressure from the Black community to provide a new school had some effect. But the Black community was also ambivalent about eliminating its Colored Schools, and therefore concentrated its protest on obtaining a new and better facility, not necessarily an integrated one. Some Black leaders, including Stewart, consistently demanded integration of P.S. 68, but they were dependent on the decision of the White majority members of the local committee. On this issue, as on others, the Black seat on the Board meant no real control over Board decisions, but simply enough access to raise and prolong consideration of an issue and some influence when the Board was closely divided.

Action favorable to the Black integrationists, however, had to await the supporting vote of a White member of the local committee. During this last decade of the Brooklyn Board's separate existence, time worked in favor of the integrationists. Pressure for professionalism, standardization, and efficiency in the school system, and conformity with neighboring New York City, steadily increased, and White members of the Board began to accept integration as part of the "progressive" package.

In the spring of 1894, when Stewart's three-year term was due to expire, Black Republicans began clamoring for his replacement by a Black Republican member of the community. This was part of a general effort by Black Republicans to persuade newly elected Mayor Schieron, a Reform Republican, to dismiss all Black Democrats and replace them with loyal Black Republicans.[17] A committee from the Colored Republican Club of Brooklyn met with Mayor Schieron to press for the appointment of Samuel Scottron to Stewart's place on the Board, and in July, when Stewart's term expired, the Mayor complied.

Scottron followed the integrationist line of his Black predecessor on the Board. During his first year in office, when Flatbush was annexed to Brooklyn, the Colored School in the new Twenty-Ninth Ward was discontinued. In February of 1896, a Scottron Resolution that P.S. 69 be made a branch of Grammar School No. 19 was adopted, but P.S. 69 remained a small basically Black neighborhood school for the primary grades. P.S. 69 had the lowest registration and attendance by far of the three Black schools. During the last year of P.S. 68's existence as a segregated Colored School, the average attendance was 142 pupils, compared to 82 pupils in P.S. 69 during that same year (see Table 1 below). In 1901, when P.S. 69 was finally discontinued, there were only 63 pupils and 3 teachers.

In general, the Black schools were costing the City more per pupil to maintain than the White schools because of the low, and steadily declining attendance at the segregated schools. Not only were many Black children choosing to attend their neighborhood White school, but many Black parents from poorer sections of Brooklyn's Black community could not afford to clothe their children for school during the cold winter

TABLE 1. Registration and Attendance at Colored Schools
in Brooklyn 1890–1895[a]

	P.S. 67 (C.S.1)		P.S. 68 (C.S.2)		P.S. 69 (C.S.3)		Total	
Year	Reg.	Aver. Attend.	Reg.	Aver. Attend.	Reg.	Aver. Attend.	Reg.	Aver. Attend.
1890	397	296	224	134	126	103	747	533
1891	356	267	252	168	134	85	742	520
1892	341	244	213	142	113	82	667	468
1893	335	223	–	–	108	70	443	293
1894	329	236	–	–	108	75	437	311
1895	345	236	–	–	117	79	461	315
1896	–	212	–	–	–	–	–	212

[a]David Ment, "School Segregation in Brooklyn, 1850–1879," unpublished paper, found at Long Island Historical Society, January 1971, (Mimeographed), p. 25. *Proceedings,* April 6, 1897, 350.

months. P.S. 69 had been considered a financial albatross for over ten years. As early as 1883 the Board had considered housing a separate White school on one of the floors of C.S. 3 (P.S. 69) to decrease financial losses. The later move to make P.S. 69 a branch of a local grammar school was also intended to minimize the loss and increase uniformity in the school system's operation.[18]

By 1897, when Scottron moved to eliminate the largest segregated Black school in Brooklyn, P.S. 67, the Board of Education appears to have accepted the inevitability of ending Brooklyn's all Black schools. Scottron's March resolution that P.S. 67 be reorganized as an intermediate school was passed without difficulty. The Black community had also gradually come to an acceptance of discontinuing segregated schools, but was understandably concerned that full integration would allow the Board to eliminate Black teachers and principals from the school system. Alarmed at the prospect of losing their last administrative position in the school system, Brooklyn Blacks attacked Scottron's proposal to remove Charles Dorsey, the controversial Black principal of P.S. 67, from his post once the school was reorganized. The issue was referred to the Committee on Teachers for further examination. By the next meeting of the Board, the Black leaders who opposed Scottron's resolution had organized a petition against dropping Dorsey and the Black teachers of P.S. 67 from the roll, and forwarded it to the Committee on Teachers.

Not only was Dorsey important in the parallel social structure of the Black Brooklynites, but his position as principal provided a unique connection between the Black community and the White authorities. His role was as important as a conduit of information to and from his Black constituency and the White school authorities as was Scottron's role in the Board of Education itself. In fact, the antagonism that developed between Dorsey and Scottron was probably generated in part by their competitive roles as educational "delegates" from the Black community.[19]

Since control of the Brooklyn schools was largely in the hands of the local committees on the Board, Scottron had more potential influence than had Dorsey and his friends. Scottron was also a member of the Committee on Teachers that set out to investigate P.S. 67. The report of this Committee was highly critical of the school. Attendance had been declining steadily for ten years. As a result, the small student body was "abnormally and unwarrantably expensive" for the City to maintain. The cost per child for Brooklyn at P.S. 67 was $55, while the City average cost per child was less than $23 per year. Although the City was spending more than twice as much per pupil at P.S. 67, the school was failing to prepare students for admission to high school. In 1896, only one student from P.S. 67 graduated, and in 1897, the highest academic average in the school was less than 55 percent. The investigation of conditions and management at P.S. 67, carried out at the request of the Committee on Teachers by the Superintendent of Public Instruction, showed that: (1) each teacher above the third grade had to teach two grades because the school was too small for a grammar or intermediate school; (2) attendance was poor, partly because children had to commute from all over the City to attend; (3) "the work of the principal so far as discipline and attention to the material wants of the school are concerned has been fairly done; but in the great matters of supervising, instructing, and assisting the teachers in their class-work, there is no evidence to show that it has been of any value"; and (4) although the teaching did seem weak, several of the teachers had ability but needed better supervision and better attendance.

Thus the Committee on Teachers concluded: "The by-law adopted by the Board some years ago, by which colored children have the right to enter any public school in the city, precludes in the judgement of your Committee, the successful maintenance of any school which attracts only colored children." Black children had successfully passed entrance examinations for high schools from integrated schools in Brooklyn, and operations at P.S. 83 had proven that Black teachers could successfully teach children of all races. Therefore, P.S. 67 had to be radically reorganized as a neighborhood school which would inspire the confidence of all residents of the area. The Committee resolved that: (1) the Scottron resolution providing for reorganization of P.S. 67 be reconsidered; (2) the principal and teachers of P.S. 67 be dropped from the Roll of Teachers; (3) the local committee and the Superintendent be authorized to reorganize P.S. 67 as a grammar school and then to turn it over to P.S. 5 as a branch of that school; and (4) the pupils of P.S. 67 be transferred to schools in their own neighborhoods.

Despite the unanimous report of the Committee, the resolutions faced opposition at the general meeting of the Board. The Board recognized the need to reorganize P.S. 67, but, after heated debate, could not agree on what was to be done with the teachers and principal and postponed decision. At the next meeting of the Board, the Committee on Teachers reported that they would accept an amendment retaining the teachers from P.S. 67, but dropping Dorsey, the principal. But the full Board still could not agree. After yet another postponement, the specific question of Dorsey's position was referred back to the local committee for P.S. 67 and the Committee on Teachers for further investigation, against the judgment of Scottron and his supporter on the Committee. In July the Board agreed to Scottron's reorganization plan, making P.S. 67 a neighborhood intermediate school, but it was not until three months later that the matter of Dorsey's reappointment was finally resolved. Characteristically, rather than overrule the committee's recommendations, the composition of the committee was altered. Scottron and his supporter were replaced on the Committee on Teachers by two members of the Board who were more compromising. The Committee then submitted a list of reappointments for six Black female teachers and for Dorsey as principal of the new school (at a salary of $1,250 per year). At the same time the Committee submitted and accepted Dorsey's resignation and application for retirement with an annuity of half his new salary per year from November, 1897.

Meanwhile Scottron was under severe attack in the Black community for his insistence that Dorsey be fired. Even the *Brooklyn Eagle* supported the attack in its March 6 editorial.[20] A bi-partisan group of Brooklyn Black notables was incensed that Scottron, a Black man, could advocate the removal of one of his own people. T. McCants Stewart lead the anti-Scottron forces. Stewart and Scottron had twice competed for the Black seat on the Board of Education. Stewart had also been a very close friend of Dorsey and had, in fact, lived with him for ten years. Scottron maintained that the deplorable conditions at P.S. 67 reflected on Stewart. He implied that although Stewart had claimed to be an ardent integrationist on the Board, he had never raised the issue of P.S. 67 because he did not want to jeopardize his friends' position as principal. Stewart, however, was backed in his support of Dorsey by most of the Black political figures in Brooklyn. The fight within the Black community became vicious. Dorsey sued Scottron for $50,000 in libel damages, and Scottron charged his predecessor, Stewart, with suppressing letters from teachers in P.S. 67 about the deplorable conditions under Dorsey's administration. During the first year of Scottron's tenure of the Board, he had warned Dorsey that the quality of his school had to be improved and the brutalization of pupils stopped. Although this warning was reported to the Board, nothing was done by Dorsey to correct the situation.

Scottron appeared to have few Black supporters for his position. On May 26, a mass meeting of Blacks resolved to ask Republican Mayor Wurster not to reappoint Scottron to the Board. In return, a delegation of three Republican Scottron supporters approached the Mayor to plead Scottron's case. Despite widespread opposition from the Black Community, Scottron was reappointed by the Mayor to a final three-year term. At this time consolidation of the cities of Brooklyn and New York was underway. For the first few years, however, the Brooklyn Board continued to have some autonomy within the Consolidated City Department of Education, and thus there remained a Black seat on the Brooklyn Board.[21]

Feelings in the Black community that Scottron had betrayed the race persisted. Scottron had served almost eight years on the Board, had been instrumental in ending Brooklyn's freedom of choice plan, and had integrated the last two legally segregated Black schools in the City. Yet, many members of the Black community, writing about the possibility of appointing a Black to the centralized Board after full consolidation, lauded Stewart and White, and denigrated Scottron, his accomplishments lightly dismissed.

Charles Dorsey, despite his apparent failings as a principal, was a well-liked and respected member of the Black elite. The attack on his competence threatened the future mobility of other Black leaders and aspiring educators. Given a racial structure in which tokenism was the rule for Black appointments, each Black appointed by Whites to a position in the White-dominated institutions of society was a symbolic figure, conferring recognition and pride upon the whole racial group. A Black leader in disgrace threatened the social standing of the whole Black community. Dorsey was not just a school principal, but a token minority group representative in a White school system. Likewise, Scottron was not simply a Board member criticizing a school principal, but a Black leader jeopardizing the whole future of Black appointments to school administrative positions. Protesting members of the Black community did not defend Dorsey's record as principal of P.S. 67; they defended the importance of the Black community banding together to maintain the few positions of influence they had.

When Brooklyn's freedom of choice plan was formalized in 1883 it represented an open recognition of both social custom and institutional organization supporting racial boundaries in the City. All over the North, Jim Crow practice had gained a new post–Civil War legitimacy, and in education, it was reinforced by the 1894 New York State Law permitting the establishment of separate but equal schools,[22] and then the *Plessy v. Ferguson* decision in 1896.

In Brooklyn most Black leaders supported racially separate schools, party clubs, churches, and voluntary associations, and used these organized Black constituencies as a political base for their activities and positions. Mnay Black parents continued to send their children to segregated schools, not only because of opposition to integrated schools from the White community, but because of pressure from the Black elite to support these Black institutions, and their own desire to have their children educated in a Black environment.

The local committee system on the Brooklyn Board was meant to be an institutionalization of the principle of close relationships between the school authorities, the school staff, and the school constituency. The appointment of the first Black member to the Board, simultaneous with a decision to formalize the continuation of Colored Schools, reinforced the Board's orientation toward decentralized decision-making on educational issues and close working relationships between the local committees and the individual public schools.

Because of the centralized structure of the Board of Education of New

York City (Manhattan), the 1883 decision to eliminate the last three remaining segregated Black schools was made at the top, written into law, and meant to be implemented immediately. Even when community pressure altered the decision and two Black schools were allowed to continue operations, the City was clearly committed to abolishing these last segregated schools as soon as Black parents agreed. In the more decentralized decision-making system of the Brooklyn Board, however, the policy on eliminating Brooklyn's last three segregated schools was one of phasing them out individually. No set standards were established by which the desegregation decision would be made. As a result, conflicts between different forces and various interests developed in almost every instance.

The final decisions to eliminate each Colored School in Brooklyn were made for a variety of reasons. The schools were indeed an economic liability for the Brooklyn Board because of decreasing attendance and increasing costs. After its initial arguments over P.S. 68, the Black community became more united in its support of integration in the neighborhood schools if Blacks could be retained in their staff positions. Once the Black seat on the Board appeared more secure, the Black member of the Board, given some constituency support, could speak out more forcefully for integrating the last schools. By the time the issue of integrating the last two schools came to the attention of the Board, consolidation legislation had been passed, and pressure to conform to the racial policy of the Manhattan Board increased.

In addition, White fears of Black dominance in the schools proved unfounded. The Black population in the City stayed between one and two percent of the total population of Brooklyn from 1870 through 1900. The relatively small, scattered communities of Blacks seemed stable enough not to threaten the racial balance of the local public schools. Both Whites and Blacks became less fearful of integrated schools. By 1890 there were more Black children in integrated neighborhood schools than in the segregated Colored Schools. Black students and teachers had been functioning successfully in the schools they attended under the freedom of choice plan, and the old P.S. 68 was operating smoothly as part of an integrated P.S. 83.

Finally, the controversies over elimination of the Colored Schools in Brooklyn took place in the context of a wider struggle over centralization of administration in the Brooklyn public school system. Many cities throughout the country were centralizing and bureaucratizing their municipal governments in response to reformist demands for less political and more scientific administration. Municipal education was a frequent target of this pressure because of the growing complexity of urban education, and the drive toward professionalism in education and administration related occupations. Brooklyn, however, and especially the Brooklyn Board of Education, defended its own politically responsive decentralized system. Despite the efforts of educational progressives, such as William Henry Maxwell, superintendent of first the Brooklyn schools and then the consolidated schools of New York, and reform-oriented Brooklyn mayors like Low and later Schieron, pressures for a smaller, more centralized Board were consistently resisted. Even after the Consolidation Bill was passed in 1896, pressure from Brooklynites forced the charter drafting committee to maintain both borough autonomy and the local committee system in Brooklyn. Brooklyn Board members, citizens groups, school principals and teachers, and journalists defended the local committee system as a particularly responsive system which avoided the excess "mechanization" proposed by reformers. The Brooklyn Borough Superintendent fought back against charges of local committee corruption by emphasizing that appointments on the merit basis alone did not guarantee good teaching.

Good government and good education, claimed the progressives, were efficient and non-partisan. Defenders of politics as valuable and necessary in municipal affairs feared progressive reforms would eliminate representation and accountability from government decision-making. The reformists, however, by claiming a monopoly on progress placed their opponents on the defensive. In 1902, Brooklyn succumbed to the centralized structure that was by then characteristic of New York City government. The Borough School Boards were consolidated into one central New York City Board of Education dominated by the more professionally oriented, and more numerous, Manhattan Board members.

Most Black leaders in Brooklyn, whether they favored more or less integration in the schools, did not identify with the reformist movement. Reformists were generally upper-class professionals, highly critical of machine politics.[23] Black notables tended to be middle class, often non-professional, and frequently achieved high positions through political connections. They were politically closer to identification with the members of the Board of Education who opposed centralization, bureaucratization, and professionalization of educational administration. Reform successes meant a loss of power for Blacks. School Boards became smaller, and the possibility of seating Blacks on the Board diminished. Appointments were made on a nonpartisan merit basis dependent on traditional scholarship achievement to which Blacks did not have equal access. Local autonomy, including a local power base, was eliminated. Integration in Brooklyn, where few Black neighborhoods were large enough to influence their neighborhood schools, meant that in education, along with other municipal services, Blacks would lose any potential for community control, Black influence on the Board, and Black staffing of the schools.

But clearly the integration versus segregation issue in education did not fall squarely within the reformist versus regular party politics conflict. Blacks also felt that segregated schools as they existed in Brooklyn did not provide equal education for their children. They resented and resisted a forced separatism that placed Colored Schools in a different relationship to the educational administration than White Schools, often catering to White racist demands for educational Jim Crow.

After consolidation, Blacks had little role in local Brooklyn politics, and turned their attention toward the Republican administration in Washington or the struggle for political control of the greatly enlarged New York City. Both the Booker T. Washington–controlled Republican political machine and the Black Tammany controlled United Colored Democracy drew support from politically active Blacks in the City. Progressives and reformers were interested in Blacks mainly as poor tenement dwellers deserving of liberal sympathy but not political influence. Thus Blacks aspiring to municipal leadership positions were forced to accept the crumbs thrown to them by the political party machines.

NEIGHBORHOOD GOVERNMENT

DOUGLAS YATES

In the 1969 New York mayoralty campaign, "power to the neighborhoods" was the battle cry of an unusual candidate, who was running, he said, to offer fresh answers to an old problem: the much lamented "urban crisis." The candidate was Norman Mailer, and since he claimed to be part visionary and part conservative, it was hard to tell whether the slogan "power to the neighborhoods" looked back to a fondly remembered past or pointed forward to an imagined future. Coming at a time in American politics when a debate swirled around participatory democracy, it was not surprising that neighborhood government was a political issue. More puzzling, perhaps, is what is meant precisely by neighborhood government; what its origins are; what its benefits and deficiencies are thought to be; what the main obstacles are to its achievement; and what general problems it raises for local democracy and community development. I will explore these questions in light of the past and present experience of decentralized, neighborhood-based government.

HISTORICAL BACKGROUND

In terms of American urban history, the idea of neighborhood government is something rather new. Demands for neighborhood self-government have not been a familiar theme in political discourse, and there is little evidence, until very recently, of programs and policies designed to give power to urban neighborhoods. Thus, while Thomas Jefferson certainly did argue for the creation of "republics-in-miniature," his little Republic was an agrarian one. Indeed, Jefferson was notoriously suspicious of and hostile to the city. Nor have other previous analysts of local democracy paid much attention to the urban neighborhood as a locus for self-government. For example, the urban reformers at the turn of the century were obsessed with the fight against corruption and wanted to shift power away from grass-roots organizations to aloof, central administrators. The main debate in this century about local government has centered on whether the city as a corporate entity should enjoy more or less "home rule" in its relationship with state government.

The practice of urban government under the great political machines also reveals little precedent for neighborhood government. While it is true that the ward bosses of legend carefully cultivated the grass roots by dispensing Christmas turkeys and patronage and by dealing with citizen complaints and problems, the point of these services was to oil a centralized political machine. Simply put, the political exchange rate in machine politics was patronage or favors for electoral support, and the currency was not used to purchase direct local democracy. Indeed, according to one historian, the essential purpose of Boss Tweed's machine, the first and most dramatic of the species, was to centralize power and therefore overcome the stalemate and inertia caused by existing governmental fragmentation. The most that can be said of the old-time neighborhood bosses is that some special ones, like the Ahearns of New York's Lower East Side, did establish little baronies. But this is testimony to the existence of feudal power, not neighborhood democracy.

Other historical examples of "neighborhood government" that might be cited by present-day advocates tend to be slight or deceiving. New York and other cities may have had Borough governments (or the equivalent), but there is a considerable difference in scale between a borough and a neighborhood. Administrative field offices, district school boards, and community planning boards existed before the late 1960's, but their functions were usually strictly bureaucratic or merely advisory. Thus, it is only with the current urban crisis and with ensuing government programs that an explicit concern with participation, decentralization, and neighborhood government has emerged. Specifically, the first traces of what might loosely be called neighborhood government were found in urban renewal, the war on poverty, and the Model Cities program. In the case of urban renewal, according to James Q. Wilson, citizen participation was limited to advisory planning and to bitter opposition of proposed renewal plans. In the war on poverty's community action program, there was a constant struggle over the meaning of "maximum feasible participation," and as a result, the degree of local participation varied sharply from city to city. In most cities, however, poverty and political mobilization, not institutionalized neighborhood government per se, were the foci of community action. In contrast, Model Cities does focus directly on the urban neighborhood, but again, the legislation concerning participation is vague and ambiguous; and as in community action, the experience of Model Cities has varied widely, from total city hall control in cities like Chicago to substantial neighborhood control in cities like New Haven.

What is clear from the historical record is that, given these shallow roots, it is only certain contemporary and dramatic events like school decentralization in New York City that have focused political discussion on community control and neighborhood government.

WHAT IS DECENTRALIZATION?

In discussing the historical background of neighborhood government, we have related a poorly defined notion to other equally vague concepts such as citizen participation and decentralization. Indeed, the central failing in the debate about neighborhood power and control is that it rests on analytical quicksand. Difficult as it may be to define "neighborhood," it is more difficult to pin down the concepts of "participation" and "decentralization," for they have been used indiscriminately to describe governmental arrangements as different as colonialism and community control. People can hardly be expected to decide whether neighborhood government is a good or bad thing, a promising policy or a totally impractical one, unless they know how the concepts are defined. The most important strand in this web of tangled concepts is decentralization. In order to give a firm meaning to this suggestive and ambiguous concept, it is necessary to ask three different questions: (1) What does the particular mode of decentralization entail in terms of power relations between the center and the locality? (2) What is being decentralized? (3) What are the reasons for decentralization?

The first question arises from the facts that there can be a whole range of power relations between the center and locality, and the relations may be obscured by superficial administrative arrangements. For instance, a strictly hierarchical administrative system, such as exists in France, decentralizes administrative offices, personnel, and the functions of intelligence gathering and consultation with citizens to departmental prefects and parish mayors. However, these local officials have virtually no autonomous decision-making power. They are, in law and practice, agents of the central administration whose authority derives from the center and who are responsible not to the locality but to Paris.

My contention would be that governmental forms increase in genuine local autonomy the more that certain structural elements are included in them (the elements are ordered in terms of increasing local autonomy and power):

1. Intelligence gathering—stationing officials in localities to find out what is going on in the field.

2. Consultation and advisory planning—seeking out the opinion of local people on policy matters.

3. Program administration—making local people the administrative agents of central government programs and policies.

4. Administrative accountability—making district or neighborhood administrators responsible for government programs and accountable to local citizens.

5. Political accountability—establishing elected officials at the local level as representatives of local interests.

6. Authoritative decisionmaking—giving neighborhood representatives the power to make binding decisions on policy matters.

7. Political resources—giving localities control over resources such that local decision making involves real stakes and capacities.

If government involves elements 1 through 3, it constitutes a form of administrative decentralization or "command decentralization," as when a platoon leader in the field is given a measure of responsibility and decision-making autonomy. If government structure includes local decision making and control over resources (elements 4 through 7), it may constitute shared center-local control or full community control.[1] In sum, it seems that these seven elements constitute one dimension along which decentralization can be defined.

A second dimension that should be considered is the number of program functions involved, or "what is being decentralized." A neighborhood health clinic serves, for example, a single function, while neighborhood multiservice centers perform several functions. In light of both these two dimensions, it is clear that none of the current decentralization experiments come close to the ideal of a general-purpose, autonomous neighborhood government. What exists currently is a variety of single-function and multifunction experiments in which neighborhoods have limited power.

There are many examples of single-function experiments in administrative decentralization, such as municipal field offices of all kinds and district-based systems of service delivery. Single-function experiments with substantial local power include neighborhood-run health clinics, community corporations dealing with poverty programs, and decentralized school boards (as in New York City). Multifunctional experiments include Little City Halls in twenty cities which provide information and receive citizen complaints. Of a multifunctional character, but with a somewhat greater amount of local power, are the Model Cities programs, multiservice centers in forty-two cities, and neighborhood corporations in New Haven. It is interesting to note that there seems to be a relationship between the number of functions decentralized and the degree of local power. In experiments existing at present, those performing single functions tend to possess relatively more local autonomy, and local autonomy seems to diminish with an increased number of functions.

The variety of existing decentralization experiments attests to, at the very least, the growing interest in neighborhood government strategies. Given this apparent enthusiasm, it is obviously important to know why government officials and community leaders wish to decentralize. That is, what answers are typically given to the nagging question: Why decentralize at all? Summarizing various written and spoken opinions on the subject, there are at least four different justifications for decentralization: (1) decentralization will increase administrative attentiveness and responsiveness to neighborhood needs; (2) decentralization will reduce the perceived distance between citizens and their government and therefore increase citizens' feelings of political efficacy; (3) decentralization will develop community cohesion and thereby focus local resources and concern on shared problems; and (4) decentralization will dramatically increase local democracy by developing local leaders and by providing wider opportunities for citizen involvement in decision making.

As against this positive view, critics of decentralization contend that it will increase racial segregation and strife, decrease due-process "fairness" and impartiality in administration, permit widespread corruption, create unchecked feudal baronies, and undermine the efficient allocation of resources (presumed to be enhanced by strong central management). To a lesser extent, critics also argue that decentralization will solve no problems; that without a massive commitment of resources to the cities, the structure of urban government makes little difference.

At present, the *a priori* and normative claims for and against decentralization have become so numerous and so passionate that one political scientist, Alan Altshuler, has devoted a book, *Community Control,* to the task of sorting out and evaluating the conflicting arguments. The key point about this debate, however, is that it gives us almost no idea about the actual impact of decentralization on an urban neighborhood. In the first place, there has been little empirical research on the impacts of existing decentralization experiences. Secondly, as has been seen, decentralization, in the form of local autonomy or community control, has nowhere been achieved, and any evaluation of existing programs will necessarily deal with halfway measures and cannot indicate the effects of full decentralization. This being the case, it is foolish to expect a clear conclusion to the decentralization debate to arise from the present clash of rhetorical claims and speculative judgments. But it is possible to speculate more rigorously by considering the obstacles to and likely problems of decentralization. For if we consider these negative factors and still judge local control to be plausible, then advocacy of neighborhood government would rest on a careful assessment of possible dangers and deficiencies rather than on wishful thinking about structural change or blind despair about the present failures of urban government.

OBSTACLES TO NEIGHBORHOOD GOVERNMENT

If one considers the context of decentralization for only a minute, one should recognize certain obstacles to increasing neighborhood power. They are (1) the costs of community organizing in time and effort, (2) community conflict, (3) city hall–neighborhood conflict, and (4) general political conflict.

First, it is a truism that political activism and citizen participation demand a considerable commitment of time, energy, and other personal resources. Doubtless, it is for this reason that the activist segment of any political community is very small indeed. Moreover, in order to persuade individuals to engage in collective action, it is necessary that the rewards of such action be greater than the personal costs. This means that serious participation is likely to occur only when neighborhood government offers visible rewards, and works to solve concrete problems. As an added complication, there are many examples of desirable collective actions where it makes sense for the individual to participate only if he knows that everyone else in the community will join with him. This is true, for example, with garbage clean-ups and campaigns to curb dogs. If one or more people do not cooperate in the effort, the impact of everyone else's effort is necessarily vitiated.

As to community conflict, it has been noted by Bell and Held that a large number of community organizations already exist in poor neighborhoods.[2] One wonders whether these organizations, with their vested interests, will find any reason to promote and ultimately defer to a more generalized system of neighborhood government. Furthermore, many of the neighborhoods are characterized by racial and ethnic cleavages and, to a lesser extent, by religious differences and age differences (as between an old guard and "young turks"). If neighborhood government is to be a successful force for community cohesion and development, the various factions and vested interests will have to join together to pursue common purposes. Unfortunately, this has not always happened in recent experience. In some neighborhoods, Puerto Rican and black groups fight ceaselessly and bitterly; in other neighborhoods, entrenched community organizations have resisted any movement to neighborhoodwide structures.

City hall–neighborhood conflict has many manifestations. In some cases, community leaders claim that central government has consistently defaulted on the promise to give specific powers or resources to the neighborhoods. In other cases, local leaders complain about government interference with and surveillance of community programs. In still other instances, neighborhood leaders report that they cannot get the central government to act on requests or make decisions on issues of great importance to the neighborhood—the result being that neighborhood policies are hamstrung by government inaction. Finally, some neighborhood governments find themselves caught between competing or warring government agencies, and their programs thereby become administrative footballs.

If the neighborhood-based organization is lucky enough to avoid these obstacles, there is still the possibility that neighborhood programs will ignite a political controversy that seriously damages the efforts at decentralization. The most dramatic political explosion over decentralization developed over the community control of schools in the Ocean Hill-Brownsville district of New York City. Before it was over, the teachers' union, City Hall, and the neighborhood had experienced a long and bloody political war, in which union rights were pitted against community authority, and charges of white racism met countercharges of black anti-Semitism. Other neighborhood programs, especially the Little City Hall Programs in Boston and New York, have also raised considerable controversy. The charge has been made in these cases that the neighborhood city halls were nothing more than political clubhouses for the incumbent mayor. The furor was such that no public money was allocated for the New York program, and the Boston program has been constantly under political attack.

FURTHER PROBLEMS AND QUESTIONS

If these obstacles are not enough, there are a number of further problems and questions that require consideration before neighborhood government is declared an unmitigated blessing.

For one thing, if neighborhood institutions are created for 150,000 or 300,000 people (as is commonly proposed in the large cities), will the citizen really feel that much closer to his government? Democratic theorists argue that a *city*, not to mention a neighborhood, should probably contain no more than 200,000 residents if anything remotely like direct democracy is to exist.[3] Or, if there is one neighborhood service center for every 150,000 to 300,000 people, will the citizen gain that much proximity and access to city services? Preliminary research indicates that, where only one such center exists in a neighborhood, only a tiny percentage of local residents will be aware of its existence.[4]

More importantly, if fresh resources are not committed to the cities, will decentralization make a concrete attack on any urban problem? And if so, on which problem? Surely new housing, parks, or subways will not be built with decentralization alone. Nor is it obvious how decentralization will make a dramatic effect on other service problems that also depend strongly on physical resources, such as garbage collection and fire protection. The problems that seem most readily treated by decentralization are those that involve social attitudes and human behavior. If a schoolchild feels alien in his own classroom, and if policemen and citizens hate each other, the community obviously suffers from a breakdown of political authority. But under decentralization, a new set of attitudes may arise that fosters citizen pride in the community and greater sensitivity on the part of public servants who are now accountable to local masters.

Following this logic, one wonders whether neighborhood government will affect those problems for which community people are both the source and the victims. Among those problems are widespread littering, turning in false alarms on fireboxes, vandalism against school property, drug pushing, and mugging. The question is: Will neighborhood governments be able to govern their own people—to establish and enforce community norms and sanctions—any better than the existing central government? Or is there a broad realm of uncontrollable, antisocial behavior that no government, whatever its location, can deal with under present social and economic conditions?

A further problem is that evidence to date suggests that citizens in poor neighborhoods do not turn out in large numbers to vote in community elections. A consequence of this in the decentralized school board elections in New York was that white Catholics were elected in wholly disproportionate numbers to govern schools in black neighborhoods. Decentralization in this case thus gave power to the wrong people, perhaps defeating the very purpose of the decentralization strategy. There is a larger point here as well. The poor have typically lost out in the one-man-one-vote and one-dollar-one-vote sweepstakes that determine who gets what in American political and economic life. Indeed, this is one meaning of powerlessness. The argument is therefore made that government should consciously protect and work for the poor and poor neighborhoods, in a paternalistic way. Advocates of community control repudiate this principle of paternalism as colonialism, or worse, racism. But it is true that decentralization does represent a partial return to a free market system in political life. If, in a racially mixed decentralized district, conservative whites win control of the neighborhood government, the poor and the blacks have no recourse. The effect of decentralization then is to establish the legitimate authority of those very forces that were viewed as the source of oppression. Clearly, too, if a central government does not redistribute resources in favor of poor districts, decentralization may produce an urban version of suburban feudalism, where the rich get richer and the poor get poorer.

The same dilemma also raises at least two contrasting alternatives regarding the encouragement of citizen participation. The first one calls for a disintegration of central government functions and powers, so that the localities can maximize their role. This view may be called the centrifugal concept of participation. The second one calls for the increased control of the central government apparatus by local groups (e.g., black minorities). This is, by contrast, the centripetal concept of participation. More concretely, the kind of local participation sought by a Rhody McCoy in Ocean Hill–Brownsville is bound to be radically different from the participation sought by Kenneth Gibson in Newark.

CONCLUSIONS

For the long-term future, neighborhood government may very well be a desirable goal. Aside from the commonly expressed justifications already mentioned, neighborhood government may constitute the "big push" that Gunnar Myrdal talks about, which will shake up a stagnant bureaucracy and also change the attitudes of citizens toward government and their own community. But it is also certainly true that the road to neighborhood government will be a difficult one, for there are several visible obstacles and a number of unresolved problems and questions. What is most important is that there is not enough knowledge about existing neighborhood government experiments to know if the road is worth taking in the first place.

As to the immediate prospects of neighborhood government, one can, I think, be more certain and more pessimistic. In New York City, where neighborhood government has proceeded further than anywhere else, there is a realization among city officials that strategies must be implemented very gradually if at all. There is a specific awareness that unions and many politicians will fight neighborhood government bitterly, and that they have the power to damage or destroy it. There is also the sense that, whereas there has been success in developing community structures, it has been very difficult to move government toward decentralization, toward more flexible administrative procedures. The new strategy in New York is to tackle the failures of government directly, before promising any new revolution in participatory democracy. More precisely, the strategy, manifest in programs like the police department's Operation Neighborhood, is to move toward command decentralization, to enhance administrative responsiveness by locating accountability and decision-making power at the neighborhood level. This is, of course, a long way from neighborhood government.

Furthermore, it is doubtful that the neighborhood government movement will take many cities by storm in the near future. In cities with black majorities or near majorities, the movement is likely to be toward centripetal participation-control of city hall. Conversely, in cities with a small black percentage of the population, the critical mass of political power may be missing that is needed to force government in the direction of local participation. It is also unclear whether neighborhood control is desired by citizens even where the power to produce it presumably exists. In Berkeley, California, for example, an electorate containing a strong black and white radical coalition was able to elect its candidates but came nowhere near winning a referendum to decentralize the police.

Finally, there is the question of whether neighborhood government is desirable for all urban neigborhoods in the same way at the same time. We must remember (and we tend to forget) that neighborhoods differ sharply in terms of their ethnic homogeneity, their level of community organization, and their assortment of needs. The New York experience has suggested that a uniform and grandiose plan will fail to distinguish among neighborhoods, and that it may be necessary to think of neighborhood government in different neighborhoods at different times.

COMMUNITY CONTROL
AND THE ENCAPSULATING
POLITICAL STRUCTURES

CHIA-LING KUO

The Chinese Exclusion Act had permanent adverse effects on the Chinese on the Lower East Side as it had on Chinese throughout the United States. It created a small, powerless population unable to exert any political influence on the political processes in New York City. This lack of political power has made it difficult for the Chinese to compete successfully with other ethnic groups for government aid, including "Great Society" programs that were designed to insure community control, and the effective delivery of social services. Chinatown cannot be understood apart from New York City politics and the city's political and administrative structures. New York City is one of the world's largest cities, and its government encompasses a vast bureaucracy that cannot effectively serve local communities, especially those ethnic communities that are politically inept in seeking benefits from the city. As Manhattan Borough President Percy Sutton explained, "The reality of government in New York City is a system of supra-structured, centralized authority operating through grossly over-funded supra-agencies, which are unable or unwilling to deliver even a minimally acceptable level of basic municipal services to the neighborhood. This despite the almost total concentration of municipal powers in the office of Mayor."[1] Black militants in the 1960s dramatized the failure of city

From *Social and Political Change in New York's Chinatown: The Role of Voluntary Organizations*, pp. 119-30, by Chia-ling Kuo. Copyright 1977 by Praeger Publishers, Inc. Reprinted with permission of Praeger Publishers, Inc.

government to meet the needs of its minority populations and demanded community control and decentralization, which involves community participation in planning and implementing services. The militants' demands found a response in President Johnson's "Great Society" program, which was a grand scheme for solving the social problems of the nation. Model cities, which were a part of the "Great Society" program, were set up in 1966 in 150 communities in an attempt to solve the problems of urban slums and to elicit community participation in planning. City governments turned their attention to social services. New York City responded by establishing a number of community agencies and organizations.

They included Neighborhood Action, Model Cities Committee, Urban-Action Task Force, Neighborhood City Halls, and Community Corporation. Urban-Action Task Force and Neighborhood City Halls have been merged into a single structure called Neighborhood Local Government. These agencies have provided better services to communities than before and have established valuable channels of communication between the communities and government officials, which have helped minimize grievances and prevent social upheaval. New York City was one of the few large cities in the nation that did not experience race riots in the period 1967–68.

Neighborhood Action was created in 1969 and is specifically designed to provide funding for capital projects selected by the community. The Model Cities Committee performs functions of city government. The mayor appoints a neighborhood director in each area, who works with an elected committee. A central Model Cities Committee, composed of city officers, is responsible for the allocation of human and material resources and also for the review of plans proposed by the community to insure that they are consistent with city policy. The director is responsible for monitoring and implementing all plans. There are three model cities—central Brooklyn, East and Central Harlem, and South Bronx.

The Urban-Action Task Force was established in 1966 to insure the provision of basic services, such as garbage collection and police and fire protection. Members of the Task Force include community representatives and the operating heads of district organizations and of the Police, Fire and Sanitation Departments. The chairman of each Task Force, a high government official, elected officials, and community leaders met regularly to discuss community complaints and demands. By 1969, there were 50 Task Forces but none in Chinatown.

Neighborhood City Halls were established in 1966 and were the extension of the mayor's office into communities. Their functions consisted of supplying applications for complaints, provision of staff and technical assistance to community groups, and initiating programs in the community.

The Community Corporation is especially designed to alleviate poverty areas by organizing and educating the poor to solve their own problems and, most importantly, to allocate funds for service projects that the local service agencies propose to conduct. In 1964, Congress initiated the War Against Poverty, and the federal government allocated $550 million in poverty areas. The Council Against Poverty was established in New York to handle federal funds, and an Anti-Poverty Operation Board composed of city officials was created to handle city funds. In 1966, the city created Community Corporation, which was to receive technical assistance from the Community Development Agency, which is a part of the Human Resources Administration. However, the Council Against Poverty remained the policymaking body for all antipoverty agencies in New York City including Community Corporation. Community Corporation sends delegates who represent social agencies in the community to the council to work with its officials in planning and budgeting. Each individual Community Corporation is run by a board of directors elected by the community. The board reviews proposals submitted to it and makes recommendations for funding to the Community Development Agency.

There are 26 Community Corporations in the city that give assistance to poverty areas where a total of 3 million people live. The Community Corporation on the Lower East Side has 24 social agencies as delegate members. In Chinatown, the Chinatown Planning Council, the Chinatown Development Council, and the Health Center are members and receive funds annually from the council through the corporation. The Community Corporation divides the Lower East Side into 13 districts, which elect 31 members for 2-year terms to its Board of Directors. At least one-third of all board members must be considered poor according to the Office of Economic Opportunity guidelines for income level.

As these agencies went into operation, it was gradually realized that local neighborhood government would not be effective because the local citizens were not adequately included in the policymaking processes, the agencies did not have the power to manage resources to meet community needs, and there was no overall structure to coordinate the activities of the agencies on the local level. To remedy these problems, Mayor Lindsay proposed a plan for local government that combined the Urban-Action Task Force, Neighborhood City Halls, and the Community Action Program into a single agency called Neighborhood Local Government. His plan was put into effect in 1970.

To qualify for the establishment of a Neighborhood Local Government, a community had to have a population of at least 125,000; and since Chinatown has a population of only approximately 65,000, it did not qualify. Its "powerlessness" in city politics were thereby increased. The plan that Mayor Lindsay proposed had the two objectives of administrative and political decentralization, the first to be accomplished by the establishment of District Service Cabinets and the second by the establishment of Community Planning Boards.

District Service Cabinets were established in five neighborhoods— Wakenfield, Edenwald in the North Bronx, Crown Heights and Bushwick in Brooklyn, Corona Heights, and Rockaway. Members of the cabinet were officials of the Departments of Sanitation, Water Resources, Park, Fire, Police, Health Services, and Environmental Protection, the Board of Education, and the Housing Authority. A district manager, appointed by the mayor, headed the District Service Cabinet and coordinated the activities of the various departments and agencies. He had the power to convene cabinet meetings and to prepare the district budget. His power was limited and lay principally in his accessibility to the mayor, and, in this sense, he was a power broker. His main function was to open up channels of communications between the neighborhood and municipal service agencies.

The Bureau of Applied Social Research of Columbia University conducted an evaluation of the District Service Cabinets of the Neighborhood Local Governments. Generally, the study considered the cabinet capable of providing mechanisms for handling and referring complaints to the proper agency, improving the relationship between city agencies and the community, providing a form for coordinating activities and programs that the community needs, and allocating resources for community projects.

The district managers met once a month to discuss mutual problems. At a meeting I attended in November 1974, the problems discussed included the difficulty of dealing with landlords and the local power elite. For example, when landlords refused to give heat, the district manager could not compel them to do so. The district manager often found the small local elite "self-seeking." For example, the Chamber of Commerce in an ethnically mixed, middle-class neighborhood complained that it had no minority representation. However, when pressed to remedy the situation, it ignored the district manager's advice. It was clear that the power of the district manager was limited in dealing with local power structures. They had no administrative power, and very often they could only steer a complaint to the department of the city concerned that failed to deliver the service.

Community Planning Boards were established in 62 community districts. Each board is made up of 50 members. Some members are appointed by the president of the borough in which the board is located. They represent various associations and organizations in the community. Councilmen-at-large from the borough also serve on the board. The board works closely with city- and state-government officials and members of Congress and receives technical assistance from the City Planning Department.

The Lower East Side did not have a Neighborhood Local Government, although it had a field-worker from the agency's central office. The field-worker's ability to serve the community was very limited. For example, if she received a complaint against the Sanitation Department, she could call up the Department and request that the matter be attended to. The Sanitation Department may or may not have complied with her request. She attended community meetings regularly and was able to alert city officials to problems that may have become serious and disrupting. Her duties consisted largely of receiving complaints and referring them to city agencies. Theoretically, all the residents in the 62 community districts have an equal voice in the local government agencies. Unfortunately, in ethnically mixed areas, there is conflict among different groups when there is an unequal distribution of power and resources. In 1975, tensions among different ethnic groups on the Lower East Side were mounting, especially between the Jews and Puerto Ricans. While Jews dominate the Lower East Side, the Puerto Ricans, who are the largest ethnic group on the Lower East Side, intend to share power with them, or, if possible, to wrest it from them. The field-worker of the Local Neighborhood Government, who was Puerto Rican herself, was helpless to ease the tensions. It was reported that in Crown Heights, Brooklyn, the Neighborhood Local Government with its larger staff, including its District Service Cabinet and the district manager, could not ease the tensions between the black and the Hasidic Jews, who were competing for control of the community.[2]

These agencies—the Neighborhood Local Government, the Community Planning Board, and the Community Corporation—were intended to serve as channels through which local communities could express their discontent and demands so that their needs could be met. However, these agencies still reflected the power of the central government, which could either withhold or deliver municipal services to the local neighborhoods. Percy Sutton proposed a plan that calls for elected Neighborhood

Councils in 49 Council Districts, which share power with the city government. According to this plan, the basic local governing unit or Neighborhood Council would have more members from separate geographical districts with populations of approximately 200,000 each. One member would serve as a chief district executive. Then the Neighborhood Council, the city councilmen, the borough president, and the city government would act as a governing body assisted by a 50-member Community Board including the district executive. The Community Board would be a nonsalaried advisory body, of which half would be appointed by the county executive and half by the local council executive. This Community Board would have the power to make decisions that affect the local communities. Under this plan, the present City Council, which exercises legislative and budgetary powers, would include the 49 members of the Neighborhood Council Districts. The Board of Estimate and the City Council would share tax-raising, expense, and capital budget responsibilities, and plan capital budget projects with the mayor. Now, only the mayor has the power to undertake such tasks. The Board of Estimate would direct City Planning, the Site Selection Board, the Franchise Bureau, and the secretary of the Board of Estimate. The Manhattan Borough president believes that his plan would provide the local Neighborhood Council with the power necessary to effectively deliver services such as snow removal, garbage collection, street cleaning, park maintenance, health care, neighborhood center, police and fire protection, day care, and youth and senior citizens' services and facilities. Most importantly, the local neighborhoods would be given a role in self-government.[3]

His plan, if adopted, would enable the local neighborhoods to participate effectively in city government and to receive adequate services. However, they could not make any more demands on the city. Moreover, the city government does not enjoy complete freedom to deal with its problems since it shares power with the state government, the federal government, special public authorities such as the Port Authority, the Metropolitan Authority, and the Urban Development Authority, and private institutions such as the Real Estate Planners, the Association for a Better New York, the Real Estate Board, the Chamber of Commerce, and Economic Development Council. Furthermore, it depends on the federal and state governments for financial assistance. Under these circumstances, the city cannot always realize the goals and the priorities it has established to meet the needs of the community. For example, in 1960, the city wanted to build a low-income public housing project, and it negotiated with the federal government for subsidies. The federal government placed such restrictive measures on its aid that, in the end, the city itself financed the project. The federal government sometimes finances projects it considers of top priority rather than those the city considers of top priority. The building of the interstate highway illustrates this. The interstate highway was supposed to provide highways within cities, but the federal government spent the funds for the benefit of the suburbs rather than on the roadways and mass transportation that the city needed. Similarly, the state also places constraints on the city in relation to programs. For instance, the state has authority for education and can reverse the recommendations of the city dealing with education. The city wanted to restructure the educational system by decentralization, but the state legislature delayed a year before enacting the legislation that did so, and when it acted, it ignored the city's recommendations.

The state public authorities are free to act without consulting the city. For example, the Urban Development Corporation can plan and build new industrial, residential, or civic facilitiês in any city in the state. It has power to issue bonds, which must be covered by revenue. Since bonds have to be paid by government subsidy, the corporation cannot build low-income housing without a subsidy from the federal, state, or city governments. The state and the city collect only one-third of all tax revenue, while the federal government collects two-thirds. This means that the city cannot impose and expand basic services and eliminate income inequality without the aid of the federal government. The city is often powerless to do what it wishes. Furthermore, the city is subject to the pressures of special-interest groups, which often render it difficult for the city to accommodate poverty areas. The interrelationships among the city, the state, and the federal governments can be viewed as continual conflicts that can be resolved only by a reallocation of resources and responsbilities among them. At the present time, the interrelationships among the city, the state, and the federal governments are very similar to those existing between the central government and local community that Bailey describes by the concept of "encapsulating political structure."

In 1975, the Neighborhood Local Government was reorganized, and its name changed to the Office of Neighborhood Services. The Neighborhood Local Government served only a few selected areas, but the Office of Neighborhood Services serves 51 districts throughout the 5 boroughs— 8 in the Bronx, 17 in Brooklyn, 12 in Manhattan, 12 in Queens, and 2 in Staten Island. The budget for the Office of Neighborhood Services for 1975 was approximately $1.5 million dollars and is financed jointly by the city and federal governments. The budget of the Neighborhood Local Government had been twice that amount.

A District Service Cabinet has been established in each district and is composed of officers on a managerial level from all major city agencies such as Police, Sanitation, Health, Parks, and other departments. The cabinet holds meetings—which are chaired by a commissioner or deputy commissioner—regularly to discuss and facilitate service delivery.

The Office of Neighborhood Services has two objectives—to enlarge the concept of decentralization and to increase the areas for services. Its policy is to coordinate existing programs rather than to develop new ones. It stresses the concept of self-help for community improvement and works with both city agencies and community organizations to solve community problems and to improve the delivery of services. Communities have direct access to the office of the mayor through the district managers who attend the meetings of the District Service Cabinets, and residents who contact the Office of Neighborhood Services have immediate access to the major city agencies. Consequently, unnecessary bureaucratic procedures or "red tape" are eliminated, there is greater utilization of local resources, and the delivery of services is much more effective.

The response of the Office of Neighborhood Services to the garbage strike in 1975 illustrates the efficiency of its organization and operations. Before the strike caused great inconvenience or a major health hazard to city residents, the District Service Cabinets in various districts organized task forces composed of officers from the Departments of Sanitation, Police, Fire, and Parks, and of city councilmen, state senators, and assemblymen, and congressmen to work out solutions to the problems caused by the strike. The task forces, in turn, established councils in the communities to cooperate with the District Service Cabinets to apply the solutions that were worked out.

The Office of Neighborhood Services has been successful in dealing with other sanitation problems in local communities. It encourages and assists local communities in block clean-up, while, at the same time, it informs the Department of Sanitation of the needs and views of local communities. In Chinatown, a Chinatown Council was established to clean the streets under the supervision of the District Service Cabinet. The council is composed of young volunteers who work with the CCBA,* restaurants, and stores. The young volunteers are trained by the Department of Sanitation and work also with the Department of Parks and are empowered to issue warrants.

---

*Editor's note—Chinese Consolidated Benevolent Association, the main traditional governing group in Chinatown consisting of family, district, merchant, and guild associations.

Youth problems are given special attention by the Office of Neighborhood Services. It provides youth specialists in each district to assist the community in a wide range of educational and recreational programs and has organized Youth Advisory Councils in each district. In the summer, the Urban Corps and Neighborhood Youth Corps provide employment for youth. The Urban Corps employs college youths to attend neighborhood meetings and develop neighborhood programs, and the Neighborhood Youth Corps provides jobs to non-college youths from ages 14 to 21 in hospitals, day-care centers, fire houses, police precincts, nursing homes, schools, and churches. In addition, the Office of Neighborhood Services has organized youth advisory councils in communities throughout the city.

The Office of Neighborhood Services is more effective than the Neighborhood local Government, since it extends over all areas of the city; and although it does not develop new programs, it coordinates existing programs essential to local communities and thereby makes them more effective. Furthermore, it has made important contributions to the solution of social problems in local communities, particularly juvenile delinquency. However, the concept of self-help, which the Office of Neighborhood Services emphasizes, has limited application to ghettos, which lack the human and material resources needed to solve these pressing social problems. More significantly, the recent budget cuts by the city government have dramatically reduced personnel in all city agencies and the number and size of their programs, thus severely limiting the Office of Neighborhood Services as an agency of social change.

While these service agencies have limited effectiveness, they provide the local communities with a line of communication to city officials. The Chinatown businessmen and American-born professionals who were appointed by the borough president to represent Chinatown on the Community Boards are given an opportunity to participate actively in U.S. political processes. Their influence on these agencies is minimal, yet they have learned through their involvement in various programs and activities the mechanics of manipulating the U.S. political system and the value of cooperating with other ethnic groups. Their outlooks have been broadened, and they have become society-oriented. Their interests have been extended beyond Chinatown, and this has led them to a recognition of the importance of forming alliances in dealing with the larger political structures. They view the newly formed Coalition of the Lower East Side Neighborhood Associations as a viable mechanism for achieving community control, and it has provided them with a power base. The members of the coalition support their projects, which enables them to assert their independence of the power structure in Chinatown.

In contrast, the CCBA officials have never joined or participated in other organizations on the Lower East Side, nor have they had working relationships with other ethnic minorities. They remain community-oriented and ethnic-centered. The officials of the CCBA expressed their views of other ethnic groups and of their conceptions of Chinatown as a community most openly in a meeting in Chinatown on July 18, 1976, concerned with the controversy between the CCBA and the Chinatown Planning Council and other social-service agencies in Chinatown over the use of a public-school building in the community that was vacated by the city. The building is a five-story structure located in the center of Chinatown and had housed Public School 23, now located at another site. The CCBA had requested the city to give the building to its Chinatown Improvement Committee to house its programs. The Chinatown Improvement Committee was formed in 1974, with the support of the City Council and the borough president, specifically for the purpose of improving the physical and social environment of Chinatown. The CCBA officials argued that in order for the Chinatown Improvement Council to achieve its goals, it should receive government assistance, including physical facilities such as the vacant public-school building.

The plans of the CCBA for the use of the building called for a cafeteria and a senior citizen center to be located on the first floor, a health clinic on the second floor, and a day-care center on the third floor. It was over its plan for the day-care center that its controversy with the Chinatown Planning Council and the other social agencies developed. The Chinatown Planning Council had established a day-care center in the building when it housed Public School 23 in space rented with a seven-year lease. The plan of the CCBA did not include provision for the Chinatown Planning Council day-care center, and, consequently, if the CCBA obtained the building, the Chinatown Planning Council day-care center would have to be either relocated or discontinued. The Chinatown Planning Council and other social agencies argued that the Chinatown Improvement Committee was not initially designed or planned to be a part of the CCBA structure but an independent community project that all the existing agencies would conduct jointly. The Chinatown Planning Council and Hamilton-Madison House, the YMCA, and the Staten Island Community College, which planned to conduct a mini-university program, together submitted an application to the city for the school building. This action infuriated the CCBA, which claimed that it had the exclusive right to the use of the building. At the meeting on July 18, 1976, an ex-president of the CCBA angrily denounced the Chinatown Planning Council for its action, stating, "When the Public School 23 school building becomes vacant, the CCBA should be entitled to use it and not the CPC.

CPC joins forces with the YMCA, Hamilton-Madison House, and Staten Island Community College to compete with CCBA. Such a strategy is the practice of the 'broker class' who uses foreign power to suppress their own people." He further stated, "Public School 23 is located at the center of Chinatown, we cannot tolerate it being used by foreigners. The action of the CPC is obvious: it intends to challenge the CCBA."[4] The same official also accused the Chinatown Planning Council staff of being non-Chinese in their speech, behavior, and values, and therefore, unable to understand the needs of the residents of Chinatown or to represent the community.

It is apparent that the CCBA does not intend to ally itself with other ethnic groups in a common cause but wishes to maintain Chinatown as a closed community. The attitudes of the leaders of the CCBA reflect a century of discrimination against the Chinese by the larger society and their exclusion from participation in it. Their view of community control is entirely different from that of the Chinatown Planning Council and other social agencies. While the goal of these agencies is to integrate Chinatown into the U.S. political system, the goal of the CCBA is to maintain the "Chineseness" of Chinatown and its independence of the larger society. Their ideological differences will keep them in continual conflict as long as U.S. domestic policy remains the same. However, the recent drastic cutbacks in social services due to the city's fiscal crisis may affect the position of the Chinatown Planning Council and other agencies in Chinatown and the Lower East Side.

The CCBA, the Chinatown Planning Council, and the other social agencies are waiting for the city to make its decision on this issue. Manhattan Borough President Percy Sutton stated in an interview that he would like all the agencies to use the building and that he felt Chinatown can have many leaders. He explained that each organization has its own constituents, and each contributes to the welfare of the community. His advice may persuade the various groups to compromise their differences because of the power he exercises in the disposition of city property.

THE CHINATOWN ADVISORY COUNCIL AND CITY POLITICS

The establishment of the Chinatown Advisory Council in 1970 symbolized the increasing importance of Chinatown in city politics. In a report on Chinatown published in 1968, the Department of City Planning of New York suggested as part of its decentralization plan the creation of a policymaking council for Chinatown.[5] The purpose of the council would be to integrate the Chinese into city politics and to encourage self-determination and citizen participation in major planning and development decisions. The council would be composed of high-level representatives of city, state, and federal agencies, local Chinese, and non-Chinese organizations and institutions such as hospitals, the Community Service Society, and the churches, and representatives of the adjacent non-Chinese neighborhoods, whose responsibility would be to provide technical advice and assistance to the community for social and physical development, and to assign and coordinate funds and work for community agencies.

Manhattan Borough President Percy Sutton who has great interest in Chinatown, established the Chinatown Advisory Council in spring 1970. It had six committees dealing with housing, employment, education, the aged, youth, and health. A wide range of topics were discussed at the council meetings, including traffic and parking, the building of a Chinese cultural center, and recreational facilities. The meetings were open to the public. The youth were encouraged to participate in the council except the radical youth group I Wor Kuen. They were quite vocal, particularly in their debates with the CCBA representative, who attended the meetings regularly.

The borough president served as president of the council and was recognized as an effective leader, but residents criticized him for some of his appointments to committee chairmanships. For example, an owner of substantial real estate whose main interest in the community was profit-making was appointed chairman of the Housing Committee. It was felt by some that the borough president "handpicked" committee chairmen when he should have conducted elections for their positions. In fact, no one volunteered to serve, and so he had to appoint the chairmen. It was generally conceded, however, that regardless of who served as president, the council would encounter difficulties due to conflicting political and economic interests.

The borough president's noteworthy achievement was to secure funds for the construction of a Chinese cultural center in Chinatown. However committees within the council were not able to deliver social services. The borough president was greatly respected and skillful in dealings with the different factions, but he was unable to unite them for a common cause. Each association that these faction leaders represent is financially independent and does not require the president's endorsement when applying to the federal, state, or city governments for funds. In fact, competition for funds between the Chinatown Planning Council and the

Chinatown Foundation* caused the dissolution of the Chinatown Advisory Council in 1973. The council has changed its name to the Chinatown Task Force with only a few selected individuals as members, and few meetings have been held since its formation.

Actually, long before the dissolution of the council, the members of the youth organizations were dissatisfied with the direction that the council had taken. They had had high hopes of making major changes in Chinatown through the council, but as events developed, it became clear to them that there was little chance for innovations mainly because CCBA members dominated the council. It was able to do so because it had 59 votes since it represents 59 family and district associations. The social structure of the community is such that the youth realized that the potential which the council had to serve as a vehicle for major social change would not be realized. The problems the council encountered were not unique. All city-government local neighborhood agencies have experienced similar difficulties with the local communities that they serve, which is clearly illustrated in the previous section "Community Control and the Encapsulating Political Structures."

Although the council no longer functions, its history and its failures reflect the difficulties the city agencies encounter. First, the city agencies are not effective in dealing with local power structures and conflict groups. Second, the Neighborhood Local Government could not provide adequate services to the community due to the lack of funds. The city itself is subject to the larger encapsulating political structures, which can either aid or withhold funds from it. Third, the city gives free rein to the community in running its internal affairs but discourages the community from seeking community control over essential services such as education and health care because of the pressure from special interest groups.

*Editor's note—Chinatown Foundation—a social service agency established by the Chinatown Advisory Council in 1971.

4

NEIGHBORHOOD CYCLES

City neighborhoods have a life cycle of their own as they move from development to growth to slum formation to renewal. The cities of today contain neighborhoods in each of these stages. However, this is not an inexorable pattern. Neighborhoods can settle in one stage or skip stages as they grow older. They can also go through the whole cycle a number of times. There are intervening variables in such factors as the type of housing, level of community spirit, and general amenities of the area. Stable neighborhoods therefore exist, but more common in our cities is the once fashionable area now a slum or the slum section undergoing revitalization.

The four selections in the chapter explore neighborhood cycles. Besides defining the pattern, the articles discuss slum formation in two areas and note the factors behind stability in another.

Edgar M. Hoover and Raymond Vernon begin their discussion by challenging the simplistic concentric zone theory of urban development. While the basic outlines of the theory have validity, they contend that there is a more complex pattern involved for the New York metropolitan region. To analyze this pattern, the authors present five stages in the evolutionary cycle of neighborhoods and note where in the region these stages are occurring. Stage 1 represents an area in which single-family houses are being built. In stage 2 there is increasing neighborhood density with the building of apartment houses—a transition stage for the community. By stage 3 the area is beginning to experience decline, with an increasing population which overcrowds existing buildups. Stage 3 signifies the start of the slum formation process. Stage 4 represents the slum fully formed but with a decrease in population density. Hoover and

Vernon see a thinning-out period after a slum area attains its highest density. Finally, stage 5 indicates renewal for a neighborhood involving primarily luxury apartment development or middle income and low income housing. The authors acknowledge that there can be variations within this cycle and present it as a generalized portrayal of neighborhood patterns.

Sam Bass Warner, Jr., in his study of the Tremont Street district of Lower Roxbury in Boston provides an analysis of a declining lower middle class area during the late nineteenth century. Housing built for the lower middle class was of a poor quality, not suited to stand up well over time. The housing of this group also crowded the neighborhood. Cheaply made housing and crowded conditions doomed the neighborhood. As the lower middle class rose in income and there were changes in housing styles, industrial jobs, and transportation services, the area fell into obsolescence for this group. The neighborhood did not have the flexibility to adjust to changing conditions. The only response for the lower middle class was to move out of the area. The working class inherited the housing, but it was poorly suited for them. Because of rents which were too high for this new income group, single-family houses were converted into multiple-family dwellings. Density increased, and the area moved toward a slum.

In Gilbert Osofsky's study of Harlem there is a similar slum formation process. Housing built for one class was not suitable for another. However, there are differences between Lower Roxbury and Harlem. In Harlem it was the building of luxury housing rather than cheap housing that caused problems. Nonetheless, there was a shift in the neighborhood from one class to another, in this case from upper to lower class residents. High rents caused conversion of single-family houses and the taking in of boarders for the lower income blacks migrating into Harlem. Increasing congestion, low wages, and unsanitary conditions moved Harlem toward a slum. Both Lower Roxbury and Harlem were essentially, with some variations, in stage 3 of the neighborhood cycle.

Roger D. Simon's article on Milwaukee's Ward 14 indicates the possibility of a neighborhood settling in one stage of the cycle. There is no inevitability about the neighborhood pattern, as various factors can affect the cycle. If Warner's Tremont Street district showed the decline experienced in an area that lacked the flexibility to accommodate change, Simon notes the stability found in an area that could adapt to changing conditions and experience upgrading. The differences between Boston's Lower Roxbury and Milwaukee's Ward 14 are discussed.

HOW NEIGHBORHOODS EVOLVE

EDGAR M. HOOVER and RAYMOND VERNON

So far, we have simply been describing some of the most conspicuous changes in the Region's over-all settlement pattern. Volumes more could be added by way of description, tracing historical trends in the particular residence patterns of different income, ethnic, or occupational groups and the changing complexion of the Region's myriad neighborhoods. But a closer examination of processes of change, if it is to be fruitful to our understanding, must be directed toward explanation and not mere description.

In the search for significant causal relations, hypothesis must play a part. Our next task is to develop a concept of the whole process of the evolution of the metropolitan population pattern which can be tested by its ability to account for the observed facts and which can serve to suggest the directions that further development is likely to take.

The shifting pattern of metropolitan residence areas has often been schematically described in terms of gradually widening concentric zones pushing out in all directions from a growing central business core like ripples from a splash. Nonresidential "downtown" land uses, pre-empting the very center of the metropolitan area almost exclusively, expand into the immediately surrounding old residential areas, and also extend an aura of blight far beyond the range of their actual land-taking.

Reprinted by permission of the publishers from *Anatomy of a Metropolis: The Changing Distribution of People and Jobs within the New York Metropolitan Region* by Edgar M. Hoover and Raymond Vernon. Cambridge, Massachusetts: Harvard University Press. Copyright © 1959 by Regional Plan Association Inc.

Housing nearest the center is mainly slum—because it is the oldest, because it is cramped, because the street traffic and other aspects of downtown development make it undesirable for residence, and because it comes to house a concentration of disadvantaged people who are shunned as neighbors by those more fortunate or longer in residence. These slum characteristics are persistent, even cumulative, since the economics of slum property deters extensive replacement, modernization, or even maintenance of the antiquated housing.

The near-central slum area, eroded from the inside and along its main streets by competing land uses, and having to accommodate an influx of bottom-income people, expands outward into the next nearest and next oldest zone, mainly by the down-grading and conversion of old apartments and houses to higher densities. This pressure, as well as over-all population growth, forces the population of the next zone to push outward in turn, and so it goes till we reach the out-crawling fringe of urban development where new houses replace farms, woodland, or golf courses.

This highly simplified picture is not unrelated to reality in the New York Metropolitan Region, but it needs a good deal of modification to take account of observed facts. In the first place, there is not just one high-density commercial center but many, of different orders of magnitude: there is not only Manhattan but Newark, Jersey City, Paterson, Passaic, Elizabeth, New Brunswick, and many other old cities. The widening ripples come, then, not from a single pebble dropped into a puddle, but from a scattered handful of large, middling, and small pebbles, each a focus of expansion. Secondly, the pattern does not really shape up into neat concentric circular zones, because of manifold variation in transport facilities, topography, zoning, and so on which "distort" the picture. Thirdly, people do not just "shove over" from one block to the next, like a row of dominoes falling, but often move to a quite different part of the metropolitan area once they decide to move at all. New residential developments too, as we have already seen, do not simply extend the built-up area into the countryside in solid sequence, but "leapfrog" across intervening vacant land in order to use sites better matched to the current demand for new housing. Finally, the housing supply responds to changing demand in several alternative ways.

We can get a realistic view of what has been happening in the New York Metropolitan Region by identifying areas in sequential stages of development. Some of the oldest communities in the Region have evolved through the whole succession while other, less "mature" parts of the Region are still in earlier stages. Our hypothesis is that the historical pattern of sequence, as exhibited in cross-section in the present structure of the Region, does have enough predictive value to be useful, if we can allow for certain evident changes in the impact of such basic determinants as means of transport.

What then are the stages of evolution we can identify, and where in the Region are they found?

Stage 1 is residential development in single-family houses. This stage, the earliest of all, is just beginning to appear in some outlying parts of the Region, is currently in full swing in the outer parts of the Inner Ring, and was passed long ago in most of the Core and in the central parts of the large Inner Ring cities, notably Newark. . . . new residential construction in the outer counties of the Region is primarily single-family. In every Outer Ring county, more than 72 percent of the new housing covered by permits issued in the first half of 1958 was in one-family structures, and all of the counties with more than half of their new housing in multifamily structures in that period were Core counties except Essex.

. . . very rapid population growth is associated with this first stage in development rather than with any subsequent increases in density that may occur through redevelopment or conversion. Thus, in the 1920's, Queens was the area in which this stage was most apparent. By the 1940's, the big boom in Queens was over, and Nassau and Bergen Counties had been joined by such Outer Ring counties as Suffolk and Monmouth in passing into the first stage. Since 1950 the zone of most active development of new residential land has moved still farther out, especially on Long Island. As recently as the early 1950's, two to three houses were being built in Nassau County for every one in Suffolk; but in each year after 1955, more have been built in Suffolk than in Nassau.

Stage 2 is a transition stage in which there is substantial new construction and population growth in the area, but in which a high and increasing proportion of the new housing is in apartments, so that average density is increasing. Much of the apartment construction replaces older single-family houses.

The zone of transition to a predominantly apartment pattern of housing can be traced in some detail in terms of the data for individual municipalities in the Land-Use Survey Area. . . . We find, first, a rather compact and inlying group of these municipalities where the process was already so far advanced by 1950 that more than half the dwelling units enumerated in the 1950 federal Census of Housing were in multi-family structures, here defined as structures for three or more households. These municipalities are all very close to New York City or are large old subcenters and their immediate suburbs. Nearly all were developed prior to the period of mass automobile commuting. In southern Westchester we find Yonkers, Mount Vernon, and Bronxville; in Nassau County, the tiny apartment community of Great Neck Plaza near the Queens line; and on the New Jersey side, most of the cities in Hudson County, the old cities of Newark and Passaic, and the suburb of East Orange adjoining Newark.

That is an indication of the extent of the outward spread of multi-family development by 1950. There has been significant further extension since then, with more communities entering Stage 2. Thus we can identify a "mature" group of places in the Land-Use Survey Area in which the proportion of units in multifamily structures in 1950 was already at least 10 percent and in which an increased proportion of multifamily units appears in the "housing starts" of the period 1951-1955. This group includes two old and sizable Inner Ring cities (Elizabeth and Paterson) and some commuter settlements with exceptionally good access to New York City or to major Inner Ring subcenters. In Westchester there is the string of commuter stops on the Hudson Division of the New York Central (Hastings, Dobbs Ferry, Irvington, Tarrytown); the Harlem Division stops of Tuckahoe and White Plains; and the New Rochelle-Mamaroneck-Port Chester sequence on the New Haven Railroad. On Long Island the well-served communities of Long Beach, Cedarhurst, Rockville Centre, Freeport, and Great Neck appear in the list. In a continuous band near Newark and Paterson we have Montclair, Orange, Clifton, and Rutherford.

To complete the picture of the transitional zone, we have to take account also of what is going on in areas closer in or farther out than our Land-Use Survey Area. In the Riverdale area of the Bronx, in eastern and southern Queens, and in Staten Island there has been active redevelopment into apartments. The same applies in the major Outer Ring centers such as Bridgeport, Stamford, Poughkeepsie, and New Brunswick, where a considerable proportion of the occupants work outside the Region's Core. Finally, there has been some new apartment development in other Outer Ring spots with special site advantages, primarily shore communities in Fairfield and Monmouth Counties.

Most of the areas where the transition process that we call Stage 2 is markedly evident, however, lie in the inner part of the Inner Ring and the outer fringes of New York City. According to our statistics for the first half of 1958, the construction of new multifamily buildings—defined now as structures for two or more families—predominated over the construction of single-family homes in a compact zone extending no farther out than a line beginning at Long Beach, on the south shore of Long Island, and extending through Hempstead, Flushing, Norwalk, Rye,

Yonkers, Maywood, Paterson, Rutherford, Belleville, West Orange, Irvington (New Jersey), Elizabeth, and Perth Amboy (plus offshoots in New Brunswick and Ossining).

Stage 3 is a down-grading stage, in which old housing (both multi-family and single) is being adapted to greater-density use than it was originally designed for. In this stage there is usually little actual new construction, but there is some population and density growth through conversion and crowding of existing structures. This stage appears most clearly in areas of recent "slum invasion" located on Manhattan's upper West Side, in sections of the Bronx and Brooklyn, and in certain old urban areas in and around Newark, Paterson, Passaic, Elizabeth, and the Hudson County cities.

Of course, the sequence to this stage from the preceding one is not always clean-cut. Thus in the down-grading stage there may be a certain amount of new housing construction too, involving the replacement of single-family homes by apartment houses at the same time that other structures are being subdivided. Moreover, Stage 2 does not inevitably lead to Stage 3: an area converted to apartments may not undergo any down-grading then or later. The Riverdale area of the Bronx, for instance, promises to hold its present quality for some time to come. The stretch of Fifth Avenue facing Central Park was almost entirely transformed from one-family residences to towering apartment buildings after about 1910 and has maintained its character. On the other hand, Riverside Drive, similarly redeveloped at about the same time, has been subject to down-grading.

The down-grading stage is often associated with the spread of districts occupied by more or less segregated ethnic and minority groups. In the spread of such districts, conversion of structures to accommodate more families plays a significant part, but not always a decisive one. Thus, the number of dwelling units in the 17-county Standard Metropolitan Area[1] with nonwhite household heads showed a net increase of about 100,000 between 1950 and 1956. Of this increase, at least 85 percent appears to have been accounted for by net shift from white to nonwhite occupancy in dwelling units that were occupied in both 1950 and 1956 and were not converted. The remainder of the increase was split fairly evenly between conversions and post-1950 construction.[2] In particular areas of the Region, of course, the relative importance of conversions in the shifting character of neighborhoods was much greater than these over-all figures might suggest.

As we look at the changes in the Region's housing stock in the perspective of the last few decades, it is not possible to sort out in hard quantitative terms the roles that new construction, demolitions, conversions, and other processes have played.[3] For the period since 1950, however, the data are more adequate. In the Standard Metropolitan Area, the number of dwelling units rose from 3,954,000 in 1950 to 4,631,000 in 1956, a 17 percent increase. This increase ... was the net result of many things—of new construction, of demolition, of conversion, of "merger" (the reverse of conversion), and still other processes. New construction, of course, was far and away the dominant element in the change, but the net addition in dwelling units due to conversions accounted for nearly one-tenth of the aggregate increase.

A considerable amount of light is thrown on the conversion process by ... figures ... comparing the characteristics of dwelling units before and after conversion with the characteristics of other dwelling units. ... the units involved in conversion were in comparatively old structures; that though only half the units were renter-occupied before the conversion process, more than three-fourths were renter-occupied when conversion was completed; and finally, that the rentals charged for the converted units were far from low when compared with the units whose status was unchanged between 1950 and 1956.*

. . . dwelling units built since 1950 were higher in value or rent, in 1956, than units that had survived unchanged in status since 1950 or earlier. Only 5 percent of the new units were occupied by nonwhite households in 1956, less than 1 percent were rated dilapidated by that time, and more than half were in single-dwelling structures and owner-occupied.

The units lost by demolition, accidental destruction, abandonment, or loss of dwelling-unit status showed the opposite characteristics. They were relatively ancient, dilapidated, tenant-occupied, multi-family, and high in nonwhite occupancy. Nearly half the units demolished between 1950 and 1956, in fact, were occupied by nonwhites in 1950, and more than 40 percent had been rated dilapidated at that time. The median rent of such units was also relatively low.

All of which brings us to *Stage 4,* the thinning-out stage. This is the phase in which density and dwelling occupancy are gradually reduced. Most of the shrinkage comes about through a decline in household size in these neighborhoods. But the shrinkage may also reflect merging of dwelling units, vacancy, abandonment, and demolition. This stage is

---

*The rent control laws in force in some parts of the Region could have produced some of these differences. Converted units and newly constructed units are not subject to such control.

characterized by little or no residential construction and by a decline in population.

To find the reasons for this thinning-out process, we shall have to retrace our steps and have another look at the families which characteristically participate in the preceding stage of slum invasion. Those families are, on the whole, recently-arrived in-migrants to the Region, with low incomes and a limited housing choice. The limitations are imposed not only by their income levels but also by restrictions and prejudices against many of them in various parts of the Region, by an inadequate knowledge of the housing market, and by uncertain employment alternatives. At the same time, these in-migrants tend to be predominantly young married couples or marriageable individuals in their twenties, that being the time of life when mobility is much the greatest for all classes of people.[4]

Households with these characteristics expand rapidly in size through the arrival of children and also, commonly, by taking in relatives or other lodgers even more recently arrived in the City and seeking a foothold. As a result, at the stage when a down-grading neighborhood is having an increase in the number of dwelling units (that is, households) per structure, it is likely also to have—either at the same time or very shortly after—an increase in the number of persons per dwelling unit.

But once settled, the main couple of the households does not characteristically move soon again. The tendency to stay put strengthens fast after people pass their early twenties. Also, . . . dwellers in central-city areas are distinctly less mobile than residents of other types of areas in the Region.

Once the in-migrant couples have settled down and raised families, the continued aging of them and their neighborhoods leads to the "thinning-out" stage characteristic of slum areas after they reach peak density— a thinning-out provided in considerable part by the shrinkage of household size.

The thinning-out stage began several decades ago in some of the Region's oldest slums, and those areas are now far less crowded than they were, both in absolute terms and in comparison with more recently created slums. In Manhattan's lower East Side the population, after having risen from 339,000 to 532,000 between 1890 and 1910, declined in the next twenty years by more than half, reaching 250,000 in 1930.

The thinning-out stage is in progress, but less advanced, in a good many other areas of New York City. . . . If we take the City Planning Department's Statistical Districts as the unit of area, it appears that population has declined since 1950 in every district of Manhattan; in all but the northern and eastern fringes of the Bronx; in all but a very few of the districts of Brooklyn; and in a number of Queens districts closest to Manhattan and Brooklyn. It also declined in the two Staten Island districts nearest to Manhattan. . . .

Further striking illustrations of the thinning-out stage are found when we examine Health Areas, which are smaller units than Statistical Districts. Manhattan has 89 Health Areas. Unpublished data from the City Planning Department, based on federal Censuses, show that, in 1950, thirteen of them had population densities exceeding 300 persons per gross acre (192,000 per square mile). In all but one of these, population declined substantially by 1957. The same was true of all five Brooklyn Health Areas with densities exceeding 150 per gross acre in 1950.

The importance of reduced household size in the thinning-out process in the highest density areas is reflected in a comparison of population and housing trends. Although population declined between 1950 and 1957 in Manhattan, Brooklyn, and the Bronx, according to federal Census reports, the number of dwelling units apparently went on increasing in each borough.

We come at last to *Stage 5*. This is the renewal stage, in which obsolete areas of housing, after arriving at Stage 4, are being replaced by new multifamily housing. Quality and the effective use of space are improved, but the over-all population density of the area affected may not change much. By and large, such redevelopment in recent years has tended to increase over-all densities somewhat in Manhattan projects and to reduce them a little in projects elsewhere in the city.

This stage has assumed importance only quite recently, but it is safe to assume that the renewal effort will grow in magnitude. It is most conspicuous in Manhattan, particularly in the oldest slum areas, though appearing also in parts of Brooklyn, the Bronx, and Newark. It takes mainly two contrasting forms: first, subsidized medium-income and low-income housing, and second, luxury apartments. So far, the unsubsidized luxury structures which have been built in the Region on the razed sites of decayed slums have appeared almost exclusively in the middle East Side of Manhattan.

Still another slum-renewal process, less important to date but with significant further potentialities in a few parts of the Region, is exemplified in Greenwich Village. Old areas of felicitous design and conveniently central location, originally high-income but deteriorated, are restored piecemeal to high-grade occupancy by extensive repair and remodeling, merger of dwelling units, and a little new construction.

To a large extent, however, Stage 5 has depended on public intervention: on the use of condemnation powers to assemble the site, on the use of public grants to bring down the site costs to levels at which medium-income rentals could be charged, and in some cases on the use of continuing operating subsidies to bring the rentals within reach of low-income families. About 500,000 people in the Region are now housed in structures falling in one or another of these categories, most of them in New York City. Though the effect of such programs on some neighborhoods has been of major importance, their impact on land use in the Region as a whole has been small. In Manhattan, Brooklyn, and the Bronx, where renewal programs of all sorts have made the greatest relative progress in the Region, the land area affected by the subsidized renewal programs adds up to about two square miles, or 1.4 percent of the total.

. . . a broad picture of the new housing construction that took place in New York City's boroughs in the 12-year postwar period 1946-1957 inclusive. Though a considerable part of the construction in Queens and Richmond was of the types characterized in our Stages 1 and 2, the greater part of the building in the three most mature boroughs (Manhattan, Brooklyn, and the Bronx) comes under our Stage 5. It was nearly all apartment buildings, and a large fraction of it was publicly financed or subsidized housing for lower-income tenants, in old slum areas. Finally, we can see that the rate of replacement of the housing stock is quite slow. The 194,000 new units of all types built in Manhattan, Brooklyn, and the Bronx during the 12-year period amounted to somewhat less than one-tenth of the total housing stock in those three boroughs, and of course some of the building represented net expansion rather than replacement. Only a fraction of 1 percent of the dwellings were replaced per year, on the average.

By taking a closer look at Manhattan we can see how the various stages of change are affecting different neighborhoods. . . . between 1950 and 1957 every Statistical District in Manhattan showed a decline in population. But if we again take smaller units of area—the 89 Health Areas of the borough—we find 14 of them registering population increases of 300 persons or more in that period. The bases for growth were different. In one Health Area in the East 60's and 70's, replacement of old buildings by new high-rise luxury apartments was the dominant factor in increasing over-all density. In six others (located in Inwood at the northern tip of Manhattan, in Harlem, and at the end of the Williamsburg Bridge), new high-rise low-income housing redevelopment was the main factor, offsetting the thinning-out that was going on in those areas during the interval. In six other areas, west of Central Park, there was little residential construction of any kind, and the increased density reflects our Stage 3 rather than Stage 5: with general down-grading, increase in Puerto Rican and Negro population, increasing size of household, and some conversions.[5]

There, then, are our five stages in the neighborhood cycle: (1) new single-family subdivisions, (2) apartment development, (3) downgrading generally associated with conversion, (4) thinning-out, and (5) renewal. Needless to say, the sequence describes what has happened only in general terms, and there are plenty of variations when we look at specific areas. For example, some fortunate areas (as already noted) have been able to stabilize their character short of the "down-grading" stage, or even short of the apartment-transition stage, in many instances by strongly supported zoning. Still other areas, like Harlem, have experienced not just a single slum-invasion-and-thin-out cycle, but several repetitions involving distinct new waves of in-migrants. . . . Moreover, we ignore the process of invasion of residential areas by nonresidential uses—developments like the transformation of Park Avenue above Grand Central from a luxury apartment area to an area of sleek office buildings. These are special cases, many of them dealt with in other portions of this volume. In terms of the amount of land area involved, they represent only minor qualifications on the general patterns developed in this chapter.

TREMONT STREET DISTRICT

SAM BASS WARNER, JR.

Despite some important exceptions, all of West Roxbury and Dorchester during the years 1870 to 1900 belonged to families of the central segment of the middle class. It was their land, and in thirty years they covered with their new streets and houses about half of its twenty-one square miles of privately held land. As their class grew in numbers, as fashions changed, or as old neighborhoods became unsatisfactory, they moved steadily outward over still vacant suburban land. The new parks, cemeteries, churches, schools, and clubs were theirs also, for these institutions depended upon the central segment of the middle class for continued use and support in order to maintain the kinds of service for which they had been established.

Lower Roxbury, the major part of the town after the highlands has been excepted,[1] was, on the other hand, the land of the lower middle class. Others lived there, to be sure. There were long residents from the days when Roxbury was a peripheral town—early suburbanites and employees of nearby mills. But lower middle class families were the driving force of this part of Roxbury. They built the new houses that sheltered the majority of the 43,000 newcomers to the district. And they did their building on an area of three square miles. This three square miles had been established by 1870 as a peripheral town of the

Reprinted by permission of the publishers from *Streetcar Suburbs: The Process of Growth in Boston, 1870-1900*, 2d ed., by Sam Bass Warner, Jr. Cambridge, Massachusetts: Harvard University Press. Copyright © 1962, 1978, by the President and Fellows of Harvard College.

Boston metropolis, and held a population of about 22,000. Within this narrow compass lower middle class families had to erect their version of the rural ideal.

In some ways it seems ridiculous to mention the rural ideal in connection with such a narrow and mean form of building as that which went up in lower Roxbury in the late nineteenth century. This was, above all, the land of the possible, not the ideal. Though customers for new houses were many, their means were sharply limited; the work had to be closely financed, closely figured, and built fast. Almost half the new dwelling construction of the three towns of Roxbury, West Roxbury, and Dorchester went on in this small area. Many men made a steady living out of this kind of construction, but of those builders about whose lives something is known, the overwhelming proportion of those trapped into bankruptcy or forced mortgage sales worked in this risky and highly competitive price range.

Like the moderately priced houses of Dorchester and West Roxbury, the houses in lower Roxbury were built from stock plans and with stock ornament. Unlike the middle-priced construction, there was here little money for an extra bay, a large porch, or a shifting about of the builder's sketches. Most lower middle class families building or buying a new house asked, "how much for how little?" The streets of three-deckers, cramped two-families and brick row houses represent what were thought to be the best buys of the day. At least 56.9 percent of the new buildings of lower Roxbury were multiple structures. These structures were owned by a family living in them, or, more usually, by some landlord of the immediate neighborhood who had put his savings in this kind of investment.[2]

If one considers the new construction of lower Roxbury in comparison to other equivalent structures, the value of this cheap building becomes clear. By and large the new streets of Roxbury were well laid out with an eye to being easy to get through and easy to clean. Each house had a full set of modern plumbing facilities, gas for light and often gas stoves as well, and, toward the end of the century, electric lights. Many new houses had central heat. In most cases the principal rooms were larger than those of the contemporary West End tenement or the rooms in South End row housing. Compared to the old wooden mill barracks of Roxbury, the new three-deckers and two-families were extravagant of space. Generally, all rooms in a rental unit had outside windows and many had sunlight and good ventilation. Where three-deckers and two-families were jammed together on narrow lots, as was frequently the case, much light and air was lost and conditions approached those of the old row housing. However, in much of the new Parker Hill district and in patches everywhere in Roxbury, lot sizes were adequate, and the light, air, and green space allotment of the new houses exceeded that of the contemporary Back Bay house.

These essential characteristics of the new housing of Roxbury were all gains in the necessaries of family life. One of the most important achievements of suburban building during the last three decades of the nineteenth century was that, even in its cheapest housing forms, it represented an advance over previous city conditions. The new lower middle class neighborhoods constituted an important step toward providing a safe, sanitary environment for all the families of Boston. This general rise in minimum standards for new housing owes most of its progress to the increase in size and in buying power of the middle class and the contemporary public health and sanitation movement which was actively supported by that class.

Nevertheless, the rural ideal, which was present in all levels of middle class thought, definitely influenced the forms new construction took. The lower middle class streets and structures were a part of one continuous spectrum of building style. If you walk today through Roxbury and Dorchester, you will notice only slight changes from street to street in ornament, house, and lot styles. Most apparent are shifts from single-family houses to three-deckers. Since the lower middle class built in areas often already developed, many of the streets of their part of nineteenth-century Roxbury are mixed in types of structures. For this reason, it is only after going some distance from an area of decidedly lower-price to one of decidedly higher-price building that you will notice a very definite change in a district's quality of plan and building. The sharpest break in house style and lot arrangement came not between the middle- and lower-priced housing but between the medium-priced and the expensive. Big houses, elaborate ornament, and expensive materials sharply distinguish an occasional street of the wealthy from the rest of the suburbs.

Since the kinds of houses appropriate to a rural setting provided most of the architectural inspiration, these styles necessarily underwent severe changes under the cramped conditions of a cheap suburban location. The landscaped rural garden and fields became a minuscule backyard, or almost disappeared altogether; the back porch and front stoop were all that remained of summer houses and shaded verandas. Today a street of three-deckers resembles nothing so much as the old row housing. But in the nineties the same street, with its tended trees and cultivated back yards, its location near the new parks and adjacent to neighborhoods of adequate yards, was an important step toward suburban life. Also, excepting one special case in lower Roxbury,[3] almost all new construction after 1873 took the form of detached houses. Again, there was a slavish copying of each shift in style in more expensive construction. All these elements point to a building process that shared one common stylistic motivation—the rural ideal.

Architecture was not the only quality held in common by the lower, central, and upper segments of the middle class. Like more expensive residences, the placement of lower middle class structures depended upon the street railway. In large measure, the dependence of the group upon crosstown service, and the relatively limited range of that service, caused the crowded land patterns of its building. Income segregation also dominated its neighborhoods. Dense building habits drove out families of higher income who had first settled the land to enjoy the quasi-rural setting of the suburbs, while the costs of new construction kept most working class families out of these districts. Finally, lower middle class neighborhoods provided an environment for the integration of families of similar income and diverse ethnic background. As in all other suburban areas, ethnic clusters of the lower middle class were temporary and dependent upon the general progress of immigrant families in the metropolitan society as a whole.

Beyond its demonstration of the uniformity of behavior at all levels of suburban construction, lower middle class building had special attributes which were of great consequence to the future of the metropolis. Lower middle class families, who depended upon crosstown transportation, were generally the last to arrive in any suburb. Because they were the final builders, their work gave a permanent set to the residential environment. The wealthy and the central segment of the middle class occupied great tracts of land, but only partially covered them. In most of their settlements plenty of room remained for new houses. When the lower middle class moved in force into a neighborhood, sheer weight of numbers brought a complete occupancy of the land. Since the terminal users of houses, the working class, were too poor to build new structures, these later generations were restricted to the inheritance of what had gone before. In this way the narrow means of lower middle class families became a permanent condition for much of the housing of the metropolis.

Limited financial ability brought two special qualities to lower middle class building: first, it crowded the land and thereby prevented later adaptation to the changing incomes and needs of its residents; second, it led a great many houses to be built to specifications which were below the common understanding of what constituted a satisfactory home. Such building was accepted by contemporaries as the best alternative of the moment, but it immediately fell to obsolescence upon any substantial change in home finance, income distribution, transportation service, or housing fashions.

The inflexibility and compromised quality of much lower middle class construction in the end gave it a destructive role in the process of city building. First it destroyed the character of existing neighborhoods by its jamming of the land, and, later, it destroyed its own good qualities by being inadaptable to future requirements. Both the general characteristics of lower middle class building and its special destructive qualities are well demonstrated by the history of the Tremont street district of lower Roxbury.

In 1870 this section was divided in two parts: a well-settled area near the South End of Boston, and a lightly settled outer part which included Mission and Parker hills. Though the outer part enjoyed good linear streetcar service it had, by 1870, failed to become as well filled with houses as equivalent sections of Dorchester. The presence of factories in the nearby Stony Brook Valley and the steepness of the hill grades had inhibited its development. Its moment of mass building awaited the results of the annexation of Roxbury to Boston, namely, complete town coverage by water, street, sewer, and gas service, without regard to the height or grade of any lot.

The inner district was partly a less expensive continuation of South End middle-income housing, partly the residence of factory hands who worked in nearby Roxbury and South End industries. Also, because downtown Boston lay only a mile and a half away, men living here could walk to most of the employment centers of the pre-streetcar metropolis. Because of its convenience, during the years 1840 to 1870 the inner parts of the Tremont street district grew rapidly in the mixed form of the old peripheral towns.

The more prosperous lived in tiny, classic revival, wooden single and double houses, and in the brick tenement and store buildings that were put up along the busy Tremont street thoroughfare. On the side streets factory owners had erected two-and-a-half- and three-story wooden barracks for their employees. Up toward Mission Hill and on the flats near Ruggles street, cheap wooden houses and brick rows of the 1860's and 1870's were the general rule. On the edge of the then unfilled Back Bay marshes, there were also an indeterminate number of shacks belonging to the shanty Irish poor.

This inner section of Roxbury developed with a great concentration of Irish immigrants, and as the colony grew it spread with heavy concentration over the whole of Mission Hill, Parker Hill, and lower Jamaica Plain. This same area during the years 1840 to 1870 held a large

German group which worked in the breweries and factories of the adjacent Stony Brook Valley and South End. The German colony prospered during the last third of the nineteenth century and, like the rest of the central middle class, migrated out from the city. In 1900 its center was in Roslindale, three miles up the Stony Brook Valley from its 1870 inner Roxbury location. The German group founded the church on Mission Hill, a church which, like St. Peter's in Dorchester, gave cohesion to the cluster which grew up around it.

Until 1846 there was no Roman Catholic church in Roxbury. Then, in the same year that Roxbury became a city, St. Joseph's Church on Circuit and Regent streets was established to serve the Catholics of Roxbury, Dorchester, Brookline, Hyde Park, Dedham, and Norwood. This site was well chosen. It lay in a new middle class section of Roxbury highlands close to the Tremont street thoroughfare and the intersection of the main arteries of Washington, Dudley, and Warren streets. By 1870 parish churches had been, or were about to be, established in all of these towns while the growth of the Catholic, especially Irish, population in Roxbury demanded new churches.

The most important of the new churches from the point of view of the development of the Tremont street district was the Redemptorist Mission Church opened in 1871 on Mission Hill at Tremont and St. Alphonsus streets. The estate purchased for the church was an historic Roxbury site. It was General Artemus Ward's Revolutionary War headquarters, the estate of General Henry Dearborn of the War of 1812, the home of his extravagant son, General Henry A. S. Dearborn, who is known for his part in designing the Mount Auburn and Forest Hills cemeteries. To this same house the Ursulines had come and had stayed for a time after the Charlestown riot and the burning of their convent. The old estate, however, had, like the whole neighborhood, fallen from the heights of fashion; for the few years prior to its purchase by the Catholic church it served as a pleasure resort. Since 1873 the new stone Church of Our Lady of Perpetual Help has looked down over the Back Bay toward the North End. Both literally and figuratively, it served as a beacon for lower middle class Irish families emerging from the tenements of Boston.

In 1870 most of Roxbury's 5,000 Irish lived in the inner part of town. Many of these were poor families attracted to pockets of cheap marshy land located on the periphery of Boston settlement. In the next thirty years such families continued to come to Roxbury where they took up old houses abandoned by middle-income groups. These families could not afford to buy new houses or pay the rents required by any but the most mean and crowded new tenement. Their presence in lower Roxbury kept down the social status of the land.

The effect of the Redemptorist Church with its popular ritual and full set of parochial services was to attract a different group of Irish settlers: the lower middle class builders. Similarly, the City of Boston's Back Bay and Stony Brook sanitary engineering projects and its aggressive street and water policies made much of the still vacant land suitable for middle class occupancy. Together, the church and the city upgraded the land about this early peripheral immigrant settlement.

During the 1870-1900 period lower middle class families moved into the Tremont street district in two waves. The Irish, then the predominant emergent group of Boston, were the largest element among the newcomers—especially so since there was an established Irish colony in the area. They constituted 44 to 48 percent of the total population, a concentration 10 to 20 percent greater than that in other wards of the three-town suburban area. However, coming with the Irish were lower middle class families of all ethnic backgrounds. A German colony continued for a time, only to be replaced in the 1890's by a wave of Canadians. A mixture of native Americans and minor immigrant groups together comprised the remaining 30 to 40 percent of the population. In the 1890's the beginning Irish settlement on the lowlands around Ruggles street began to be taken over by the next emergent group, the Jews. Throughout the three last decades of the century, the whole area served primarily as a "zone of emergence" for lower middle class immigrant families. Between 70 and 80 percent of its population was first and second generation foreign born.

In the postwar building boom which lasted through 1873 cheap row houses filled the vacant lots on the streets off lower Tremont street and up the side of Mission Hill. In the next two decades, especially in the 1885-1895 boom, inexpensive housing of one kind or another covered most of the outer section from Mission Hill to the West Roxbury line. Two new parishes had to be created to supplement the services of the Redemptorists, while their church became one of the most active and important in all Boston. On the rolling hills to the south of Centre street, small singles and two-families predominated; on the north side of Centre street the three-deckers marched almost uninterrupted from the botton of the Stony Brook Valley to the very peak of Parker Hill.

These uplands held the potential of some of the handsomest sites and best views of any Boston residential district. However, because the lower middle class had to keep costs to a minimum, and because the general custom of the day dictated narrow frontage lots set on grid streets, all the site potential disappeared beneath rows upon rows of wooden structures all squeezed on small lots. The view became the house opposite; the natural setting was the street, the sidewalk, an occasional street tree, and sometimes a backyard patch of grass or garden.

Not only was this pattern of lower middle class building destructive of nature, it was destructive of itself. It was so finely adapted to the disciplines of the moment that it could not be adjusted to future conditions save through the process of crowding and conversions which only made an already unsatisfactory housing environment even worse. Though the streetcar opened to the lower middle class more land than it had ever before been able to reach, the supply was too little for so large a number of families. These families not only competed with each other, but with industrial and commercial users who were also attracted by the convenience of the inner suburbs.

What one type of user did not purchase, another did. Apartments were built over and behind the stores and three-deckers, and wooden tenements took up the vacant spaces between the factories. This competition for space kept land prices high, the highest of all the sections in the suburbs. Under these conditions each family could afford but little more land than it had controlled in the central city. Cost discipline further required the cheapest known kinds of construction, so that most of the new inner suburbs came to be filled with the cheapest acceptable statements of the housing fashions of the day. Once a small area was filled with houses, factories, and stores, there was no way it could respond to a further rise in income or standards among its resident families—they had to move on to fresh land and new neighborhoods.

Similarly, a successful factory frequently required more space, but the pattern of building was so dense that few manufacturers could find room to expand. The Dennison Manufacturing Company in 1880 set up a factory in Roxbury highlands at Vale and Thornton streets. It was an industrial island surrounded by houses. As this stationery company prospered, like the families of Roxbury, it moved further out in the suburbs. The Western Electric Company purchased a square block of land in lower Roxbury but chose instead to build on a much larger parcel in the more distant suburb of Watertown. The once famous Prang's Lithographic Company and the piano factories of the South End and Roxbury chose these locations when their lots were on the edge of the city and land was at once plentiful and moderately convenient to labor and transportation. These companies neither expanded nor moved, and after many profitable years they ultimately closed their doors. The process of consolidation and increased scale of business which went on through-out the nineteenth and twentieth centuries left Roxbury with many vacant old industrial buildings unsuited for continued use in their original manner.

By the 1890's Boston's metropolitan region stretched five to ten miles from the downtown. Roxbury no longer offered cheap space on the periphery of the region; instead, it was a convenient location for service and distribution industries that wanted to be close to the cheap labor of the inner metropolitan region and handy to the lines of metropolitan distribution. The vacated industrial space of the early years was now filled with users of unskilled labor. As old factories closed or moved, the skilled workers and small businessmen of the district became stranded in their neighborhoods, which were but from ten to thirty years old.

Lower middle class neighborhoods were, thus, attacked from several directions at once. Changes in housing fashions and transportation brought rapid obsolescence. When these changes occurred, new families of similar income to the original builders could, and did, choose new land and new neighborhoods to live in, rather than taking their places in those already built. Moreover, since land in lower middle class neighborhoods was so densely covered, rising families could only move out if they wished to express their economic progress and gain the housing advantages their new standard of living allowed them. At the same time, the process of industrial change which tended to shift from highly skilled, highly paid employment to ever lower skills, encouraged low paid, low status workers to move into neighborhoods previously dominated by the lower middle class. The cumulative effect of all these forces brought a rapid decline in the social status, personal income level, and housing condition of lower middle class districts. According to contemporary observers, by 1900 all of lower Roxbury, then just completed, underwent a shift from a lower middle class to a working class district, and that under the pressure of industrial change and changes in housing preference those families who could afford to leave were rapidly abandoning the area. New low income families, in order to keep rents down, were converting single houses to multiple use, and doubling up in existing multiple dwellings. After but a few years as an acceptable lower middle class neighborhood, lower Roxbury was becoming a slum.

Today the old Roxbury areas of lower middle class building are in an advanced stage of decay and disrepair. Families still occupy the houses because they are inexpensive. All of these structures have not declined equally rapidly, however, a fact which suggests that there may have been more to the rapid decline of the area than the major forces of population and industrial movement reveal. The differing fate of two late nineteenth-century housing experiments indicates that in an important sense there were satisfactory and unsatisfactory ways to cheapen a housing fashion.

Off Centre street, at the outer edge of the Tremont street district, just beyond the old shoe factory and the breweries, Robert Treat Paine erected 116 cheap houses in the 1890's. Today, this project is in a neighborhood of well-maintained structures. It was the outgrowth of twenty years' experience in building model houses for the lower middle class. Paine, a descendant of a signer of the Declaration of Independence, and a successful corporation lawyer, retired from practice in the 1870's in order to devote himself full time to philanthropic activity. He is justly famous for beginning the Associated Charities movement in Boston. In an age that relied on charity for almost all its social welfare, this movement rendered great service. It brought some order and cooperation among the fragmented charitable organizations of the city.

As a "friendly visitor" in the South End, Paine came upon the contemporary problems of housing, the crowded tenement and the equally crowded row house conversion. He tried in all his charities to ease the burden of the "substantial workingman," the man who despite thrift and middle class aspirations frequently lived in economic jeopardy and tenement squalor. To this end Paine organized unemployment, accident, and sickness benefit groups, educational associations, and a cooperative savings bank. Like most men of his day, he felt that individual homeownership was one of the basic elements of satisfactory middle class life. This conclusion led him to experiment with providing safe, sanitary houses at prices the substantial workingman could afford.

In 1874–75, in the inner Tremont street district, Paine built a few brick row houses on Ruggles street. Then, nearby, from 1886 to 1890 he undertook a large scale project off Madison Park on Greenwich, Warwick, and Sussex streets. Paine, his brother, and his father-in-law supervised the construction and held the mortgages. They put up Philadelphia-style single-family row houses, then the current fashion in philanthropic housing. These were narrow two-story brick structures with about 600 to 800 square feet of floor space, and minuscule pieces of land which provided a rear service alley and enough private space to hold the trash barrels and a baby carriage. To keep land costs down further, narrow alleys were used instead of the standard 40-foot street. The total effect of this subdivision is that of a miniaturized Back Bay executed with all the grace and scale of the old South Boston workingmen's alleys. In support of these mean and unfortunate structures, it must be remembered that such houses were then being put up by the thousands in Philadelphia by purchaser-managed cooperative building companies. Furthermore, such houses were then standard stock in trade of English philanthropic builders.

Paine's Sussex street houses could be purchased by substantial workingmen for $2,500 apiece, $1,000 in cash and a $1,500 mortgage at 5 percent for five years. Now, seventy years after the event, it is difficult to establish exact price comparisons, but Paine's terms seem to have been usual for suburban houses. The short-term straight mortgage was general. Most mortgagors counted on renewing it several times before finally paying the principal. Indeed, Paine ultimately assigned most of his mortgages to the Boston Safe Deposit and Trust Company. However, the very usualness of the price and terms of Paine's model houses suggests that they were no special bargain. If the substantial workingman were willing in 1886 to sacrifice the convenience of lower Roxbury for a more distant location, he could buy an equally small detached wooden single house with the same capital and get more land and a full sized suburban street. Such limited alternatives led most lower middle class families into renting. They rented old houses, or took parts of the new doubles and three-deckers, moving farther and farther out from Boston as increases in transportation service allowed.

Though Paine's houses and narrow streets may have been suitable for Philadelphia, where there was a long and continuous tradition of row housing, in Boston these buildings had a strong philanthropic air. They were brick and fireproof and had a full set of plumbing facilities, but for all their safety and sanitation they remained mean, cramped row houses built a full decade after the main body of the middle class had ceased building row houses for itself. Like the wooden barracks and tenements of the neighborhood, these houses were suited to the momentary needs and capabilities of their inhabitants—all too suited to them, and not at all suited to their aspirations.

The choice of location was equally suitable and equally unfortunate. In the 1880's much of inner Roxbury was already well established as a lower middle class quarter, so well established that in a few years, as transportation service advanced, large numbers of lower middle class families would leave this inner suburb for more ample surroundings. When they moved, they would leave behind them outmoded and cramped houses which were so small that a mere doubling up of poor families in each structure created conditions similar to those in the North End tenements.

Because Paine had built minimal structures, and built without regard to some of the important middle class aspirations of the day, his houses suffered the fate of all the other homes in the area. For the last forty years they have served as slum dwellings, and, despite Paine's careful construction, they are falling to the ground.

Paine's next undertaking marked a considerable advance in understanding and execution. In this case, instead of building model philanthropic houses, he tried by large-scale planning to improve on ordinary cheap construction. A division of his cooperative bank, the Workingmen's Building Association, served as the central finance and planning agency. This organization purchased several large parcels off Centre street in the outer Tremont street district and laid out its streets and lots in the then advanced method of romantic landscape architecture. This was a cheap project, so no handsome yards and vistas resulted, but the streets do follow the contours of the land and are designed to make a traffic cul-de-sac. By this method more lots with usable space were secured than would have been possible if the current grid street pattern were adopted. Such site planning was just then coming into vogue for expensive subdivisions in Brookline and other parts of greater Boston.

The houses themselves came in several styles of detached frame single and two-family structures. A variety of contemporary ornament was also offered. The house lots were very small but there was a green space to the rear and a little ground and a standard planted suburban street to the front. These houses were more than twice as big as the little row houses of the 1880's and they sold for twice as much. The financing was done by the then still novel amortizing mortgage which reduced the risk both to borrower and lender. The whole suburban "cottagey" effect of this hundred-house subdivision was underlined with street names of "Round Hill" and "Sunnyside."

Had a site been chosen at greater distance from Boston, cheaper land would have allowed a more generous solution, but all developers feared that a distant subdivision might stand vacant for a few years while the main path of building caught up to it. Both Paine and his customers thought in terms of what were then the existing neighborhoods of the city.

Nevertheless Paine's second project was a substantial and permanent contribution. Through the Workingmen's Building Association he succeeded in building at comparable prices a better planned and slightly more landed neighborhood than ordinary private developers were then able to provide. He did this in a place and at a time when the three-decker was the almost universal statement of lower middle class building. Today that class has largely deserted this section of Roxbury. A federal housing project has been required to clean up the 1870 housing of the neighborhood. All around the area, the once popular three-deckers are in disrepair or a state of partial collapse. Paine's houses are still kept up, and they are kept up because for sixty years they have been the best choice of the neighborhood. They have been the best choice because they were more in keeping with the housing aspirations of Bostonians than any of the other cheap alternatives of the 1890's.

The success of Paine's experiment suggests that slum housing is one of the prices that a society pays for allowing any major amount of its building to proceed at a level below its common understanding among the middle class as to what constitutes a satisfactory home environment. Since much late nineteenth-century building depended upon the financial abilities of very restricted family incomes, it could not have taken any other form than it did. Its cheapness of construction and meanness of land plan, however, have already brought the destruction of neighborhood land and housing values and, so far, two generations of family life set in an environment which for forty years has been incompatible with middle class standards.

HARLEM
GILBERT OSOFSKY

In the last three decades of the nineteenth century, Harlem was a community of great expectations. During the previous quarter-century it had been an isolated, poor, rural village. After the 1870's however, it was transformed into an upper and upper-middle-class residential suburb—Manhattan's first suburb.

Prosperity had come to Harlem before.[1] Throughout the colonial period its lands brought wealth to farmers. The estates of some of America's most illustrious colonial families were located there—Delanceys, Beekmans, Bleeckers, Rikers, Coldens, Hamiltons, and others. The stamp of respectability and distinction colored Harlem's name, and later settlers recalled its past glories proudly: "Who among [you] then," a lecturer on the history of the community said in 1882, "with Harlem's . . . history before you, and the goodly prospects in store, are not proud of being called Harlemites. . . . The spirit which animated their [the founders'] breasts," he concluded romantically, "is rooted in the soft rich soil of Harlem. . . ."

For some two hundred years the village of New Harlaem remained remarkably stable. Most of its small population, following the general ethnic patterns of New York City's population (as it would continue

Specified material abridged and adapted from *Harlem: The Making of a Ghetto* by Gilbert Osofsky. Copyright © 1963, 1965, 1966, by Gilbert Osofsky. Reprinted by permission of Harper and Row, Publishers, Inc.

to do in the future), descended from Dutch, French, and English pioneers.

[Osofsky continues his discussion of Harlem as a village community with many large estates during the colonial and early national periods.]

Harlem's decline began when its lands, worn out after centuries of use, lost their former productivity. . . .

Into this decaying community came groups of people to whom the once productive soil seemed less forbidding. Those in search of cheap property bought land there and built one- and two-story frame houses. Others, including many newly arrived and destitute Irish immigrants—some of whom remained in Harlem to see the twentieth century—squatted on the forsaken land or lived in mud flats at the river's edge. They created Harlem's shantytowns and lived in two-room cottages pieced together with any material that could be found: bits of wood, twigs, barrel staves, old pipes, tin cans hammered flat. . . . And so it remained until the pressure of urban population growth and the subsequent need for living space restored value to Harlem lands.

[The author goes on to note that Harlem still continued to maintain its beauty and serve as a rural retreat for the rich. The area was far from the city and its rudimentary transportation system kept it isolated and fairly unsettled.]

The phenomenal growth of Harlem in the late nineteenth century was a by-product of the general development of New York City. From the 1870's on, the foundations of the modern metropolis were laid. This urban revolution was characterized by improvements in methods of sanitation, water supply, transportation, communication, lighting, and building. As the city expanded, so did its population. In 1880, for the first time in its history, and in the history of any American city, the population of Manhattan alone passed the one million mark (1,164,673), and "New Immigrants" had just begun to arrive. This increase in population coincided with an expansion of commercial and industrial activity, and both made serious inundations on living quarters in formerly staid residential sections. The only way for the island city to grow was northward. Many older residents and older immigrants, attempting to avoid the bustle of the new metropolis and escape contact with its newest settlers, looked to Harlem as the community of the future: "In our family, we were always careful to explain that we lived in Harlem, not in New York City," a man whose family moved uptown in these years recalled. "It was our way of avoiding contact with such uncouth citizens as might be found downtown. . . ." The neighborhood would become "the choicest residential section of the city," predicted another resident. "Upper Seventh Avenue in Harlem has become one of the finest streets in New York. . . . Rows of trees and pretty gardens . . . lend to it a semi-suburban aspect."

Harlem expanded gradually in the 1860's and was annexed to New York City in 1873. The city filled some 1,350 acres of marshland in 1870, sold them to the public, and constructed houses over them. A few city fathers in the heyday of the Tweed Ring appropriated promising lands for themselves and built fashionable homes there. The turning point in Harlem's history came in 1878–1881. During these years three lines of the elevated railroad came as far north as One Hundred and Twenty-ninth Street and, by 1886, the elevated line came even further north. Rows of brownstones and exclusive apartment houses appeared overnight: "Business grows, blocks and flats go up with apparently so little effort, that the average Harlemite is in a continuous swim of development and prosperity," the local newspaper commented in 1890. Practically all the houses that stand in Harlem today were built in a long spurt of energy that lasted from the 1870's through the first decade of the twentieth century. . . .

Speculators made fortunes buying Harlem land, holding it for a short while, and reselling at great profit. Builders purchased land, constructed houses and sold them as soon as they were completed. They used the profits for reinvestment.

[Osofsky then discusses specific speculators and the efforts of earlier Harlem property owners to reclaim their land.]

People generally took it for granted that Harlem would develop into an exclusive, stable, upper- and upper-middle-class community: "a neighborhood very genteel." The newly built elevator apartment houses, many equipped with servants' quarters, rented for prices that could be paid only by the wealthy.

[The author continues by describing some luxury apartment houses and other Harlem amenities.]

The people attracted to this "residential heaven" were obviously older and wealthier New Yorkers—"people of taste and wealth." Few neighborhoods in the entire city at the turn of the century had so disproportionate a number of native Americans or immigrants from Great

Britain, Ireland, and Germany, including German Jews, living in it. In 1902, of the 103,570 families in the Twelfth Ward, only 10,786 could be classified as "New Immigrants." Many late nineteenth-century Harlemites were born in downtown Manhattan or immigrated to America in the years 1830-1850, and subsequently moved to the community after 1870. One man came to visit a friend in Harlem in 1889 and was surprised "to see so many downtowners who have come here to live. It looks as if everybody will be rushing up here from downtown before long," he said. A future director of the Harlem Board of Commerce moved to the neighborhood in the 1880's and was surprised to meet so many Greenwich Village friends there. The homes of municipal and federal judges, mayors, local politicos (including Tammany boss Richard Croker), prominent businessmen, and state politicians (Chauncey M. Depew, for example), were scattered throughout Harlem. Their children attended Grammar School 68, "referred to as the 'Silk Stocking School' of the City" because its "pupils were practically all from American families, and . . . more or less prosperous people."

[The next part of the book continues to describe the wealthy element in Harlem but also the poorer sections that were developing in the 1880's and 1890's as a result of Italian and black migration into the area.]

Harlem life altered radically in the first decade of the twentieth century. The construction of new subway routes into the neighborhood in the late 1890's set off a second wave of speculation in Harlem land and property. Speculators who intended to make astronomical profits when the subway was completed bought the marshes, garbage dumps, and lots left unimproved or undeveloped in the 1870's and 1880's. Between 1898 and 1904, the year that the Lenox Avenue line opened at One Hundred and Forty-fifth Street, "practically all the vacant land in Harlem" was "built over," the *Real Estate Record and Builders' Guide* noted in 1904. "The growth of . . . Harlem . . . has been truly astonishing during the last half dozen years."

The real estate boom created a wave of new building activity in Harlem dominated primarily by speculators, although some individuals made long-term investments. It was taken as business gospel that investments would be doubled and trebled after the completion of the "tunnel road." "Even a 5-story single flat in Harlem would net . . . at the end of . . . three to five years . . . at the utmost . . . a very handsome unearned increment," a realtor concluded. "It would be impossible to err." Another supposed expert in urban real estate maintained that no "other class of public improvements had such a great, immediate and permanent effect upon land values as rapid transit lines. . . ."

Speculation in Manhattan land along the routes of new transportation facilities originally occurred when charters were granted to horse-car companies in the early nineteenth century. Trafficking in city lots throughout urban America proved often more lucrative than speculation on the western frontier.

[Osofsky's discussion of speculation and building continues with an emphasis on the Jewish community.]

More luxurious apartment houses were built around 1900 in West Harlem, along Seventh and Lenox Avenues in the One Hundred and Thirties and One Hundred and Forties, the first section of the neighborhood to become Negro Harlem. Contemporaries called these blocks "the best of Harlem." This section of the community suffered most from inaccessibility in the 1880's and 1890's, and hardly an edition of the local newspaper in the 1890's failed to demand improved transportation facilities there. To contemporaries this "old, old story of rapid transit" would make Harlem "even more popular than it is as a place of residence. . . ."

Speculation in these properties was probably more widespread and involved larger expenditures than realty manipulations in other sections of Harlem or the city. Two brothers, John D. and Thomas F. Crimmins, for example, bought the entire blocks of One Hundred and Forty-fourth and One Hundred and Forty-fifth Streets between Lenox and Seventh Avenues in 1895, thinking the "Lenox Avenue electric car" would "greatly enhance the value of the property." In keeping with the traditions of the neighborhood and the type of homes constructed in the 1880's it was believed richer people who wanted "high-class flats," "costly dwellings," and who earned enough to afford them, would come to West Harlem. Many of the newly constructed buildings were equipped with elevators, maid's rooms, and butler's pantries. In 1899 William Waldorf Astor erected an apartment house on Seventh Avenue at a cost of $500,000. Sunday real estate sections of New York City newspapers at the turn of the century bristled with full-page advertisements and pictures of the elegant homes in West Harlem. The revived building activity of these years created the physical foundations for what became the most luxurious Negro ghetto in the world.

Speculation in West Harlem property led to phenomenal increases in the price of land and the cost of houses there—increases inflated out of all proportion to their real value. . . .

The inevitable bust came in 1904–1905. Speculators sadly realized afterward that too many houses were constructed at one time. West Harlem was glutted with apartments, and "excessive building . . . led to many vacancies." No one knew exactly how long it would take to construct the subway, and many houses built four and five years in advance of its completion remained partly unoccupied. The first of them to be inhabited by Negroes, for example, was never rented previously. Rents were too high for the general population ($35–$45 per month) and precluded any great rush to West Harlem even after the subway was completed. There was a widespread "overestimation of . . . rental value," a contemporary remarked. When the market broke, landlords competed with each other for tenants by reducing rents, or offering a few months' rent-free occupancy to them. Local realtors unsuccessfully attempted to eliminate these cutthroat practices.

By 1905 financial institutions no longer made loans to Harlem speculators and building-loan companies, and many foreclosed on their original mortgages. The inflated prices asked for land and property in West Harlem "solemnly settled beneath a sea of depreciated values." In the aftermath of the speculative collapse, and as a consequence of the initiative of Negro realtors, large numbers of colored people began to settle in West Harlem.

[The author goes on to discuss the Afro-American Realty Company and the opening of Harlem to blacks.]

But not all property owners were ready to open their houses to colored people. It seemed unbelievable to some that theirs, one of the most exclusive sections in the entire city, should become the center of New York's most depressed and traditionally worst-housed people. Some owners banded together in associations to repulse what they referred to as the Negro "invasion" or the Negro "influx." The language used to describe the movement of Negroes into Harlem—the words "invasion," "captured," "black hordes," "invaders," "enemy," for example, appear repeatedly in denunciations of Negroes—was the language of war.

In the 1880's and 1890's Harlemites annually celebrated the historic Revolutionary Battle of Harlem Heights. These patriotic fetes were symbols of community pride, and pamphlets were widely distributed informing the neighborhood of the dignitaries participating in them. In the early twentieth century, however, Harlem's residents gathered not to preserve the memory of a Revolutionary conflict, but to fight their own battle—to keep their neighborhood white.

Most of the formal opposition to Negro settlement in Harlem

centered in local associations of landlords. Some were committees representing individual blocks, others were community-wide in structure. Property-owners on West One Hundred and Fortieth, One Hundred and Thirty-seventh, One Hundred and Thirty-sixth, One Hundred and Thirty-fifth, One Hundred and Thirty-first, One Hundred and Thirtieth, One Hundred and Twenty-ninth Streets, and so on, in descending order as the Negro community spread southward, and along the avenues, signed restrictive agreements. Each swore not to rent his apartments to Negroes for ten or fifteen years—till when, it was thought, "this situation . . . referred to . . . will have run its course." "The premises, land, and buildings of which we . . . are the owners . . . shall not be used as a . . . Negro tenement, leased to colored . . . tenants, sold to colored . . . tenants . . . or all [other] persons of African descent," one agreement reads. "Each of the parties," another maintains, "does hereby covenant and agree [not] to . . . hereafter . . . cause to be suffered, either directly or indirectly, the said premises to be used or occupied in whole or in part by any negro, quadroon, or octoroon of either sex whatsoever. . . ." Some covenants even put a limitation on the number of Negro janitors, bellboys, laundresses, and servants to be employed in a home. Following a pseudo-legal procedure which was supposed to make these agreements binding, each signer paid all the others a fee of one dollar. The finished products were notarized and filed at the County Clerk's Office in the New York City Hall of Records, where they may be read today. The streets covered by such restrictive codes were known in the Negro community as "Covenant Blocks," and Negroes took pride in being the first colored landlords or tenants to live in them: "to knock [the covenants] into a cocked hat," one said. "Although organizations to prevent the settling of colored citizens in certain . . . sections of Harlem mushroom overnight," the *Age* quipped, "the colored invasion goes merrily along."

[Other efforts to stop black movement into Harlem are noted.]

The basic cause of the collapse of all organized efforts to exclude Negroes from Harlem was the inability of any group to gain total and unified support of all white property owners in the neighborhood. Without such support it was impossible to organize a successful neighborhood-wide restrictive movement. Landlords forming associations by blocks had a difficult time keeping people on individual streets united. There also continued to be speculators, Negro and White, who, as in 1904 and 1905, sought to exploit the situation for their own profit. They bought tenements and opened them to Negroes to try to force neighbors to repurchase them at higher prices. Nor was it possible, and this is the major point, to create a well-organized and well-financed movement of Negro restriction (the HPOIC* plan called for the contribution of one-half of one percent of the assessed valuation of all property to a community fund) in the disrupted and emotional atmosphere that pervaded Harlem in the first two decades of the twentieth century. The very setting in which whites were confronted with Negro neighbors for the first time led to less than level-headed reasoning. The first impulse of many "in a rather panicky state of mind" was to sell at whatever price their property would bring and move elsewhere. Realtors called this "panic selling" and, in spite of efforts to prevent it, it continued. Between 1907 and 1914, two-thirds of the houses in or near the Negro section were sold—practically all at substantial losses to the original owners. Since the already weak real estate market was flooded with property in a short time, and only a relatively few Negroes were wealthy enough to buy— "there was no market for real estate among the newcomers"—prices continued to depreciate rapidly: "realty values have tumbled by leaps and bounds." "The coming of Negroes to this locality without any financial backing brought about a decided change, as the colored people . . . were unable to adhere to the standard formerly observed by the whites," a Harlem banker wrote. "Hence there was a deterioration in values. . . ." In the 1870's and 1880's fortunes were made in soaring Harlem land prices; by 1917 white realtors tried to encourage interest in the neighborhood by advertising how cheap property had become: "Changes in the character of Harlem population," a member of the Harlem Board of Commerce wrote, have led "to remarkable bargains, both for rental and purchase. . . . Such properties in good condition can now be purchased at less than the assessed value of the land alone." In the 1920's, as will be shown, this situation changed radically.

[The author continues by discussing the development of black ghettos in other cities during the same period and the uniqueness of Harlem in that it was a symbol of wealth.]

Harlem was originally not a slum, but an ideal place in which to live. For the first and generally last time in the history of New York City, Negroes were able to live in decent homes in a respectable neighborhood,

---

*Editor's note—HPOIC—Harlem Property Owners' Improvement Corporation—a white group opposing black settlement in Harlem.

"the best houses that they have ever had to live in": "It is no longer necessary for our people to live in small, dingy, stuffy tenements," *The New York Age* said in an editorial in 1906. Harlem was "a community in which Negroes as a whole are . . . better housed than in any other part of the country," an Urban League report concluded in 1914. "Those of the race who desire to live in grand style, with elevator, telephone and hall boy service, can now realize their cherished ambition."

It was expensive to live in "grand style." The rents paid by Harlem's Negroes were higher than those charged in any other Negro section of New York City, and they continued to rise rapidly after World War 1. In 1914 the average Negro family paid $23.45 per month for apartments in Harlem, and rents in the most elegant houses were much higher. As Negroes moved into the neighborhood they complained of being overcharged by landlords, and, as a rule, most were paying higher rents than their incomes would warrant. Although the cost of living was certainly high by the standards of a low-income group, few of Harlem's rentals, prior to World War 1, were extortionate. Houses were originally constructed for the well-to-do, "the class above the ordinary." "Harlem tenements," one Negro wrote, "were built for persons of larger incomes than Negroes receive."

[The movement of the black upper and middle-class into Harlem before World War 1 is noted.]

As Harlem became a Negro section, its "modern Houses" and "better homes" attracted many people from the older Negro sections of Manhattan. Negro women in the Tenderloin hoped "to marry and go get a home in Harlem." Negro businessmen, finding customers moving uptown, sold their property and moved northward. "The massing of the large Negro population in the Harlem district," a journalist observed in 1910, "has been the making of many successful Negro . . . businessmen." San Juan Hill (usually called Columbus Hill after the First World War) "was fast pouring its people into Harlem [as the] exodus from the downtown districts continues with great activity." By 1920, the former Negro sections of Manhattan were terribly rundown backwash communities inhabited by Negroes who, as a rule, desired to live in Harlem but could not afford to pay the high rents charged there.

[Osofsky continues by describing the movement of black churches into the area, the activity of black real estate companies and, in general, the resettling of various black institutions in the neighborhood. He also

notes the reaction of white businessmen as this transformation of Harlem occurred.]

The creation of a Negro community within one large and solid geographic area was unique in city history. New York had never been what realtors call an "open city"—a city in which Negroes lived wherever they chose—but the former Negro sections were traditionally only a few blocks in length, often spread across the island, and generally interspersed with residences of white working-class families. Harlem, however, was a Negro world unto itself. A scattered handful of "marooned white families . . . stubbornly remained" in the Negro section, a United States census-taker recorded, but the mid-belly of Harlem was predominantly Negro by 1920.

And the ghetto rapidly expanded. Between the First World War and the Great Depression, Harlem underwent radical changes. When the twenties came to an end, Negroes lived as far south as One Hundred and Tenth Street—the northern boundary of Central Park; practically all the older white residents had moved away; the Russian-Jewish and Italian sections of Harlem, founded a short generation earlier, were rapidly being depopulated; and Negro Harlem, within the space of ten years, became the most "incredible slum" in the entire city. . . .

The Harlem slum of the twenties was the product of a few major urban developments. One of the most important was the deluge of Negro migration to New York City then. . . . If one is looking for a dramatic turning point in the history of the urbanization of the Negro—"a race changing from farm life to city life"—it was certainly the decade of the twenties. Between 1910 and 1920 the Negro population of the city increased 66 percent (91,709 to 152,467); from 1920 to 1930, it expanded 115 percent (152,467 to 327,726). In the latter year less than 25 percent of New York City's Negro population (79,264) was born in New York State.

[Osofsky then provides a detailed look at the sources of black migration into New York.]

The rapid settlement of a heterogeneous Negro population coincided with another important population change—the migration of whites from all sections of Manhattan to other boroughs. For the first time since Dutch settlement, Manhattan's population declined in the 1920's as first- and second-generation immigrants moved to nicer residential areas in the Bronx, Brooklyn, and Queens. Many of the homes they left behind had deteriorated significantly. By 1930 a majority of New York City's foreign-born and second-generation residents lived outside Manhattan. As whites moved out of Manhattan, Negroes moved in.

[The author continues by discussing Italian and Jewish out-migration from Harlem and the expansion of the black sections as well as the arrival of Puerto Ricans in the neighborhood. He further notes the heterogeneous aspects of the black community by commenting on West Indian blacks and their immigration into Harlem.]

The most profound change that Harlem experienced in the 1920's was its emergence as a slum. Largely within the space of a single decade Harlem was transformed from a potentially ideal community to a neighborhood with manifold social and economic problems called "deplorable," "unspeakable," "incredible." . . .

The most important factor which led to the rapid deterioration of Harlem housing was the high cost of living in the community. Rents, traditionally high in Harlem, reached astounding proportions in the 1920's—they skyrocketed in response to the unprecedented demand created by heavy Negro migration and settlement within a restricted geographical area. "Crowded in a black ghetto," a sociologist wrote, "the Negro tenant is forced to pay exorbitant rentals because he cannot escape." In 1919 the average Harlemite paid somewhat above $21 or $22 a month for rent; by 1927 rentals had *doubled,* and the "mean average market rent for Negro tenants in a typical block" was $41.77. In 1927 Harlem Negroes paid $8 more than the typical New Yorker for three-room apartments; $10 more for four rooms; and $7 more for five rooms, an Urban League survey noted. Another report concluded that the typical white working-class family in New York City in the late twenties paid $6.67 per room, per month, while Harlem Negroes were charged $9.50.

Realty values which had declined significantly prior to World War 1 *appreciated* in Harlem in the twenties. Harlem experienced a slum boom. "The volume of business done in the section . . . during the last year is . . . unprecedented," *Harlem Magazine* announced in 1920. "Renting conditions have been very satisfactory to the owners and the demand for space . . . is getting keener every year [due] to the steady increase in the negro population," a *New York Times* reporter wrote in 1923. There was, in the language of a Harlem businessman, an "unprecedented demand for Harlem real estate." For landlords—Negro and white (Negro tenants continually complained that Negro landlords fleeced them with equal facility as whites)—Harlem became a profitable slum.

High rents and poor salaries necessarily led to congested and unsanitary conditions. The average Negro Harlemite in the 1920's, as in the 1890's, held some menial or unskilled position which paid low wages—work which was customarily "regarded as Negro jobs."

[A description of black occupational and income levels, as compared to whites, is then offered.]

Added to the combination of "high rents and low wages" was the fact that Harlem's apartment houses and brownstones were originally built for people with a radically different family structure from that of the new residents. Seventy-five percent of Harlem's tenements had been constructed before 1900. The Negro community of the twenties, like all working-class peoples in times of great migration, continued to be most heavily populated by young adults—men and women between the ages of 15 and 44. Family life had not yet begun for many Negro Harlemites—as it had for older Americans and earlier immigrants who lived in the community previously. In 1930, 66.5 percent of Harlem Negroes were between the ages of 15 and 44, contrasted with 56.5 percent for the general population of Manhattan and 54.4 percent for New York City at large. Harlemites who were married had few children. In 1930, 17.5 percent of Harlem's population was under 14; the corresponding figure for New York City was 24.5 percent. The number of Harlemites under the age of 15 declined 14 percent between 1920 and 1930, as whites left the neighborhood. There was a corresponding decrease of 19 percent for those over 45 years of age.

What all these statistics mean is simply that apartments of five, six, and seven rooms were suitable for older white residents with larger families and larger incomes—they obviously did not meet the needs of the Negro community in the 1920's. "The houses in the section of Harlem inhabited by the Negro were not only built for another race," E. Franklin Frazier noted, "but what is more important, for a group of different economic level, and consisting of families and households of an entirely different composition from those which now occupy these dwellings." "Unfortunately," Eugene Kinckle Jones of the Urban League stated, "the houses built before [the Negroes'] arrival were not designed to meet the needs . . . of Negroes." "The class of houses we are occupying today are not suited to our economic needs," John E. Nail said in 1921. Negro Harlemites desperately needed small apartments at low rentals: "One of the community's greatest needs [is] small apartments for small families with a reasonable rent limit. . . ." Few realtors were philanthropic enough to invest their capital in new construction;

older homes, properly sub-divided, produced sufficient income. Only a handful of new houses were built in Harlem in the 1920's.

A variety of makeshift solutions were found to make ends meet: "What you gonna do when the rent comes 'round," has been an old Negro song. The most common solution was to rent an apartment larger than one's needs and means and make up the difference by renting rooms to lodgers—"commercializing" one's home. In the twenties, approximately one white Manhattan family in nine (11.2 percent) took in roomers, contrasted with one in four (26 percent) for Negroes. Most lodgers were strangers people let into their homes because of economic necessity. It was difficult to separate "the respectable" from "the fast." "The most depraved Negroes lived side by side with those who were striving to live respectable lives," a contemporary complained. Urban reformers blamed many of Harlem's social problems on this "lodger evil."

Every conceivable space within a home was utilized to maximum efficiency: "Sometimes even the bathtub is used to sleep on, two individuals taking turns!" Negro educator Roscoe Conkling Bruce wrote. Boarding houses were established which rented beds by the week, day, night, or hour. A large number of brownstones were converted to rooming houses: "Private residences at one time characteristic of this part of the city have been converted into tenements. . . ." One landlord transformed apartments in nine houses into one-room flats, a state commission investigating New York housing reported. Space which formerly grossed $40 a month now brought in $100 to $125. People were said to be living in "coal bins and cellars."

[Osofsky continues his discussion of the housing problem in the neighborhood.]

All these factors combined to lead to the rapid decline of Harlem. . . .

People were packed together to the point of "indecency." Some landlords, after opening houses to Negro tenants, lost interest in caring for their property and permitted it to run down—halls were left dark and dirty, broken pipes were permitted to rot, steam heat was cut off as heating apparatus wore out, dumb-waiters broke down and were boarded up, homes became vermin-infested. Tenants in one rat-infested building started what they called "a crusade against rats." They argued that the rats in their houses were "better fed" and "better housed" than the people. Some common tenant complaints in the 1920's read: "No improvement in ten years"; "Rats, rat holes, and roaches"; "Very very cold"; "Not fit to live in"; "Air shaft smells"; "Ceilings in two rooms have fallen"; "My apartment is overrun with rats"; and so on. There were more disputes between tenants and landlords in Harlem's local district court—the Seventh District Court—than in any municipal court in the five boroughs. Traditionally, municipal courts were known as "poor-men's courts"; Harlemites called the Seventh District Court the "rent court." Occasionally, socially conscious judges of this court made personal inspections of local tenements that were subjects of litigation. Without exception what they saw horrified them: "Conditions in negro tenements in Harlem are deplorable"; "Found few fit for human habitation"; "Negro tenants are being grossly imposed upon by their landlords"; "On the whole I found a need for great reformation"; were some of their comments. One municipal official accurately called the majority of Harlem's houses "diseased properties."

HOUSING AND SERVICES
IN AN IMMIGRANT NEIGHBORHOOD
Milwaukee's Ward 14

ROGER D. SIMON

One need not be an environmental determinist to recognize that housing and services played a role in adjustment to urban life. As Roy Lubove pointed out: "Depending on the aspirations and life styles of individuals or groups, differential environments might be accommodative or dysfunctional. . . . Environment performs enabling and constraining functions. It provides or inhibits satisfactions throughout the life cycle." To date neither historians nor social scientists have demonstrated a precise relationship between the urban physical environment and social conditions or social change. In fact, both have been eager to point out that statistical associations do not prove causation, as indeed they do not. However, it would be fallacious to conclude that no relationship exists between physical environment and social behavior. It would also be erroneous to assume, however, that such relationship as might exist is confined only to those living in the very worst housing and suffering the most abject misery.

The importance of studying the physical environment also derives from its permanence. The housing stock, streets, open spaces, and water and sewer networks, once in place, must serve for generations, perhaps centuries. And yet, the aspirations, tastes, incomes, and family patterns

The original version of this article appeared under the title, "Housing and Services in an Immigrant Neighborhood: Milwaukee's Ward 14," by Roger D. Simon, published in *Journal of Urban History*, vol. 2 no. 4 (August, 1976) pp. 435–448 and is reprinted herewith by permission of the publisher, Sage Publications, Inc.

of an area's residents change considerably. The adaptability of the physical environment to such social and economic change is a determinant of the quality of urban life.

We know relatively little about the factors affecting the quantity, quality, and spatial distribution of a city's housing stock or the timing of installation of essential services. Our knowledge of such matters as subdivision, lot sales, and transportation expansion is based on examples from a limited number of places, notably Boston and Chicago, and we know little of how patterns vary among neighborhoods of one city, among different cities, and over time.

It has been fourteen years since the publication of Sam Bass Warner's outstanding *Streetcar Suburbs,* which initiated the investigation of some of these issues. But except for a handful of studies of tenement and ghetto conditions, surprisingly little has been done to build upon this seminal book. Students of the "new urban history" have focused instead upon social and residential mobility, two very important but nonetheless distinct issues. We have learned much of value from the mobility studies, but in terms of examining the city, they have told us little of the physical environment which encased the mobile Americans.

This article will examine one peripheral neighborhood on the south side of Milwaukee which the city designated as Ward 14. Between the mid-1880s and the first decade of the new century, one and two family dwellings covered the area. The new residents were overwhelmingly first generation Polish immigrants and their families. Almost half of these family heads were unskilled laborers with a limited income. Subdividers and builders anticipated and responded to the needs of those families, who were most likely to move into the new ward. The narrow lots, small frame homes, and the absence of water or sewer mains were a function of the need to keep down costs as much as possible.

The manner in which the ward developed provided the residents with a remarkable opportunity to manipulate the physical environment to meet their needs. The primary mechanism for this was home ownership. The long run result was a stable, lower middle class neighborhood. This was in striking contrast with the lower Roxbury section of Boston, for example, which, according to Sam Warner, rapidly deteriorated.

Before examining the new neighborhood, we must consider the context in which it emerged. First settled in the 1830s, Milwaukee by 1880 had grown into a city of 115,000 people. Although it was still dependent on its port and its processing plants, heavy industry had already taken hold. In the ensuing thirty years it was among the country's fastest growing major urban centers. By 1910 its population stood at 373,000, making it the twelfth largest city and the fifteenth largest metropolitan area in the country. This rapid growth meant that new homes and neighborhoods had to be created for all segments of the population. The city simply lacked a sufficient supply of older housing which the more affluent segment of the population could pass down to lower income groups.

Immigrants and their children dominated Milwaukee's population as they did in other large cities, but there was a distinctive feature of the immigrant community which influenced the city's growth. Two ethnic groups accounted for almost three-quarters of the foreign stock. German immigrants had provided an overwhelming share of the city's population since its earliest days. As late as 1910, half of the foreign-born were Germans. Milwaukee did not attract as large a share of the so-called "new immigrants" as it had of earlier groups from northern and western Europe, but it did attract large numbers of Poles. In 1910, 22% of Milwaukee's foreign-born were Polish-speaking. That was twice the combined population of Milwaukee immigrants whose native tongue was Yiddish, Italian, or Czech.[1] The significance of this imbalance was that the two major groups could easily dominate entire neighborhoods and sections of the city.

The immigrants turned to Milwaukee's growing industrial sector for employment. The city was a major diversified fabricating and processing center with iron and steel, machinery, motors, milling, packing, tanning, and brewing among the leading industries. In 1910, 56.9% of all employed males over age ten were engaged in manufacturing or mechanical pursuits. Among the largest cities only Buffalo and Detroit had a higher percentage similarly engaged. Thus, Milwaukee also had an exceptionally large population of artisans and laborers. Much of the new housing and the new neighborhoods accommodating the city's rapidly growing population would be built for this segment of the work force.

In addition to the characteristics of population which affected neighborhood formation, Milwaukee's geographic and topographic features also influenced residential patterns. Because a wide river valley cut Milwaukee in half, many of the factories, yards, and mills were able to move away from the immediate vicinity of the central business district and the harbor area without moving to the periphery. Other major industrial installations were located along the lake shore south of the harbor entrance and along the banks of the Milwaukee River; thus, large portions of the city were within walking distance of some industrial employment.

As a result of this diffusion of industrial establishments and because of the city's relatively small size, Milwaukeeans relied much less heavily on mass transit than did residents of other cities. In the early twentieth century, the most frequent streetcar riders lived in those cities with special topographic problems, such as San Francisco and Pittsburgh, or in the very largest cities. In 1902, for example, Boston averaged 246 streetcar rides per inhabitant, while Milwaukee averaged only 156. The extent to which the streetcar facilitated or restrained the sorting out of population was more limited in Milwaukee than in cities where mass transit was more heavily used. Table 2 shows the rank of Milwaukee among all cities over 200,000 in 1910 along these measures.

TABLE 2. Milwaukee's Rank Among U.S. Cities Over 200,000 in 1910 on Selected Measures[a]

	Rank
Population	12
Metropolitan Area Population	15
Percentage Increase in Population, 1880–1910	7
Value Added by Manufacture, 1909	11
Percentage of Male Work Force in All Manufacturing Occupations	3
Percentage of Work Force in White Collar Clerical Occupations	15
Percentage of Population Foreign Born	9
Percentage of Population of Foreign Stock	1[b]
Persons per Acre	3
Persons per Dwelling	15
Percentage of Homes Owned	8
Streetcar Rides per Inhabitant, 1902	21

[a]There were 28 cities with more than 200,000 people in 1910.
[b]Tied with New York for the same rank.

During the commercial era of Milwaukee's growth, most of the population and business activity concentrated north of the wide Menomonee Valley. The south side lacked an early aggressive promoter to match those of the town's other section, and its low lying lands were not drained for some years. It was the least prestigious location in the city. The area attracted primarily artisans and unskilled laborers of German, Irish, and Scandinavian origin, who lived together in ethnically mixed, low density neighborhoods.

In the late 1860s the first Polish immigrants moved into the south side and increasingly came to dominate that section of the city. By the first decade of the twentieth century, Ward 14, at the far southwest periphery, housed half of all the city's Poles. Further, over 80% of the families living in the ward were of Polish stock. Here was an immigrant neighborhood which was overwhelmingly dominated by a single group, and contained a substantial portion of the city's population of that group. Yet, it was a peripheral neighborhood of new homes on quiet residential streets, with small front yards and an occasional tree. Neither tenement houses nor huge triple-deckers were anywhere in sight.

To trace the development of this area and to understand its character, it is necessary to examine it at a disaggregative level. The analysis which follows is based upon a 10% random sample of the facing street blocks of Ward 14. Data were collected on every property in each sample block with respect to subdivision, house construction, and residents. The installation of new services on each block was also examined.

The area designated as Ward 14 lay between 2 and 3.5 miles from the center of town. In the 1870s it was largely beyond the built-up area of settlement. The city did not even annex the southern half of the ward until 1889. In 1887 the Cream City Railway Company built a horsecar line along Forest Home Avenue, the ward's northwest border, as far as the cemetery. Service remained irregular on the route until the early 1880s. In the middle of the decade a second route penetrated the ward as far as the House of Correction. In the 1890s that route was extended further south and another line paralleled the ward's eastern border.

With the extension of the city limits and the streetcar lines, subdividers moved into the ward and carved up the land into house lots. They worked systematically, moving outward from areas of existing settlement. The subdividers imposed a rectangular grid pattern on the area. Consequently, both the blocks and the house lots were long and narrow. Most north-south blocks contained 38 to 44 house lots with dimensions usually of 30' wide by 120' deep.

There were two major open spaces in the ward which influenced its development. The larger of the two was Forest Home Cemetery, a 188-acre tract in the southwest corner opened in 1871. In 1890, the Park Commission purchased a 26-acre parcel in the middle of the ward around a small lake. They named it Lincoln Avenue Park, but shortly changed it to Kosciuszko Park. The homes along the park's border were more substantial than the average, and usually housed families a bit higher up the socioeconomic ladder. In 1910, when the ward was almost completely built-up, the Park Commission bought a 14-acre site that had escaped development because of its hilly terrain. They named it Pulaski Park.

Forest Home Cemetery and the city's House of Correction, which was near the northeast corner of the ward, attracted a few inhabitants to the area in the 1870s. Land costs were relatively low because the ward was still beyond the built-up section of the city. At the time of the 1880 federal census there were only 53 families on the sample blocks, clustered in the northeast corner. Forty-six of the 53 family heads were unskilled workers or factory operatives. Fifty-one listed their birthplace as Germany or Prussia, although at least 23 of them had Polish surnames.

In the twenty-five years after 1880, subdividers, builders, speculators, homeowners, and tenants transformed Ward 14 from an outlying, lightly settled periphery of open spaces into a dense and complex urban neighborhood. The sample blocks which housed 53 families in 1880 contained 456 in 1905. The ward as a whole became the most populous in the city, with 25,300 residents in 1905.

The new housing stock of Ward 14 was characterized primarily by its modest size. Small, one-story cottages dominated the landscape. The average size of the dwellings built on the sample blocks from 1888 to 1929 was 1,054 square feet in exterior dimensions. Some homes started out as only four-room dwellings measuring 20' x 30'. Bedrooms in such cottages often measured 7' x 9' or less. These small homes lacked the porches or fancy trim of large houses going up in other sections of town. A few wooden steps to the front door was all that could be expected. A half-finished dirt basement was a common feature; although in numerous cases the original cottages were raised and the basement converted into a first floor, making a two-story house. This did not necessarily mean a two-family house, however. In some cases the property owner later erected a second home at the rear of the long, narrow lots. Eighteen percent of the homes on the sample blocks eventually shared their lots. Most of the rear dwellings, however, clustered in the older, northern portion of the ward.

Quite clearly, the homes of Ward 14 were built in anticipation of a low income population. The Polish workers already in the vicinity were, in many cases, themselves the builders. Here was new construction at the absolute minimum standard, and it would provide a very minimum environment for the residents, at least in the early years.

In 1905 not only did Polish immigrants dominate the ward, but so did unskilled laborers. Fifty-five percent of all the household heads on the sample blocks lacked a skill, and 46% of the total were both unskilled and Polish-born. Table 3, based on the published state census of 1905, compares the percentage of major immigrant and occupational groups for the city and the ward. It indicates the magnitude of over-representation of Poles and the unskilled. Thus, while 5.7% of the city's population came from Polish lands, 34% of Ward 14 residents were Poles. Factory hands and laborers together accounted for 19.5% of Milwaukee's work force, but 53.3% of the ward's. Conversely, native-born persons, Germans, white collar workers, and most skilled artisans tended to avoid the area.

Table 4 shows the percentage of heads-of-household on the sample blocks in 1905 by birthplace and ethnic group in each socio economic category. The table demonstrates the concentration of Poles as unskilled laborers. The table also reveals that native-born children of Polish parents

TABLE 3. Percentage of Population and Work Force of Milwaukee and Ward 14 in Selected Ethnic and Occupational Categories, 1905

	Milwaukee	Ward 14
	Percentage of Total Population in Each Category	
U. S. Born	71.1	60.0
German Born	16.5	5.4
Polish Born (German Section)	4.6	30.4
Polish Born (Austrian Section)	.2	.6
Polish Born (Russian Section)	.9	3.0
	Percentage of Work Force in Each Category	
Physicians and Lawyers	1.0	.1
Agents and Commercial Travelers	2.1	.5
Foreman	1.9	.3
Bookkeepers and Stenographers	3.5	.4
Clerks and Salesmen	8.9	2.9
Skilled Building Trades Workers	7.3	6.0
Tailors	5.4	4.7
Mechanics	4.6	2.4
Smiths and Metal Workers	5.7	10.0
Factory Hands, misc.	6.3	16.0
Laborers, not specified	13.2	37.3

SOURCE: Wisconsin, Secretary of State, Tabular Statements of the Census Enumeration, 1905 (Madison, 1906), 171–173, 446–451.

did somewhat better than second generation Germans. This is not surprising since the ward was almost exclusively Polish. Opportunities for service jobs or a petty proprietorship by Polish sons were probably greater than for Germans.[2]

Unskilled immigrants, like all unskilled workers, received low pay, put in long working hours, and sustained considerable periods of unemployment. How then could they afford to live in new, single family cottages in a peripheral residential neighborhood? Certain characteristics of Milwaukee's socioeconomic and morphological structure provide part of the explanation, but the needs of the immigrants themselves and the nature of the physical environment also illuminate the processes at work.

There were distinct advantages to locating along Milwaukee's periphery. Land values tended to decline with distance from the city's center. This differential had special appeal to two overlapping groups: large households and homeowners. Large households, usually those with a number of growing children, could obtain more space for their money,

TABLE 4. Percentage of Each Ethnic Group of Sample Heads-of-Household by Socioeconomic Group, Ward 14, 1905

| | U.S. Born of U.S. Born Parents | German Born Parents | | Polish Born Parents | | |
		German Born	U.S. Born	Polish Born	U.S. Born	All Others
High White Collar	0	0	0	1.0	0	0
Low White Collar	40.0	16.4	0	7.0	15.4	33.3
Skilled	20.0	31.1	58.8	26.5	50.0	66.7
Semi-Skilled	20.0	13.1	0	2.6	7.7	0
Unskilled	20.0	37.7	35.3	62.1	26.9	0
Unknown, Retired, Unemployed	20.0	1.6	5.9	1.0	0	0
N	5	61	17	343	26	3

SOURCE: Sample data.

both inside and outside the dwelling, near the periphery. Thus, households in the child-rearing stage of the family life cycle were disproportionately present in Milwaukee's peripheral wards at the turn of the century. Ward 14 reflected these city-wide trends. The ward had more children of school age and a higher percentage of such children in its population than any other ward in the city.

A peripheral location would appeal to would-be homeowners because of the greater availability and wider selection of house lots and new homes to be found there. Equally important, however, was the overlap between large families and homeowners. Large families could obtain needed space at a better price by buying rather than by renting. Smaller families had less need for an entire dwelling and could more conveniently rent. Moreover, it took time for families to acquire sufficient funds even for a minimum down payment, and it also took some time to accumulate children. Among Milwaukee's twenty-three wards, Ward 14 ranked fourth in percentage of homeowning families, and first in percentage of homeowners carrying a mortgage.

The relationship between household size and tenancy status of the families on the sample blocks is clear within the ward. Table 5 shows the percentage of each group of households, by size, in each tenancy status. It indicates that while 64% of households of one to four persons rented, only 27.7% of the largest group did so. These relationships also held for other peripheral wards in Milwaukee developing at the same time.

TABLE 5. Percentage of Households on Sample Blocks, by Size, in Each Tenancy Status, Ward 14, 1904

Household Size	Unknown	Owned			Rented	Number of Cases
		Unencumbered	Mortgaged	Encumbrance Unknown		
1–2	6.3	7.8	18.8	3.1	64.1	64
3–4	2.0	14.7	18.6	0	64.7	102
5–6	.9	10.7	43.8	.9	43.8	112
7 or more	.6	18.1	52.4	1.2	27.7	166

SOURCE: Sample data.

Home ownership was also desirable because it conveyed to the owner a sense of status, as well as economic security. In Poland, as in other areas of eastern Europe, land ownership brought social standing in the community. Further, ownership was important because it provided a measure of control over one's immediate environment. Edith Abbott, the social worker, found that immigrants in Chicago purchased homes partly because landlords sometimes refused to rent to them if they had a large family. Some immigrants wanted a relative and his family in the same or nearby building—not always feasible in rented quarters.

In order to own their homes—despite the low pay and insecure employment often associated with unskilled labor—the Polish families of Ward 14 made considerable sacrifices which seriously eroded the quality of their environment, at least for a short time. But their practices resulted in a more satisfactory environment in the long run. Moreover, the families were only able to reap the maximum benefit from their hardships because they were homeowners. The sacrifices were subletting parts of their dwelling and delaying the installation of vital urban services.

Families in Ward 14 lived under crowded conditions within their dwellings. Households often took in boarders, or another family. Frequently, one family lived in the basement while the other occupied the upstairs. The dirt floor basements were damp, dark, and poorly ventilated, but on occasion the family which owned the dwelling lived in the basement and rented out the upstairs because of the greater income it produced. A state investigator, noting these conditions, observed, "the houses in most cases are painted and kept in fair repair because the landlord is there himself and simply subletting other rooms to pay off the mortgage." Another commentator, specifically referring to the conditions in Ward 14, argued, "the higher interests of the family are too often sacrificed in a struggle to purchase the home."

Meeting the mortgage payments also meant keeping down other housing expenses, such as tax liabilities, as much as possible. A variable element of property taxes in the period were the special assessments levied for improvements on the block. The city levied special assessments against abutting property owners for most or all of the cost of laying water mains and sewers, grading and paving streets, and installing sidewalks and curbs. The property owners and the city both participated in the decision to proceed with new services on a given block. Most improvements to a block required a petition from a majority of abutting owners before work could be planned; an elaborate procedure was necessary to get around that restriction. In all cases, the Common Council, whose members were elected on a ward basis, had the final say, and they did not usually impose their will on the owners.

Because the property owners in Ward 14 were predominantly residents, and because they could exert considerable influence over these special assessments, we can examine the timing of installation of new services as an indication of the level of services which the population could afford and the quality of the new physical environment. To measure this we can employ the concept of a threshold population. The threshold population is defined here as the percentage of house lots which contained a structure when the city decided to install the service. Looking at three basic services—water mains, sewers, and graded streets—the thresholds for Ward 14 were: water mains: 46.7%; sewers: 47.4%; and improved streets: 45.9%. In other words, the housing development of those blocks was almost half completed before the services arrived.

These threshold percentages are more meaningful when we compare them with two other peripheral neighborhoods in Milwaukee developing in the same time period at similar distances from the central business district. One neighborhood in the city's northwest corner housed mainly working class and lower middle class skilled artisans, shopkeepers, and white collar clerical workers. Just over half of the household heads were German immigrants, and an additional 27.0% were native-born of German parents. The city designated this corner of the city as Wards 20 and 22. A second area, Ward 18, in the city's northeast corner, contained mainly professionals, proprietors, and white collar clerks of American and British parentage. Like Ward 14, Wards 20-22 and 18 had high rates of home ownership and a disproportionate share of children in their population. Wards 20-22 received its services at an early stage, when it was between a fifth and a quarter developed. The extremely low

TABLE 6. Threshold Populations[a] for Provision of Water Mains, Sewers, and Graded Streets, Selected Milwaukee Wards

	Ward 14	Wards 20-22	Ward 18
Water Mains	46.7	21.2	4.0
Sewer Pipes	47.4	23.4	5.1
Graded Streets	45.9	26.1	5.0

[a]The threshold population for a given block was the percentage of platted lots improved upon by the end of the calendar year before the city installed each service. The figures here are the mean percentages for the sample blocks in the indicated wards.

thresholds for Ward 18 indicate that, for the majority of its new residents, a graded street with water mains and sewers already in place was the minimum standard for a new suburban neighborhood.

There were social costs: Ward 14 had the highest death rate in the city. Partly this reflected the high proportion of children in its population in an era of appalling infant mortality. The causes of high death rates are complex, and involve a good deal more than congestion and bad water. Crude death rate per thousand is a weak measure of health conditions, but it is suggestive. In 1900 the crude death rate per thousand for Ward 14 was 16.3. The rate for the city was 13.4; for Ward 18: 12.1; and for Ward 20-22 area: 13.4 The composition of the death rates reveal more about the impact of delayed services. Mortality from diarrheal diseases among infants is particularly suggestive of the costs of impure water, although it was certainly not the only reason for deaths among those children. In 1900, the crude death rate per thousand from acute intestinal diseases for persons under one year of age in Ward 14 was 3.16. That compares with rates of 1.35 for the city, 1.42 for Ward 18, and 1.22 for the Ward 20–22 area.

At the turn of the century Ward 14 was a new neighborhood built by and for a particular socioeconomic group striving for a greater stake in the society. Although this study did not trace individual career patterns, over time, we can examine the continuing evolution of the Ward 14 area. The particular residents have changed, but the neighborhood could, and does, continue to serve the same kind of people.

Ward 14 represented an environment suited to the needs and aspirations of its original residents. By 1940 home ownership in the area was widespread and well above the city average. But overcrowding remained, and 45% of the dwelling units either shared bathroom facilities or had none. Between 1940 and 1970 the area continued to upgrade. The population declined, but not the number of dwelling units, indicating a decongestion in the housing. (It did not necessarily indicate an aging of the population, because the percentage of children was greater in 1970 than 1950.) The percentage of units lacking some plumbing dropped to 7.9% and the percentage of owner-occupied units rose. During those 30 years the socioeconomic character of the population remained quite stable. Examining housing value, family income, and educational attainment of the adult population, we find that the ratio between the medians for the city and for the ward changed little. Although the percentage of the Polish-born fell with the end of immigration, the share of this group in the area remained far above the city average. As late as 1970, 19.8% of the population of the census tracts in the area was of Polish stock. This was four times the proportion of Polish stock persons in the city.[3]

Unfortunately, we do not know enough about many urban neighborhoods built at the turn of the century to make extensive comparisons with Ward 14, but we can compare the ward with the streetcar suburbs of the Roxbury and Dorchester sections of Boston which developed at the same time. Many of the unskilled laborers of Ward 14 would not have located in Roxbury or Dorchester, because Boston had a larger stock of old housing near its center, and because, with a much larger population and area it was more reliant on its mass transit network. In 1910 the Boston Metropolitan District had three times the area and 3.5 times the population of the Milwaukee District.

Boston laborers who could move away from inner city neighborhoods moved to lower Roxbury, which had the best transit service and some heavy industry. Although lower Roxbury was about the same distance from downtown Boston as Ward 14 was from downtown Milwaukee, Roxbury was considered a close-in district, and land values consequently were correspondingly higher. Therefore, it was built over with two and particularly three story dwellings housing as many families. The large three-deckers cut out much of the light and fresh air which were among the suburb's principal attractions. In Milwaukee the houses were overcrowded, but the smaller cottages did not so overcrowd the land; this is a critical distinction. As the Polish workers saved their money, they retired their mortgages, took over their dwellings, and improved and invested in their property. The housing stock provided the opportunity for single family owner occupancy, the obvious housing preference of middle class Americans in the twentieth century. This was never the case with the double and triple deckers of Roxbury, which, by definition, contained rental units. Furthermore, by 1900, when greater numbers of lower middle class and working class families were entering Roxbury, there was an increase in doubling-up and dividing of homes into more units. This congestion *within* the dwelling was only compounded by overbuilding on the land. According to Sam Bass Warner, "after but a few years as an acceptable lower middle class neighborhood, lower Roxbury was becoming a slum." Population pressure and reliance on mass transit resulted in a housing stock in Roxbury with much less capacity to face the changes occurring during the twentieth century.

The conditioning factors affecting the formation of Ward 14 were, first of all, those created by the city. Milwaukee was new, thus it lacked a large supply of old housing. Also, an exceptionally large share of its population was of immigrant stock and was also in the industrial work force. But the locations of industrial employment were sufficiently diffused that workers did not have to choose between high cost central locations or reliance on the streetcar.

The second group of conditioning factors were those directly bearing on the ward. Polish immigrants dominated the south side, and so new homes at the southwest periphery would be occupied by that group. The processes of subdivision and street layout were similar to developments elsewhere in Milwaukee and in other cities. But the homes were extremely small, and were crowded with boarders, lodgers and second families living in basements. Water mains and sewers did not come with streetcar expansion or first residents. On the average, they came when the block was half completed.

The residents of Ward 14 were able to exert some control over their environment because they were able to gain a tenuous form of home ownership. Ownership allowed them to house a second family in their dwellings and to realize the income it produced. It also enabled them to hold off on services which were undoubtedly good for their health, but which would nonetheless deprive them of a very scarce resource: their savings. It enabled them to forge an environment capable of being continually upgraded. Although there was doubling-up and there were some rear dwellings, the units were kept in good repair. The long term achievement was a stable, lower middle class residential neighborhood.

5

NEIGHBORHOOD RENEWAL
AND REHABILITATION

Stage 5 of the Hoover and Vernon neighborhood cycle indicates renewal for an area. There are a number of strategies for improving a neighborhood. The two selections in this chapter analyze renewal and rehabilitation schemes and include different approaches to dealing with neighborhood residents. The controversy surrounding urban renewal is noted, and questions concerning the type of neighborhood that will be created and who will live there are discussed.

Bob Kuttner examines renewal plans for Southeast Baltimore, a multi-ethnic working class neighborhood. In this area the neighborhood residents, organizing against the city's destructive highway and renewal plans, revitalized and preserved their community. Rather than see their neighborhood demolished through renewal or themselves forced out through upper middle class renovation, the residents of this area were able to create a stable working class community.

A different outcome occurred in Atlanta. Clarence N. Stone analyzes that city's renewal program. The low income Bedford-Pine neighborhood was scheduled for renewal with the planned displacement of almost a thousand families. Concerned that renewal would change their neighborhood into a non-residential section or into an area for the upper middle class, this community, as in southeast Baltimore, fought back, but with less success. The tensions and conflicts within the neighborhood and the response of city government are described and offer a good comparison to the events in Baltimore.

ETHNIC RENEWAL
BOB KUTTNER

On a recent morning, Mrs. Matilda Koval led her brigade of neighborhood women on an inspection tour of a dingy alley near Patterson Park. As her troops, called Community Taking Action, rounded the corner row house, garbage came pouring out the window. "Who do you think you are?" the grandmotherly Mrs. Koval shouted. She phoned downtown to the city health inspectors, who fined the culprit $40.

Mrs. Koval's shock troops are part of a remarkably successful campaign to restore this community of 19th-century row houses. Patterson Park lies at the heart of Southeast Baltimore, the city's old ethnic quarter. At Patterson Park, a ragtag band of irregulars held off the British in 1814, but Southeast Baltimore has succumbed to waves of foreign invaders ever since. Poles, Ukrainians, Italians, Greeks, Germans, Czechs, Finns, and their children live there today. (Mrs. Koval is Ukrainian.) The area's 90,000 residents also include nearly 10,000 blacks, and even a colony of Lumbee Indians from North Carolina.

The Patterson Park women are a constituent unit of the area's federation of block clubs, church groups, ethnic fraternities, and union locals; it is called the Southeast Community Organization (SECO), and it is spearheading the larger community's revival. SECO's allies include Baltimore's enlightened housing Commissioner, Robert Embry, and several penitent local bankers eager to shed their "red-lining" image. Southeast Baltimore has become an obligatory pilgrimage for the country's growing band of neighborhood preservationists. A tour of the area reveals renovation of entire blocks. There are community self-help projects, new schools, and lesser amenities like curbs, street lights, and clean alleys. Several score "urban homesteaders" have taken title to dilapidated row houses for a dollar each on condition that they restore them and live in them for three years.

There is no purity hereabouts, yet Southeast Baltimore is just the sort of ethnic community Jimmy Carter was addressing. It is understandable that he tripped. The delicate equities of retaining the white working class in reviving city neighborhoods without at once excluding blacks poses an issue too slippery for even Carter to finesse. Yet, the furor over the candidate's gaffe should not obscure the more important point. Belatedly, there is growing recognition of neighborhoods as the basic cells in the urban organism.

Public policy has conspired against neighborhoods like this for a generation. Housing subsidies, mortgage flows, and tax shelters all favored new suburban expansion. Bankers looked skeptically at the aging row houses; urban renewal demolished them. Federal highways carried millions to the newly fashionable suburbs, often literally over the ashes of the old neighborhoods. Racial tensions in the 60's accelerated their decline.

But scarcity economics is beginning to reverse the trend. Suddenly, the higher cost of housing, energy and transportation has priced the new suburban split-level beyond the means of four out of five Americans. (In the Baltimore suburbs, the average new home sells for better than $40,000.) An obscure bankers' term—red-lining—has emerged as an unlikely *cause célèbre*. The logic of neighborhood preservation is irrefutable. Nearly half the cost of new development is infrastructure—land, roads, sewers, public utility systems. In city neighborhoods these already exist. Not only is rehabilitation cheaper, but thanks to declining standards and rising costs, a properly maintained 19th-century house is probably a better investment than a brand-new ticky-tacky creation. In Southeast Baltimore, a sturdy row house costs $12,000.

The attraction of city living in a restored town house, of course, is hardly news. Indeed, once an old neighborhood like Brooklyn Heights or Washington's Capitol Hill becomes fashionable, prices skyrocket and a renovated upper-middle class neighborhood displaces an existing blue-collar community. Significantly, the revival of Southeast Baltimore is primarily a renaissance of the existing ethnic neighborhood and not an invasion of brownstoners. Only in the area's oldest section, Fell's Point, are chic pubs beginning to compete with workingmen's saloons, as wealthy newcomers buy in.

Five years ago, Southeast Baltimore was another familiar declining neighborhood. On the area's western fringe, the Victorian town houses of once-elegant Washington Hill had been divided into cramped flats by absentee landlords. The Hill was designated an urban-renewal area and set for demolition.

Farther east, near the city line, blight was beginning to threaten the neat row-house communities of Highlandtown and Canton. The last neighborhood doctor was moving out. The area's main shopping street was looking shabby and losing trade to the new shopping malls five miles to the east. South of Washington Hill, the historic waterfront district, Fell's Point, was about to be cut by a six-lane expressway. Some 350 homes along the proposed route had already been torn down. Dozens more had been condemned by the city.

"It all began with the fight against the road," according to Southeast Baltimore's best-known daughter, Barbara Mikulski, who has since become a national spokeswoman for ethnic causes. In those years, she was teaching social work. Mikulski and several others organized a protest coalition called SCAR-Southeast Community Against the Road.

"For the first time we all rejected the philosophy that says put it in somebody else's neighborhood, just don't put it in my neighborhood," Mikulski recalls. Through court fights and a bond-issue rejection, SCAR managed to delay the highway. By 1971, SCAR had grown into SECO, and Barbara Mikulski was on the City Council, after ousting an incumbent who supported the highway.

"My predecessors were known for delivering small favors," Mikulski observed. "For going along with City Hall, they were rewarded with patronage goodies. When the Mayor said put the road through Fell's Point, they didn't object." As in other big cities, ethnic machine politics delivered jobs for neighborhood people, but little for the neighborhood itself.

"When people started organizing against the road, they began looking at official city-planning maps," said Joe McNeely, the director of SECO's staff. "They found the city had literally written this area off. No new capital improvements were planned because the city had a 20-year projection of declining population. No new school had been built here in 30 years. It was a logical place to put a highway." In short, expectation of decline created decline.

In what McNeely calls "our confrontation phase," the neighborhood used direct-action tactics reminiscent of Chicago organizer Saul Alinsky. Mothers with baby carriages blocked traffic to force diversion of truck traffic from residential streets. A protest campaign culminating in a wheelchair march blocked plans to close the area's only public nursing home. A running battle with zoning officials resulted in lower-density zoning to discourage conversions of row houses to flats. And SECO's affiliate in the Washington Hill section ousted a landlord-dominated citizens' advisory board for the urban-renewal area, and persuaded Commissioner Embry to drop the plan to level the area in favor of a community-designed program to convert four blocks of blighted Victorian town houses into 200 middle-income co-op apartments.

About the time of the highway fight, other Baltimore groups were finding that lending institutions would not make mortgage loans in many city neighborhoods, thus accelerating their decline. A Jesuit priest, the Rev. Vincent Quail, who ran a housing assistance center out of a ghetto storefront, launched a campaign against several savings-and-loan associations. Father Quail, who has a fine sense of irony, began with Loyola Federal Savings and Loan. "I told the president of Loyola Federal," Father Quail recalled, "that he was a greater disgrace to the memory of St. Ignatius than I." Eventually, the community groups opposed to redlining persuaded Embry's Department of Housing and Community Development to open an official investigation of red-lining.

All over the country, older working-class neighborhoods were encountering the same problem. Banks, like highway planners, had little use for the old neighborhoods. If the houses were more than 30 years old, if racial change seemed around the corner, mortgages on reasonable terms were not to be had.

The Federal National Mortgage Association (F.N.M.A., known as Fannie Mae) also slighted the row-house communities. Fannie Mae replenishes savings institutions' capital by purchasing mortgages from lenders for cash. It was well known in the business that if the age of the house plus the term of the mortgage exceeded 60, Fannie Mae's computer would spit out the offered mortgage and demand additional information. The mortgage might not be rejected, but if you wanted an uncomplicated relationship with Fannie, better to keep out of the old neighborhood.

After the 1968 riots, the Federal Housing Administration's stepped-up activity in the inner city only made things worse. F.H.A., which had always been a suburban creature, came roaring into the red-lined neighborhoods, only to become the natural ally of blockbusters. Speculators, armed with commitments of F.H.A. mortgages written wholesale, stampeded white residents into panic-selling and turned over entire neighborhoods from white to black at inflated prices.

In March 1972, at a national conference of ethnic groups held at a parochial school on Chicago's Northwest Side, red-lining foes from diverse cities discovered they were fighting the same battles against blockbusters, lenders, and the F.H.A. The conference was conceived by a fortyish housewife and mother of six named Gale Cincotta, who has since emerged as La Pasionaria of red-lining. A platinum blonde of huge proportions, she is the daughter of Greek and Latvian immigrant parents who ran a restaurant on Chicago's West Side. Her husband, who is Irish and Italian, manages a filling station.

"Every issue I've ever worked on affects my family," said Gale Cincotta with conviction. "If there's an abandoned building, it's on my block. If somebody is mugged on the corner, it's my husband. If the schools are lousy, it's my school."

The other guiding presence at the 1972 conference was Msgr. Geno Baroni, a craggy priest who runs an organization called the National Center for Urban Ethnic affairs. In his study at Catholic University in Washington, Monsignor Baroni has a ceramic figurine of an angel carrying a picket sign that reads "Ethnic is Good." Baroni's gospel is that ethnic cohesiveness is a legitimate and powerful force that should be mobilized to preserve neighborhoods. If working-class ethnics have their own turf, Baroni argues, they can make common cause with their black neighbors. As a white cleric who spent a decade in Washington's worst ghetto before moving on to ethnic organizing, Baroni retains the confidence of both groups.

There is a danger, of course, that "neighborhood preservation" can turn into preservation against black encroachment. Admittedly, in some communities, like Mrs. Cincotta's Austin section of Chicago, an early target of ethnic protest was racial blockbusting. And in a sense one man's blockbusting is another's equal opportunity. But that simple conclusion does an injustice to the preservationists. In most cities, the coalitions opposed to red-lining have been well integrated: That would not have been possible if blacks had seen disguised racism in the preservation movement.

In fact, this is probably the most thoroughly integrated protest since the early civil-rights days—more so, since it is integrated out of common self-interest rather than the limousine liberalism of upper-middle-class white support groups. The movement against red-lining has enlisted the same class of city people found in street confrontations over busing. But in this case, black and white homeowners are fighting banks instead of each other.

In many areas, like Chicago's suburb of Oak Park, Cincinnati's Bond Hill, Boston's Jamaica Plain, or Seattle's Mount Baker, the preservationists are endeavoring to save their neighborhood's integrated character. In other places, like Southeast Baltimore, the community renaissance draws its strength from its cohesive ethnic composition. People like Patterson Park's Matilda Koval cherish the old-fashioned cohesion and convenience of the old neighborhood and refuse to be pushed out. The main enemies are blight, absentee-ownership, and declining city services, not black neighbors, and the community's ethnic identity is an obvious source of strength.

Baltimore's black city Councilman Clarence Burns, who represents the district next door to Southeast Baltimore, says, "I have no complaint with SECO; I see them as friends. . . . Obviously what they do helps white people more because their area is mostly white, but it spills over into our neighborhood." His view is not universally shared among Baltimore's blacks, however. Parren Mitchell, the congressman who represents inner-city Baltimore, says neighborhood revival "means prices are going to rise. That will exclude many black people. . . . For most of Southeast Baltimore, preservation means preservation of the white ethnic community."

Since 1972, Mrs. Cincotta, Monsignor Baroni, and allied groups like SECO have gradually fashioned a network dedicated to old neighborhoods. They have become self-taught experts in the esoterica of mortgage finance, appraisal, code enforcement, and zoning. Perhaps because it is supported by neighborhood people fighting for immediate goals rather than theoretical reforms, this network has had surprising success. The city of Chicago and the Illinois Legislature now have mortgage-disclosure laws aimed at discouraging red-lining. Last year, when Congress balked at new regulatory proposals of any kind and even Ralph Nader's consumer-advocacy agency was stalled, the neighborhood groups persuaded Congress to enact a similar national law to inhibit red-lining. The bill, sponsored by Senator William Proxmire, the banking committee chairman, marked the first time in memory that citizens' groups took on the powerful banking lobby and won.

In 1972, however, red-lining remained an almost unknown word and an unproved allegation. The forces opposed to red-lining scored an early major success in Baltimore, where Commissioner Embry's own 1973 investigation confirmed that most of the city's lenders were indeed arbitrarily writing off entire neighborhoods. Further, in a city where the bulk of the homes are narrow, prewar row houses, many banks automatically rejected mortgage applications on houses more than 20 years old or less than 18 feet wide, Embry found.

Thanks to an accident of timing, the city's statistics on mortgage investment appeared just when Maryland's bankers were lobbying the State Legislature to lift Maryland's 8 percent usury ceiling. Interest rates had soared; banks could no longer make 8 percent loans and stay in business, they claimed. As it turned out, the vote was close, and the Baltimore city delegation held the balance. In a shrewd stroke, Embry, the community groups, and the city representatives seized the chance to shake down the banks. The usury ceiling would not be lifted until the banks stopped red-lining Baltimore. Eventually, the banks agreed to increase city mortgage lending by at least $45 million, to remove all artificial limitations on the age, width, or location of a property, and to evaluate all mortgage applications on their merits.

With the city's bankers in a receptive mood, SECO organizers turned to an approach pioneered in Pittsburgh, called neighborhood housing services. The idea is to contain and reverse neighborhood blight by throwing every known preservationist remedy into a small area on the edge of spreading deterioration. For the project, SECO selected the transitional 12-block area north of Patterson Park. Under the plan Neighborhood Housing Services was established as a community corporation with a board of local residents and bankers. For its part, the city agreed to increase basic services in the area: garbage collection, rat extermination, curb and pavement improvement. Responsibility for code enforcement, which has had poor results elsewhere when city inspectors descended on unprepared neighborhoods, was delegated to Mrs. Koval's local block-improvement association.

The N.H.S. staff, led by former SECO organizer Tom Adams, has inventoried the entire neighborhood. For its own office, N.H.S. restored a corner storefront on East Fairmont Avenue that had been vacant for 20 years. Adams can recite from memory the ownership status, history, and last selling price of nearly every house in the neighborhood. In order to convert absentee-owned or vacant properties into owner-occupied homes, Adams uses the same skills as the speculators, but to benign purpose. He has a rehab specialist on his staff, and often helps renovators to find tradesmen. Adams had found that many landlords are eager to sell out if N.H.S. can find them a buyer, especially if the code inspectors are on their trail.

"There are a lot of myths, like the myth of the gouging landlord," Adams said on a recent walk around the neighborhood. "Most landlords in an area like this are small-timers. They're not making much money because whole houses rent for $125, and the market is soft. When we call them, they often want to sell. I don't think of creative code enforcement as harassment. We're just helping them to make a decision."

The N.H.S. project, which includes a mortgage specialist on loan from a bank, has helped tenants buy out landlords, brought new families into the 12-block area, helped homesteaders to revive boarded-up shells, and secured home-improvement loans for several long-time residents. In its first nine months, N.H.S. obtained 49 loans from banks and granted another 39 from a high-risk fund capitalized by government and private donors. Twenty-seven vacant row houses have been homesteaded; another 20 were restored with aid from the city. In the original N.H.S. target area, home ownership has increased from 30 percent to 70 percent.

Howard Scaggs, the chain-smoking bank president who serves as voluntary chairman of N.H.S., has turned into an unabashed booster of the neighborhood. His own savings-and-loan association, which made 10 suburban loans for every one in the city in early 1974, was putting most of its mortgages in the city a year later. "Supposedly," said a SECO staffer, "the bankers come in to teach the community about mortgages. But it also turns into a consciousness-raising thing for the bankers."

Scaggs waxes lyrical about Patterson Park. The N.H.S. "model block" facing the park, he says, "looks just like Georgetown, Washington, D.C."

It almost does. The block contains the area's finest town houses—and also a funeral parlor. The houses are being tastefully restored, with formstone removed, and trim refinished to reveal natural wood. But Patterson Park is no Georgetown. It is too unfashionable, happily, which keeps prices at bargain levels. On our walk, Tom Adams pointed to the row house across the street from the N.H.S. office. "That sold for seventeen, plus eight thousand to restore it," he said. Seventeen thousand? "Seventeen *hundred*." Adams grinned.

On the same block, we visited a sanitation worker who had fixed up his house with an N.H.S. loan. The man proudly showed off his new furnace. "You know what I really want to do, Tom," he confided as we were leaving; "I'm saving up $300 to put on formstone. What do you think?"

Adams nodded tactfully. Though home-improvement fever may have a different meaning here from that in chic Victorian neighborhoods where prices are zooming, it is just as infectious. In its strategy for reviving the larger Southeast community, SECO marries occasionally militant tactics with the traditional values most radical organizers would shun: home ownership, thrift, ethnic and church ties, and unrelenting civic pride. "We promote hell out of the neighborhood," says Joe McNeely.

The result is something of a cross between Cuban or Chinese style block-committee peer pressure and old-fashioned Rotarian boosterism.

One of SECO's most successful ventures is a monthly tour of the neighborhood conducted by residents for representatives of the several city agencies responsible for garbage collection, code enforcement, rat control, roads, sidewalks, and sewers.

"It used to be that we'd complain and they'd shift us from department to department," said Mrs. Elaine Smith, a SECO vice president from the Upper Fell's Point area. "Now we get all the agencies to walk through with us once a month and they can't tell us to call somebody else."

After each tour, the city sends the Upper Fell's Point Community Council a progress report of work done. Like the women in the N.H.S. area, Mrs. Smith also operates her own code-enforcement program. On a recent tour, she encountered the owner of a dilapidated row house and scolded him about the peeling paint.

"I've lived here four years," the man said testily. "Nobody tells me when to paint my house."

"I've lived here 40 years," replied Mrs. Smith. "Paint your damn house."

"I get cussed out now and then," she said afterward. "They say, 'Who's paying, SECO? The city?' But we make our point. We had a house last week with 40 violations. He was fined $250."

Since its confrontation phase, SECO has also established a community-development corporation, which is engaged in several joint ventures with the city, including an ambitious project to restore a two-block area that was mostly absentee-owned and half-vacant. The city housing department is restoring a row of 13 houses on one block for use as public housing or sale to homeowners. On the adjoining block, several houses are available for homesteading. A final section will be developed as rental housing by Southeast Development, SECO's subsidiary. When the project is finished, a pivotal two-block section of the community's western fringe will be cleaned up and repopulated by a racial and economic mix of renters and owners, helping to shore up the entire area. In order to keep prices from rising too rapidly as the area revives, SECO has a grant from the Ford Foundation to buy attractive properties before speculators move in.

In all of these ventures, SECO's de facto alliance with city housing officials is an enormous asset. As early as 1969, Commissioner Embry pioneered a program to acquire 1,500 of Baltimore's 5,000 vacant row houses to be renovated for use as scatter-site public housing. Embry's department has the power to acquire abandoned or badly blighted properties through tax delinquencies, condemnation or negotiated sale. Depending on the property's condition and location, the department may offer the house for homesteading, or do its own renovation job for public housing or private resale.

"This approach is fantastic," says Embry, who confesses he was dubious at the outset. "It's fast, and it doesn't displace anybody. Instead of destroying neighborhoods, it saves blocks, and it doesn't concentrate poor families the way conventional public-housing projects do." The plan to use renovated row houses for public housing has slowed down, however, partly for lack of Federal money and partly out of a frank fear of inundating ethnic Baltimore's fragile revival with masses of low-income minority families.

On the race issue, SECO treads a necessarily narrow line. It has lost a faction on its right for being too integrationist, and one on its left for being "co-opted" by city officials and bourgeois values. Almost by definition, preserving a neighborhood's ethnic heritage means resisting rapid racial change. Neighborhoods like Southeast Baltimore have natural barriers to racial change, which SECO leaves alone. Realtors have never been active in the area; houses change owners mostly by word of mouth. The area resisted the waves of blockbusting that overwhelmed the less cohesive Irish and Jewish neighborhoods of Northwest Baltimore in the late 60's, and the neighborhood's tough reputation helped. "If block-busters had come in here," said Councilwoman Barbara Mikulski with a touch of bravado, "they would have gotten the hell beat out of them."

SECO's organizers are quite aware that they would lose substantial credibility with the community if the residents of the restored row houses turned out to be 90 percent black. "We try to be sensitive to the neighborhood's ethnic character," says N.H.S. Director Tom Adams. Yet Patterson Park's very first homesteader was a black man, and he was welcomed.

In its battles to improve local schools and promote community improvements, SECO has made common cause with the community organization based in the black neighborhood a mile to the north. Councilwoman Mikulski maintains a close tactical alliance with that neighborhood's three black legislators. On the explosive school busing question, SECO's annual community congress has voted to accept busing-in of black children from poorer neighborhoods, but to strenuously resist busing-out. That approach is the basis of Baltimore's current desegregation plan, which the U.S. Department of Justice considers insufficient. "We simply cannot afford to have our kids bused out of here," Joe McNeely contends. "It would bring down the neighborhood."

What is ultimately needed, the new preservationists argue, is a national neighborhoods policy to reverse the decades-old suburban bias. Several states, including New York, recently adopted programs to discourage red-lining. Baltimore has an office of urban homeownership. Seattle has a Mayor's urban reinvestment task force. The Federal Home Loan Bank system has adopted the Neighborhood Housing Services program, and brought it to neighborhoods in 18 cities. Philadelphia's large banks voluntarily scrapped their neighborhood-based system of appraising property and liberalized their underwriting standards for lending mortgage money on old houses.

At the same time, though mass transit is slowly gaining on highway subsidies, Federal spending priorities still reflect the suburban momentum. Under the block-grant approach introduced in the Nixon years, Baltimore's Federal money for community development drops from $32 million to $18 million a year. The tax code still makes it more lucrative for an urban developer to demolish a sound building and make his money depreciating the new structure built on the site. When Congress passed a tax credit last year to stimulate housing, it was frankly intended to assist suburban homebuilders.

But scarcity economics may finally succeed in fostering neighborhood revival where enlightened self-interest failed. To the children of the old neighborhood who are moving back, the $12,000 average price of an East Baltimore row house is a powerful incentive. And why is the housing so cheap? Commissioner Embry says it's because Baltimore is a working-class town, without the civil-service elite or the management cadres that drive up prices in New York and Washington.

Joe McNeely of SECO has another thought. His office on the second floor of a church school looks out across a rubble-filled alley to a block of row houses SECO is helping 13 homesteaders to restore. In the distance is a panoramic view of downtown. Why is the housing here so cheap? McNeely smiles slowly, "Who would want to live in East Baltimore?"

ATLANTA'S NEIGHBORHOOD RENEWAL

CLARENCE N. STONE

In November 1965 the Bedford-Pine Survey and Planning application got federal approval. The consequences were unanticipated. A routine newspaper item on the proposed project, containing a reference to the displacement of 966 families, became the subject for concerned discussions among two white merchants and three black ministers of large churches serving the neighborhood. One of the ministers was also a state legislator representing the area. Each of the ministers pastored a church that had been displaced by an earlier wave of urban renewal. The five men, all quite aware of what had happened to other neighborhoods, determined to challenge the city's renewal plans. They did not attempt to work through city-wide black leaders, but chose to operate as a strictly neighborhood group. While they as individuals had extensive contacts in the area, they wanted a more formal and broadly based organization. They contributed money to organize a protest under the name of U-Rescue: Urban Renewal Emergency, Stop, Consider, Understand, Evaluate.

The strategy that the U-Rescue founders decided on was to hold a mass meeting for the neighborhood in one of the churches and invite city officials to attend. The group, because of its composition, could

From *Economic Growth and Neighborhood Discontent: System Bias in the Urban Renewal Program in Atlanta,* pp. 107–12, 153–64, by Clarence N. Stone. Copyright 1976 The University of North Carolina Press. Reprinted by permission of the publisher.

make use of church announcements to arouse the neighborhood, but they also publicized the meeting by distributing pamphlets that contained the leading statement, "Learn about the danger of losing our Neighborhood because of Urban Renewal." In addition, on the day of the meeting, they rented a sound truck to go through the neighborhood and urge full attendance. An overflow and wrought-up crowd resulted. One of the ministers, an especially passionate orator, proved highly effective in building feeling further as he talked of Atlanta's "urban removal" program, of unkept promises to maintain the residential character of areas, and of the many cases of personal hardships caused by displacement he had witnessed. Several individuals spoke out—homeowners of long standing, proprietors of small businesses, and others who made it clear that they had important stakes in maintaining the neighborhood. An attitude of "you can't trust City Hall" permeated the proceedings.

The news media gave the meeting extensive coverage, and the morning newspaper presented a "task force" report on the proposed project. The "task force" was prepared by reporters and was based largely on interviews with U-Rescue leaders and other neighborhood residents. Under headings such as "It Hurts When They Must Up and Move," reporters offered descriptions of the potential impact of the renewal project on families in the area.

The initial mass meeting was followed by three others, and a series of resolutions to the city was unanimously adopted. The first set of resolutions contained U-Rescue's basic platform, which in brief was:

1. The creation of a citizens' advisory committee to serve as a liaison between the neighborhood and urban renewal office;
2. No change in the area from a residential neighborhood to nonresidential purposes;
3. No replacement of substandard dwelling units with housing beyond the financial means of the people displaced;
4. No widening of a street (Bedford Place) eastward, which would have an adverse effect on one of the small churches in the area (Little Friendship Baptist Church).

The resolutions were carefully worded not to be entirely negative in tone; they expressed general approval of the idea of eliminating blight and specific approval of the new school and adjoining playground.

Drawing on public records in City Hall, U-Rescue strengthened its position first by detailing past instances in which the city had planned to redevelop an area for residential purposes and subsequently either had amended the plan to permit other reuses (the stadium area) or had left land undeveloped (Rockdale). U-Rescue broadened its leadership into a twelve-member executive committee reflecting various political, business, and church groups from the neighborhood. Despite some initial aloofness, city officials came to be convinced that U-Rescue represented genuine grassroots resistance to displacement and that the leadership of the organization had the skill and the incentives to fight effectively against any large-scale clearance.

The city's renewal planning worried the U-Rescue leadership in two respects. While the Survey and Planning application called for the area to remain predominantly residential with rehabilitation in most of the neighborhood, the displacement figure of 966 was regarded as much too high. But, more than that, U-Rescue genuinely feared that the designated area of clearance, a strip along the western edge of the project near the civic center, was only a prelude to total clearance. They saw the civic center as part of a Chamber of Commerce/CAIA/Uptown Association* move to extend the business district all the way to Boulevard Street, the easternmost boundary of the proposed project. They also realized that the Uptown Association wanted to create a wide commercial zone extending into the northern portions of the neighborhood. (A little later they were confronted with ambitious expansion plans by Georgia Baptist Hospital in the southern portion of the project area.) Furthermore, with the Egleston-site experience clearly in mind, they feared that a majority of the Board of Aldermen harbored anti-black sentiments and would be quite willing to support efforts to move blacks to Atlanta's Westside.

To gain some assurance that the proposed project would not disrupt the neighborhood, U-Rescue followed a procedure of meeting privately with aldermen and with the city's planning and redevelopment staff. Since various city officials were also invited to attend mass meetings in the neighborhood, assurances given privately thus had to be repeated publicly. U-Rescue regarded the mayor as someone who had to be dealt with gingerly and therefore not to be put on the spot. Consequently, attention centered on Rodney Cook, chairman of the aldermanic urban renewal committee, and on the two aldermen who resided in the ward

---

*Editor's note—CAIA—Central Atlanta Improvement Association, an organization of businessmen with interests in the central business district (founded 1941). Uptown Association, a group similar to the CAIA. Eventually the CAIA absorbed the Uptown Association and became Central Atlanta Progress, Inc.

containing Bedford-Pine. U-Rescue pursued a hard line with the alder-men. In effect, the aldermen were told to be at the mass meetings and state their commitment to maintaining Bedford-Pine as a residential neighborhood for its current population. U-Rescue would construe failure to make this public commitment as opposition to its goals.

Once the general commitment was secured, U-Rescue began to negotiate with Alderman Cook and the Housing Authority over specific points. The city's initial position, as expressed by Alderman Cook, was allegedly one of "don't worry, we'll take care of you." He admitted that some business interests had brought pressure on the city to clear the area for commercial redevelopment, but he maintained that this pressure had been resisted. The city, Cook argued further, would not have committed $2,000,000 or more for a school and park in the middle of the area if it had plans to change the neighborhood from residential to commercial purposes. However, U-Rescue was not at all sure that new housing would be available at a price that would serve current neighborhood residents. To statements that there was nothing to worry about, U-Rescue responded with a demand that the organization wanted to be consulted and in-volved in the planning of the project. The Housing Authority countered with the suggestion that in place of U-Rescue a large advisory committee for the neighborhood be created. U-Rescue's leadership insisted that the organization would not under any circumstances disband and that, if they served as a neighborhood advisory committee, they ought to be able to make recommendations that would be followed. In short, U-Rescue took the stance that unless they were effectively involved in renewal planning, they would "raise hell." Specifically, U-Rescue's leaders felt that they possessed both voting power in local politics and the capacity to invoke federal regulations.

The city appointed and accepted U-Rescue's leadership as a liaison committee, one that could speak for the neighborhood as redevelopment was planned and executed. In addition there was early agreement to the point that, while the project would consist largely of rehabilitation, the clearance portion would be staged on a block-by-block basis. The Reverend J. D. Grier, spokesman for U-Rescue, and Alderman Cook joined in making a statement that the city would seek to develop pro-cedures whereby one area would be cleared and developed before the next area was cleared. In this way, as people were displaced, there would be housing available in the neighborhood for them to relocate in.

U-Rescue followed up its victories on general points with victories on particular points. A proposed widening of Bedford Street, the street form-ing the boundary between the Bedford-Pine project and the Buttermilk Bottom project, was postponed indefinitely at U-Rescue's request. When the chairman of the Aldermanic Parks and Recreation Committee stated that the proposed park of twelve acres was not large enough, that it should be twenty-five acres or none, U-Rescue was able to veto the suggestion and maintain the original size.

U-Rescue's most substantial victory, however, was that of gaining the city's agreement to build public housing in the project and to place it in an area covering the northeast sector of the project. Unable to persuade the city to decrease the amount of displacement, U-Rescue turned its attention to the type of residential development that would occur. The organization presented to the Urban Renewal Policy Committee a resolution calling for public housing to "be placed on site within the Bedford-Pine Urban Renewal Project area." The U-Rescue resolution also explicitly demanded that "as soon as the number of families in the area eligible for low-rent housing can be determined . . . not less than this number be scheduled for construction." Finally, the resolution requested that a 650-unit reservation from the Federal Public Housing Administration be obtained to meet the area's needs. The city did agree to 350 units and also suggested that at a later time moderate-income units could be built under the 221(d)3 program.

Opposition from within the business community appeared, not against the request for public-housing units, but against the location of units along North Avenue—the northern boundary of the renewal area. Even before U-Rescue had been formed, the Uptown Association made clear its desire to have the south side of North Avenue, that is, the portion in the Bedford-Pine renewal area, included in a Ponce de Leon/North Avenue commercial corridor. The Uptown Association engaged in prolonged and determined opposition to low-income housing in that location; on one occasion, the Uptown Association generated a proposal to build a new post office facility in the area planned for housing. Next, the Uptown Association suggested that the renewal project be held in abeyance until public housing could be built elsewhere, either in the project or in an outlying area. City officials rejected both overtures.

U-Rescue's leadership had purposefully selected the North Avenue site for housing in order to prevent further commercial incursion into the neighborhood. Both the proposal for an enlarged park and for the post office facility were viewed as threats to the residential character of the neighborhood. Conversely, public housing in the northern edge of the project was seen as a reasonably good guarantee that the area would remain residential. Although the Uptown Association had staunch support for its position on the Board of Commissioners of the Housing Authority, U-Rescue exerted its influence with the Board of Aldermen, in particular with the chairman of the renewal committee. A divided Urban Renewal Policy Committee supported the North Avenue public-housing site.

In Georgia Baptist Hospital, U-Rescue faced another threat to the residential character of Bedford-Pine. Situated in the southeast sector of the project, Georgia Baptist Hospital first requested a total of thirty-five acres of land for expansion purposes. Although U-Rescue initially opposed selling any renewal land to the hospital, the organization did accede to the sale of fifteen acres, most of which was commercial property and already in nonresidential use. The compromise provided the hospital with land deemed quite adequate for its immediate needs and at the same time generated no real resistance by U-Rescue, because residential displacement was minimal. However, two years later when the Housing Authority proposed expanding the eastern boundary of the renewal project to encompass land sought (purportedly privately) by the hospital for further expansion, U-Rescue strongly and successfully opposed the suggestion.

Overall, U-Rescue prevailed or at least gained significant concessions on most of the points at issue in Bedford-Pine renewal. By contrast, the Uptown Association, while it had attained a much desired objective with the construction of the civic center in Buttermilk Bottom, was rebuffed in its attempts to extend nonresidential reuses into the Bedford-Pine project.

U-Rescue's accomplishments are best appreciated by considering the interests arrayed against the maintenance of Bedford-Pine as a predominately low-income neighborhood of essentially undiminished population. The Uptown Association, which was especially closely identified with one bank and one department store, included on its board of directors representatives of five banks and two other financial institutions, a major department store, and a major national corporation, several "small" but important businesses, attorneys and other professionals, and real estate companies of varying sizes. In brief, the association represented the portion of the CAIA oriented toward the upper sector of the business district. U-Rescue was strictly a neighborhood organization; the twelve-member executive committee was composed of black church and political leaders and black and white businessmen who, without exception, represented small owner-operated businesses dependent upon the immediate vicinity for their customers.

A strictly neighborhood-based organization was thus able to gain important concessions from the city and thwart the demands of an influential element in the business community. Further, while U-Rescue had no active allies, the organization did receive sympathetic and extensive coverage from the news media, editorial endorsements of its general renewal objectives, and timely expressions of support from some business figures on the CACUR* and from the Urban Renewal Committee of the Chamber of Commerce. Compared to the Localities Committee of the 1950s, U-Rescue had made a major breakthrough in the local political scene.

[Moving beyond one section of the city, the author goes on to analyze the organizational efforts in low-income neighborhoods around the city aimed at presenting an alternative to the mayor's and business community's view of renewal. He then proceeds to discuss the last years of Mayor Ivan Allen's administration in terms of whether changes in the priorities of renewal actually occurred as a result of neighborhood pressure. Stone continues by returning to an analysis of the Bedford-Pine area.]

Until a program moves beyond the stages of being a plan, a proposal, or a declaration, the program has not really been tested. Program execution is the battleground on which a policy must ultimately prove itself. Costs and competing priorities once hidden begin to surface. Victories gained at an earlier time can again be contested. And new conflicts among affected groups emerge. Program execution is thus strategically important ground in the group contest to influence public policy.

The previous chapter has shown that general plans to renew nonaffluent neighborhoods and rehouse slum dwellers were not followed by successful efforts to execute these plans. City officials were unwilling to devote the time, allocate the resources, and incur the resentments needed to push the program forward. Neighborhood groups and the proponents of improved housing opportunities lacked the capacity to maintain the initial momentum toward a new policy direction. In contrast, at an earlier time, when efforts to expand and upgrade the CBD were stymied by the noncooperation of city departments and by the opposiiton of various neighborhood groups, forceful counteraction from the business community bestirred city officials and unblocked CBD renewal. Later, Mayor Allen made stadium and civic center construction items of top priority in his administration and surmounted many obstacles to move

---

*Editor's note—CACUR—Citizens Advisory Committee for Urban Renewal.

the necessary redevelopment projects ahead rapidly. Yet the mayor made no comparable exertion of leadership on behalf of neighborhood renewal and rehousing goals.

The present chapter continues the consideration of program execution. It contains a detailed examination of redevelopment and rehousing activities in one neighborhood, the Bedford-Pine area. This area was singled out for an in-depth study of implementation for two reasons: (1) Bedford-Pine was a project in which both neighborhood and non-neighborhood interests had substantial stakes; and (2) the Bedford-Pine project was the first neighborhood project on which protests had an impact, and it was therefore further along in the execution phase than other neighborhood projects.

The reader may recall . . . that a neighborhood organization, U-Rescue, had worked out with the city an urban renewal plan that supposedly would protect the interests of low- and moderate-income residents. The present chapter shows, however, that agreed-upon objectives suffered as planning gave way to execution. Open neighborhood dissatisfaction reoccurred, but it was dissatisfaction that had relatively little impact on city officials. As with the larger relocation and redevelopment program for the city, housing for the Bedford-Pine area was built neither in the numbers nor on a time schedule that matched the early hopes of neighborhood residents.

MAJOR DEVELOPMENTS

In August of 1967, the city submitted an Early Land Acquisition application to build public housing, install temporary housing units for relocation purposes, and along Boulevard, the eastern edge of the project, rehabilitate apartments and do some spot clearance. In April 1968, after a lengthy review, federal officials in Washington at first denied approval to the temporary housing. (The city could, of course, have undertaken the temporary housing on its own, but without federal approval the city would have to bear the entire cost.) With strong urging from the city, including the mayor, federal renewal officials reversed their position and did approve the inclusion of the temporary housing in the project activities. However, before the city completed all of the steps required to implement the Early Land Acquisition, new federal legislation was enacted. The NDP* established by the 1968 Housing

---

*Editor's note—NDP—Neighborhood Development Program.

Act, as a new version of urban renewal, was regarded by federal officials as especially suited for areas such as Bedford-Pine. The city was persuaded to convert the Bedford-Pine project to NDP, with the result that new planning applications had to be prepared and additional hearings held. Meanwhile the visibility of U-Rescue within the neighborhood waned.

When conflict finally surfaced, opposition to city actions was voiced not by U-Rescue but by dissident social action agencies. Two of these agencies, somewhat ironically, were based at Emory University, a predominantly white institution located in the Atlanta suburbs.

An Upward Bound course at Emory in the "Urban Crisis" led to "lab work" in one of the unredeveloped remnants of the area originally known as Buttermilk Bottom. The urban-crisis laboratory was a small neighborhood overlapping the old boundary between the Buttermilk Bottom and Bedford-Pine projects (the two were combined into one project in August, 1967). Ed Ducree, director of Emory's Upward Bound program, had good command of the rhetoric of black militancy and also had a flair for dramatizing issues. Under Ducree's leadership, a center for several service activities in the neighborhood, called Crisis House, was established in the southern portion of the renewal project. Crisis House was also in contact with the Emory Community Legal Services Center (sponsored by Emory University and funded by the Office of Economic Opportunity), which had an office nearby; and, for a time, Crisis House was assisted by some Vista workers. A Catholic charitable organization, the St. Vincent de Paul Society, was also working in the Bedford-Pine area, but its activities were concentrated in the northern portion of the renewal project.

During 1968, the head of the St. Vincent de Paul neighborhood office and the director of the Community Action neighborhood center in the area made efforts to encourage wider citizen participation in the renewal process. In collaboration with the renewal project office, which was located in the neighborhood, a number of meetings were held during the year, but none was based upon a mutual understanding of what the term "citizen participation" meant. The project office gave the residents minimal information, and let them know that the major decisions about the area had already been made and could not be changed. One group specifically sought to have a small church (Little Friendship Baptist Church) in a clearance portion of the project preserved as part of the neighborhood, but they were told that it was too late to change plans. When some residents pressed the project office for specific examples of what they could participate in, the project office cited as examples the design and decorating features of the new public housing for the area. Some residents complained about the condition of rental property in the area, but they were informed that the Housing Authority could do nothing about code enforcement and that the only service available through the project office was information on where displacees could relocate. One of the larger meetings with residents was not attended by the project director, who left the handling of questions from residents to a Housing Authority trainee serving temporarily in the project office. Block chairmen in the Community Action program, who were important links with poorer residents, did attend meetings for a time, but eventually stopped going to them. The block chairmen came to believe that the meetings had no clear purpose. Insofar as they could see, the meetings consisted of explanations as to why resident questions and requests could not be attended to, and were therefore pointless.

None of the meetings with residents involved U-Rescue, and the Community Action representatives were for the most part unaware that U-Rescue existed. In a statement before the Georgia Advisory Committee to the United States Civil Rights Commission, the head of the local St. Vincent de Paul office charged that U-Rescue failed to represent the poorer elements in the neighborhood. He said that the organization was composed mostly of homeowners who "don't associate with the people down in this area." He added, "They . . . do not communicate."

The absence of more extensive neighborhood participation was challenged finally, but not through the Community Action program. In November, 1968, Ed Ducree and a number of residents from the Crisis House vicinity made the challenge during the public hearing on the inclusion of Bedford-Pine in NDP. Decree voiced concern about proposals to move residents out of the southern portion of the Bedford-Pine project and to convert the area to nonresidential uses. He stated further that a board of black people represented the area and that they wanted to keep their neighborhood and rebuild it.

Since the area under discussion was not proposed for action in 1969, the chairman of the Planning and Development Committee (the aldermanic committee on urban renewal), Rodney Cook, attempted to cut off the Crisis House testimony with the statement that Ducree's presentation was "not relevant." Ducree retorted, "I'm not finished. You wait until I finish what I have to say. This is the old game you boys have been playing for a long time. You say I'm out of order because you don't like what I say." Cook returned, "I'm the chairman and I'll make a statement when I want to make a statement." Decree then charged, "It's dictatorship." He added that he wanted the aldermen to be aware of the problems and again stated that some citizens were not involved in the planning process. U-Rescue representatives were present, but they kept a distance from Ducree both during the meeting and later. They acknowledged no shortcomings in the representation of neighborhood interests.

Despite the heated nature of the exchange, Cook called Ducree the following day and invited him to discuss the neighborhood further. During the subsequent discussion, Cook, along with the director of redevelopment, assured Ducree that plans were not fixed for the southern portion of the project and that the city was willing to consider a proposal from Crisis House.

Ducree did not follow through. Without a tangible program around which the residents could be rallied, personal animosities came to the forefront, and Crisis House could no longer mobilize overwhelming support from the surrounding area. Since the Emory Community Legal Services Office was an available ally, Crisis House gave some thought to bringing a suit to prevent the execution of the urban renewal project. Ducree, however, expressed qualms about working with whites—the Legal Services staff was white. Moreover, at that point Ducree's stated preference was for using confrontation rather than legal tactics. The issue lapsed, however, for Ducree became occupied mainly with Upward Bound and other matters outside the area.

During the summer of 1969, dissatisfaction among Bedford-Pine residents once again welled up, this time in the northern section of the project in which the St. Vincent de Paul Society was most active and in which some clearance was taking place. The long-promised temporary housing for displacees was opened at the end of May, but only a few units were ready for occupancy. Only sixty units had been purchased, and, of these, ten were three-bedroom units and the rest two-bedroom units. It soon became apparent that not only were the number of units far short of what was needed to keep residents in the neighborhood, but that families were carefully screened before they were placed in the temporary units. Obviously, large families could not be housed in such small units, and "problem" families were excluded.

The publicly stated position of the Housing Authority was that everyone was to be accommodated in temporary housing or at least other housing in the neighborhood. Even large families could be accommodated, it was said in response to public queries, by combining two of the two-bedroom units. However, the in-house policy was that screening was necessary to make temporary housing a success, and that proper maintenance depended upon housing only the smaller and most desirable families as tenants. Both the St. Vincent de Paul and the Community Action workers in the area discovered that the real policy was one of relocating in outlying public-housing projects all larger families and families with any history of social problems. These families, of course, retained the option of refusing that alternative and relocating themselves in private dwellings.

Neither the St. Vincent de Paul Society nor the Community Action office was willing to make an issue of the de facto relocation policy. Both agencies felt that they needed the cooperation of the renewal office, and, in fact, both organizations had service activities housed in facilities provided by the renewal agency. The position of the St. Vincent de Paul Society was that raising an issue might help one or two families in the short run, but that project office cooperation would be lost for long-term service efforts. The St. Vincent de Paul Society, moreover, had only recently weathered one conflict with the Community Action program and was not eager to become embroiled in another controversy.

The Community Action staff was also operating under constraints. The agency's director made it known that he regarded Community Action as essentially a referral agency, dependent upon cooperation from other agencies. In 1969, operating under a budget cut, Community Action felt especially dependent on other agencies. Without exception, the staff working in the Bedford-Pine area recognized that residents needed to be organized to make demands, but also without exception the staff saw community organization as an activity not proper for the Community Action program. From above, they were told that their principal objective was, as one staff member said, "to work *with* and cooperate *with* other agencies." From below, they sensed no pressure. Rather, they saw the low-income residents as apathetic, as unwilling to attend meetings, and, in general, as a dependent population with much to lose if they antagonized the various social service agencies.

Thus, while both the St. Vincent de Paul Society and the Community Action staff were fully aware that residents were apprehensive about the renewal program and while both were dissatisfied with the Housing Authority's relocation policy, they believed that no substantial gains could be made by raising an issue. At this time, the summer of 1969, the two agencies were working closely with one another, but neither saw the other as an ally "with weight." Both saw the Housing Authority as the only agency in the area with sufficient resources and staff to provide social services directly and indirectly on a significant scale, and each saw itself as without the power needed to compel a change in Housing Authority practices. Social agency "constituents" were not regarded as a force that could be mobilized, but simply as people who were, in the words of one staff member, "submissive and shy." One anti-poverty worker described the mass of Bedford-Pine residents as having "no power—they don't vote; they are poor, uninformed, non-mobile, alcoholic, et cetera."

In August of 1969, the relocation program came to the direct attention of the Emory Community Legal Services Office. With some assistance from the St. Vincent de Paul Society and after a lapse of several months, a Legal Services lawyer was able to obtain from twelve families in the area depositions with which to challenge the city's relocation practices. In March of 1970, a class-action suit was brought, charging the city with failing to meet relocation obligations under the Workable Program. The legal brief stated: "The city has undertaken a program to reduce the supply of (low to moderate income) housing, stem in-migration of low income citizens, disperse the resident constituency of low income citizens and erect protective barriers for downtown commercial interests." The suit further challenged the city's stated policy of only partially enforcing the Housing Code. In particular for urban renewal areas, the city's policy was one of selective enforcement on the grounds that "it is necessary to use all of the city's housing for its residents, even if presently dilapidated." Finally the court action sought to prevent the city from expending funds on nonresidential purposes, in particular for the expansion of Georgia Baptist Hospital and its affiliates.

Working with the Emory Community Legal Service Office, Ed Ducree again became active and initiated two open meetings in the neighborhood. However, both meetings—in comparison to the U-Rescue protest meetings in the earlier years—were lightly attended. Moreover, at the first meeting, one of the U-Rescue leaders expressed his opposition to the suit against the city. For the second meeting, Ducree persuaded a number of activists in various militant organizations to attend. The new chairman of the aldermanic Planning and Development Committee (Rodney Cook had run unsuccessfully for mayor in the fall of 1969 and was no longer on the Board of Aldermen after January, 1970), an attorney from the Housing Authority, and a representative from the Georgia Baptist Hospital were invited to and did attend the meeting to hear residents' grievances. However, in the face of harassment from some of the audience, the two city officials and the Georgia Baptist Hospital representative walked out of the meeting.

In a rump session, Ducree then planned to break into a meeting of the Housing Authority commissioners the next day and to present a list of demands. Accompanied by a few people from the neighborhood (including some of the St. Vincent de Paul staff) and by a newspaper reporter and some black militants, Ducree brought off the dramatic confrontation that he had been considering for some time. The group broke into the meeting of the Housing Authority Commission. Some physically imposing militants stood at the door while Ducree presented a list of demands and made a shrill speech in which he announced that they were going to "hold trial for criminals [that is, the Housing Authority]." A black member of the authority was singled out as an "Uncle Tom" and was subject to an especially bitter verbal attack. The commissioners themselves were flustered by the incident, but the Housing Authority director began to talk in a calm and reasoned manner about the individual demands presented.

The demands of the Ducree group were far-reaching. Some were very general, such as the demands that no more renewal money be spent for nonresidential renewal and no additional houses be torn down until the poor had adequate places to live. Some demands were quite specific. For example, the group asked that commercial land, including a supermarket serving the area, not be sold to Georgia Baptist Hospital for redevelopment. Taking advantage of the fact that Bedford-Pine had been converted to NDP renewal, the Ducree group also called for the replacement of U-Rescue with an elected committee to represent the neighborhood. Several of the demands related to housing directly—the group called for the enforcement of the housing code inside renewal areas (the city's policy was not to enforce the code in areas marked eventually for clearance) and the making of retroactive relocation payments "to all people moved by urban renewal who were eligible but did not receive them." The group also sought to reduce housing costs in the area by calling for the Housing Authority not to charge rent on "the 30 slum houses" it owned in Bedford-Pine until the houses were brought up to code "and then [to] charge public housing rent rates." They also asked the Housing Authority to recommend to the Board of Aldermen the passage of a rent control ordinance covering the rehabilitation portions of renewal projects. Finally, to drive home the point that the city had neglected neighborhoods for other priorities, the Ducree group called for the city to provide emergency housing "for all people living in unhealthy or hazardous dwellings in urban renewal or model cities areas by using the Atlanta Civic Center until relocatable housing is sufficient to the need"; and the group asked for the civic center to be made available, free, for community meetings.

The Housing Authority offered no concessions on the major questions relating to land use, but several demands relating essentially to procedural matters were acceded to. Rent was stopped in the thirty Bedford-Pine houses, even though some of the units were not substandard. U-Rescue, it was agreed, would cease to be recognized as the

Project Area Committee, and an election would be held. Nine months elapsed, however, before the election was held. Retroactive relocation payments were also agreed to, but rent control received no consideration beyond a promise to look into ways of preventing slum owners from raising rents on deteriorating properties in renewal areas. The civic center, it was pointed out, was not under Housing Authority control and therefore could not be offered by them for community meetings, but later an effort was promised to secure the civic center for the election of the Project Area Committee. Code enforcement was also a City Hall function not under Housing Authority jurisdiction, but the Housing Authority promised to and did successfully urge the city department to step up its activity in the area. Without a program of supplemental housing assistance, however, the code enforcement effort led to increased housing costs for and worked hardships on some area residents.

The major negotiating point concerned the provision of emergency relocation facilities. The use of the civic center was, of course, never really considered by either side and was brought into the discussion only as a symbol of the imbalance in the city's renewal program. What the Housing Authority did work out with federal consent was a plan through which two of the new outlying public-housing projects were made available to Ducree for relocation purposes. Ducree formed an organization called the People's Housing Authority, which was given a contract for handling the relocation responsibility for Bedford-Pine, including the direct conduct of moving operations for residents. The Housing Authority agreed to pay moving expenses both to the outlying projects and back into the Bedford-Pine area when new housing was built. Displaced residents were promised priority for new Bedford-Pine units as they became available. Serving still as the director of the Emory Upward Bound project, Ducree had limited time to devote to the actual relocation operations, and the business affairs of the People's Housing Authority were soon ensnarled by some serious mismanagement. The organization became defunct long before facilities were available to move people back into the area. Whether intended that way or not (and they probably were), the relocation arrangements served mainly to divert Ducree from further use of confrontation tactics.

New efforts were made through the Emory Community Legal Services Office to stop the expenditures of renewal funds for nonresidential purposes and to commit City Hall to a housing policy that would increase the supply of low-income housing in all parts of the city. But neither legal action nor direct contact with the mayor's office yielded any significant results. Specific requests for increased participation in the federally-subsidized Section 23 Leased Housing program, for the representation of poor blacks on the CACUR, for the establishment of an emergency housing fund, and for the obtaining of an additional supply of temporary housing of the relocatable type yielded no better results than requests for broad policy changes. The mayor (Sam Massell had succeeded Ivan Allen by this time) showed some interest in a proposal from his own staff to require that Georgia Baptist Hospital provide free clinic services for people in the neighborhood. Beyond that, the only matter that the mayor showed concern about was the representation of poor blacks, but he indicated that he was interested only in the names of individuals who were proven leaders with supporting constituencies.

The Emory Community Legal Services lawyer did obtain full access to city records on relocation and related matters, and sought to handle hardship cases by working with Housing Authority officials. Court procedures proved so cumbersome that the lawyer found it more productive to seek administrative remedies. At the same time he realized that work on individual hardship cases did not lead to replanning of the project area in order to meet the broad needs of the neighborhood's low-income residents. One person working part time could not perform all the legal and historical research required to challenge the city's plans. As allies, he could count only on Ed Ducree and the head of the St. Vincent de Paul Society. The former could devote only a portion of his time to Bedford-Pine, while the latter had to balance opposition to Housing Authority plans against the need for cooperation from the authority's project office. Without funds for publicity and canvassing, it was not possible to rally neighborhood support. Limited resources and political weakness thus dictated the strategy of seeking to relieve individual hardships, even though the basic character of neighborhood renewal went unchallenged.

In the meantime, during the summer of 1970, the Community Relations Commission held open hearings in the Bedford-Pine area. Complaints about high rents, substandard housing, and inadequate services and facilities were aired once more. The summer did see the groundbreaking for Bedford-Pine's first permanent public housing. Of the 353 units planned, 283 would serve the elderly. In December of 1970, when an election was finally held for the Project Area Committee, leaders of the old U-Rescue organization dominated the new committee. Some of the Community Action block chairmen were also elected to the PAC, but they offered no challenge to city policies. Social agencies had reverted to the practice of aiding people on an individual basis, and with the coming of winter protest activity ceased.

More than five years had elapsed since residents had first become alarmed over the possibility that the neighborhood would be disrupted and depopulated. Attempts were made to secure the residential character of the area; but, despite the earlier efforts of U-Rescue and the later efforts of various social action agencies, rebuilding and rehousing never kept pace with displacement activities. Although the original objective of keeping the neighborhood intact as a home for a generally nonaffluent population was never publicly repudiated, many of the very poor were quietly moved away.[1]

CONCLUSION

A number of reasons could be offered for the failure of Bedford-Pine renewal to meet its stated objective of rehousing residents within the neighborhood. The complexity of intergovernmental relations, the shortage of federal funds, and the transitory nature of leadership in a slum community could, for example, be cited as contributing factors. But such particular reasons assume importance only in the light of underlying and continuing conditions that have characterized low-income neighborhoods in Atlanta through the time period encompassed by the present research.

A program goal may be displaced either because a powerful group with overriding interests is able to reshape policy or because the group originally intended as the beneficiary of the program is too weak to sustain a policy effort on its own behalf. Bedford-Pine faltered at least as much for the latter reason as for the former. There were, to be sure, competing interests. But these competing interests, as exemplified by Georgia Baptist Hospital, registered gains, not because they were able to defeat neighborhood groups in head-on conflicts, but rather because they were capable of maintaining a persistent and multifaceted effort on behalf of their land expansion and other needs. Low-income residents, by contrast, proved to be an unsteady source of pressure on city officials. Although mobilized from time to time in varying numbers to attend public meetings or hearings, residents were seen even by the social agencies working in the neighborhood as apathetic and dependent. The agencies themselves were short on resources and on numbers of residents who could be induced to act in furtherance of organizational goals. In their capacities as the clients of public agencies—clients who had neither the information nor the material wherewithal to pursue alternative courses of action—low-income residents had much to lose individually. Potential collective gains could not always be readily perceived. As the consumers of publicly provided social services, slum dwellers represent an especially difficult group to organize. Under any set of circumstances, organizing consumers is a substantial task; but consumer organization becomes nearly impossible when the group is poor, dependent, and not highly educated.

Because many of the neighborhood residents had multiple and pressing needs, social agencies working in the area were themselves inclined to pursue actions to meet the immediate needs of residents rather than to seek fundamental and long-term solutions to neighborhood problems. The social agencies were also disinclined to engage in controversy. Their own needs were great, and they forewent active dissent rather than lose opportunities to enhance their own service-providing capabilities.

While several groups in the project area realized that the Housing Authority was guided more by a general public relations concern than by a concern with neighborhood housing needs, project area residents were too weak politically to challenge the Housing Authority. Besides, since many area residents believed that the most they could do was to delay the inevitable, they felt that they might eventually need relocation assistance from the Housing Authority. Some therefore concluded that they would be better off individually if they did not antagonize the agency.

The two aldermen from the ward that included Bedford-Pine had been drawn into initial controversy over renewing the area as allies—at least publicly—of U-Rescue. Both aldermen were white, lived in neighborhoods well to the north of Bedford-Pine, and failed to keep in close touch with the renewal situation. The two aldermen were contrasting political types: one had essentially a "good government" orientation and the other had a more traditional orientation. Neither knew very much about what was occurring in the neighborhood. Neither was on the Planning and Development Committee. The alderman with the "good government" orientation assumed that the renewal of the neighborhood was essentially a matter of promoting rehabilitation, and in the absence of any cues to the contrary from the chairman of the Planning and Development Committee, he believed that relocation was being handled to the satisfaction of all concerned. He had no ties with groups in the neighborhood, and moved primarily in white-collar and Republican political circles. The other alderman was more the old-style, ward-oriented politician, but he did nothing more than talk occasionally with some of the U-Rescue leaders. He was knowledgeable about the civic center, but knew little of the relocation situation.

The mayor's office and the Housing Authority staff were the city officials most immediately concerned with Bedford-Pine renewal, and at no time did they indicate anything less than full sympathy for the goal of rehousing residents within the neighborhood. However, Mayor Allen did not make Bedford-Pine redevelopment an item of top priority as the stadium and the civic center had been, so that neighborhood redevelopment was not pursued with a sense of urgency by his staff. No deadlines were set, and no systematic set of follow-through actions was undertaken. The Housing Authority staff, as employees of an agency esteemed neither by the larger community nor by the residents of low-income neighborhoods, was especially eager to avoid bad publicity around the use of temporary housing for relocation purposes.

What part business influence had in the course of events is difficult to determine. There was no overt business opposition to the originally agreed-on rehousing plans for Bedford-Pine. City officials knew that some individual businessmen favored minimal low-income housing for the area, but no business demand was articulated (that is, during the time period considered here).[2] If there was business pressure, it was indirect. Administrative officials were sure that they were expected to handle rehousing efforts in a manner compatible with the nearby presense of the civic center. And, of course, Georgia Baptist was expressly interested in expanding its facilities and in decreasing the low-income population of the area generally. In the absence of some indication from the mayor or other top level officials that rehousing Bedford-Pine residents was a matter of high priority for the city, program administrators understandably proved to be less than vigilant guardians of rehousing opportunities for large or problem-ridden families. The rehousing of Bedford-Pine residents within the neighborhood faltered, then, partly because the renewal of the neighborhood was not a high priority program for city officials and partly because Bedford-Pine residents lacked the organization and resources to maintain a steady and unrelenting pressure in support of their housing goals.

NOTES

Keller: THE NEIGHBORHOOD

1. Ruth Glass (ed.), *The Social Background of a Plan* (London: Routledge and Kegan Paul, 1948), p. 18.
2. D. D. McGough, *Social Factor Analysis, Community Renewal Program,* City of Philadelphia Community Renewal Program, Technical Report no. 11, October, 1964 (mimeographed), p. 54. H. L. Ross also found food shopping to be a local activity; church attendance, work, and entertainment, less so. Clearly non-local activities were shopping for clothing or furniture. H. L. Ross, "The Local Community: A Survey Approach," *American Sociological Review* 27, 1 (February, 1962); see also *Neighborhood and Community* (Liverpool: Liverpool University Press, 1954), pp. 93, 95, 104.
3. A. Schorr, *Slums and Social Insecurity* (Washington, D.C.: U.S. Department of Health, Education and Welfare, 1963), p. 41. See also the observation that younger age groups may use clubs near at hand but adolescents already "prefer to go farther afield." J. H. Nicholson, *New Communities in Britain* (London: National Council of Social Services, 1961), p. 137.
4. Glass, op. cit., p. 41. Compare with the following observations: "There is good reason to believe that the level of functioning of local areas in cities is limited, but there is in all probability considerable variation in the sense of community and the nature and type of social functioning among different types of areas within a city." Mary W. Herman, *Comparative Studies of Identification Areas in Philadelphia,* City of Philadelphia Community Renewal Program, Technical Report no. 9, April, 1964 [mimeographed], p. 14. Janowitz suggests the term "community of limited liability" to connote the partial and selective character of residents' orientation to local areas. See Ross.
5. See Theodore Caplow, Sheldon Stryker, and Samuel E. Wallace, *The Urban Ambience* (Totowa, N.J.: Bedminster, 1964), p. 201; N. Foote, J. Abu-Lughod, M. M. Foley, and L. Winnick, *Housing Choices and Housing Constraints* (New York: McGraw-Hill, 1960), p. 184. "To attract upper class residents, an area should contain, in addition to the homes they want, a church, a club, an inn, railroad connections, and have something like a horseshow." (D. E. Baltzell, *Philadelphia Gentlemen* [New York: The Free Press, 1958], p. 205).

Goldman: BUFFALO'S BLACK ROCK

1. M. Goldman, *Buffalo's Black Rock: A Neighborhood and the City*, Ph.D. dissertation (SUNY/Buffalo, 1973), 22–41.

2. That the majority of the neighborhood businesses were locally owned can be derived by reading the neighborhood newspaper, by studying the names of the businesses as listed in the annually published city directories, and by examining the city atlases which list the owners of each piece of property. By correlating the information in the city directories with that in the atlas, a fairly accurate assumption about local ownership can be made. These assumptions are reinforced by the impressions gained from extensive reading in the local newspaper.

3. The city atlas, published intermittently throughout the nineteenth century, indicates whether the land was subdivided and/or developed. By looking at the atlas of 1874, conclusions can be drawn about the states of development before the completion of the Belt line.

4. For the complete story of the growth and development of Assumption Parish, see Goldman, Ch. 4.

5. *The International Gazette,* May 7, 1891. The members of the Black Rock Businessmen's Association, to a man owners of such locally based businesses as taverns, groceries, butcher shops, etc., had little to gain economically from greater integration with the rest of the city. While they clearly had some belief that business values in general might rise with greater integration, what motivated them more than economic self-interest was the intangible, yet deeply felt sense that somehow integration was simply good for Black Rock. The business activities of the members of the Association are mentioned in practically every issue of the *International Gazette.*

6. Brenda K. Shelton, *Reformers in Search of Yesterday: Buffalo in the 1890's.* (Albany, 1976), 49. The author points out that "there was no single department of Public Works in Buffalo. Instead the Aldermen shared with a variety of elected and appointed officials the responsibility for streets, garbage removal, sewers and related matters."

7. Population figures by ward can be tabulated by studying the manuscript censuses taken by New York State in the following years: 1855, 1866, 1875, 1892, 1905. These records are available at the County Hall of Erie County, located in Buffalo, New York.

Hurst: INTEGRATION, FREEDOM OF CHOICE, AND COMMUNITY CONTROL IN NINETEENTH-CENTURY BROOKLYN

1. U.S. Bureau of the Census, *Eleventh Census: Population I,* 470 and 422; *Twelfth Census: Population I,* 631. One study of the early history of Bedford-Stuyvesant (then Bedford Village) showed the area to be one-third Black in 1790. By 1930 Bedford-Stuyvesant was only 12% Black although the proportion of Blacks increased thereafter. Nancy Haber, "A History of Bedford-Stuyvesant," unpublished paper, Long Island Historical Society, n.d.

2. According to the Census of 1890, there were 65 Black professionals in Brooklyn. Out of this number, 24 were music teachers and 21 were professors and teachers of other subjects. *Eleventh Census: Population II,* 640.

3. "Back where I was growing up, the 'successful' Lansing Negroes were such as waiters and bootblacks. To be a janitor at some downtown store was to be highly respected. The real 'elite,' the 'big shots,' the 'voices of the race,' were the waiters at the Lansing Country Club and the shoeshine boys at the state capitol." Malcolm X, *The Autobiography of Malcolm X* (New York: Grove Press, Inc., 1964), 5. See also Alan H. Spear, *Black Chicago: The Making of a Negro Ghetto, 1890–1920* (Chicago, 1967), 54, where he describes a similar class of Black elite in Chicago.

4. For a review of the economic status of Blacks in New York City during the last half of the nineteenth century, and a discussion of the nature of the Black elite and the gap between the Black middle and lower classes, see Gilbert Osofsky, *Harlem: The Making of a Ghetto* (New York: Harper and Row, 1963), 3–7. Whites and some Black Elites tended to glorify the situation of Blacks at mid-century compared with their status at the end of the century. See, for example, J. Gilmer Speed, "The Negro in New York," *Harper's Weekly,* December, 1900, 1249–50.

5. One way of determining Black elite status in Brooklyn was membership in a society restricted to those who were born in North or South Carolina, Virginia, or New York. These societies were founded in the 1890's, perhaps as an attempt to preserve the socially elite position of the Black bourgeoisie who felt threatened and degraded by the influx of lower-class Blacks from the deep South. They also served to reaffirm the Americanism of the Black man and thus distinguish him from the recent foreign immigrants. The *Brooklyn Eagle* referred to this upper crust of Black society as "the colored 400 of Brooklyn." *Eagle,* September 16, 1892, 13.

6. "Brooklyn seems always to have shown less race antagonism than Manhattan . . . and it has been in Brooklyn for the past three generations that the well-to-do colored families with their children have chiefly been found." Mary White Ovington, *Half-a-Man: The Status of the Negro in New York* (New York: Schocken Books, 1969; originally published 1911), 173.

7. Joseph Connally Flora, "The Centralization of Professional Administration in the Brooklyn, New York, Public Schools, 1887–1902," unpublished dissertation, Teachers' College, Columbia University, 1971, 13. According to an authorized history of the New York Public School, "regarding any particular school, the local committee was practically supreme." The constant criticism of the local committee system by centralization-minded reformers generally centered around its conduciveness to local pressure and personal corruption. A. Emerson Palmer, *The New York Public School: Being a History of Free Education in the City of New York* (New York: Macmillan Co., 1905), 178.

8. "The colored children who are in attendance upon Nos. 80 and 81 are but a small minority of the whole number of colored children who avail themselves of our system and attend the schools throughout the city in common with whites, between whom and the colored children no distinction whatever is made; and in the opinion of this Board it will be to the advantage of the system and of the colored scholars themselves, to assimilate Nos. 80 and 81, in practice as well as in theory, to the other Grammar Schools, at the earliest practicable date." Quoted in Palmer, 178.

9. In 1968 the Supreme Court recognized that freedom of choice plans could have the effect of maintaining segregated school systems. In *Green vs. County School Board,* Justice Brennan affirmed that "'freedom of choice' is not a sacred talisman; it is only a means to a constitutionally required end—the abolition of the system of segregation and its effects. If the means prove effective, it is acceptable, but if it fails to undo segregation, other means must be used to achieve this end." Supreme Court using the language of *Bowman v. Country School Board,* 382 F2d 326, 333 (CA 4th Cir. 1967) (concurring opinion), in *Green v. Country School Board,* 391 U.S. 440.

10. *Age,* March 28, and April 18, 1891. A third candidate, Dr. Peter Ray, a wealthy druggist like White, was chosen as the nominee of the Colored Citizens Central League of Brooklyn, but Ray himself supported Scottron, a fellow Republican, for the position. The nominations were made by small groups of politically active Blacks through their party clubs. There appeared to be little discussion of the candidates' policy preferences. Blacks were more concerned with the nominees' party affiliation, status in the community, and acceptability to the White authorities. Whites made their decision on the basis of partisanship. The mayor's choice was always seated by the Board.

11.   Brooklyn, Board of Education, *Proceedings*, 282; *Age*, April 25, 1891. On the Tuesday following the meeting of the Board of Education at which Stewart's name was presented, members of the Colored Central League joined with Reverend W. H. Dickerson, who was in the midst of a personal feud with Stewart, and packed the meeting of the sedate and prestigious Brooklyn Literary Union (Black). Dickerson and the others almost, but not quite, succeeded in defeating Stewart's bid for reelection to the presidency of the Literary Union. *Age*, May 9, 1891.

12.   In fact, in the eight years of *Proceedings* of the Board of Education from 1890 to 1898, although there was a Black member of the Board all during those years, there was no entry under the Black member's name that did not refer to some matter dealing with the Colored Schools

13.   ". . . the new school house on Bergen Street and Schenectady Avenue was built for the relief of P.S. 68, and upon the joint request of certain white and colored citizens, was made large enough to accommodate all the children residing in the vicinity of said school with the understanding that P.S. No. 68 as now organized would occupy the entire new school house, and that the pupils and any additional teachers needed therein would be classified and employed without regard to race or color." *Proceedings*, October 6, 1891, 648.

14.   Brooklyn, *Proceedings*, April 5, 1892, 68–69, 281; *Eagle*, April 8, 1892, 8; April 30, 1892, 8; *Proceedings*, May 3, 1892, 288, 339–344. Stewart stressed in his argument the fact that the Board's original decision to integrate was based on approval of delegations from both the Black and White communities.

15.   Brooklyn *Proceedings*, March 7, 1893, 183–187. ". . . from and after this date P.S. No. 68 be and hereby is abolished and the pupils thereof sent into P.S. 83. The local committee of P.S. No. 83 in conjunction with the Superintendent of Public Instruction is hereby authorized and directed to organize four new classes therein, and transfer and appoint thereto the four class teachers now in P.S. 68."

16.   C. Simis, at that point Stewart's leading ally, and Stewart himself supported Aegesta Back as Head of the Department, but Georgiana Putnam was appointed instead. Brooklyn, *Proceedings*, June 6, 1893, 381–83. The local committee then brought charges against Putnam, but the Committee on Teachers did not sustain the charges. Putnam, however, was granted sick leave for two months, which may have been the concession made to the local committee. Ibid., December 5, 1893, 706; March 6, 1894, 210.

17.   *Eagle*, May 20, 1894. It was not, of course, only Blacks who argued for a change of municipal appointees when the Mayor's office changed from one party to another. School Board appointments in Brooklyn were particularly noted for their partisan nature during this period. Flora, 128.

18.   In a plea to Mayor Seth Low in 1883 to maintain C.S. 3 for Black children only, Black Reverend George E. Smith promised to personally see to it that Black children filled up the school. Reverend George E. Smith to Seth Low, March 16, 1883, "Brooklyn Board of Education," Box 163, Columbia University, Special Collections, Seth Low Papers.

19.   Today in Southern counties where integration is avoided through "freedom of choice" plans, the Black principal plays a similar role and is often one of the strongest supporters of maintaining segregated schools. One reporter has characterized the relationship between a Black principal and the White superintendent of schools in the South as being "the smoothest, if most pernicious, inter-racial working relationship in a rural county." Taylor Branch, "'Freedom of Choice' Desegregation: The Southern Reality," *Washington Monthly*, 1, 10 (November 1969), 74.

20.   *Eagle*, March 6, 1897, 6. The *Eagle*, however, alleged that Dorsey himself did not object to being retired, but that the principal wanted an annual pension of his full salary. Ibid., March 23, 1897, 16.

21. Scottron's last reappointment was in July, 1900, for a three-year term. New York City, Borough of Brooklyn, *School Board Proceedings,* July 3, 1900, 448.
22. This law was repealed, at the urging of Governor Theodore Roosevelt, in 1900. *Laws of New York,* One Hundred and Twenty-Third Session, 1900, Chapter 492, p. 1173.
23. The upper class basis of the reform movement is best analyzed by Samuel P. Hayes in "The Politics of Reform in Municipal Government in the Progressive Era," in *New Perspectives on the American Past,* ed. by Stanley N. Katz and Stanley I. Kutler, II: 1877 to the Present (Boston: Little Brown and Co., 1969). Flora's study confirms Hayes's thesis as it applies to the reformers pressuring for changes in Brooklyn's educational administration, Flora, 125.

Yates: NEIGHBORHOOD GOVERNMENT

1. Sherry Arnstein's article, "A Ladder of Citizen Participation," *Journal of the American Institute of Planners,* 35: 216–224 (July, 1969), presents another way of labeling the progression from weak to strong decentralization. The point of my analysis is to show the structural prerequisites to different kinds of participation.
2. Daniel Bell and Virginia Held, "The Community Revolution," *The Public Interest,* No. 16 (Summer, 1969), pp. 155–158.
3. Robert Dahl suggests that a population range of 50,000 to 200,000 is best suited for widespread citizen participation in a city. See his "The city the future of democracy," *American Political Science Review,* 61: 967–970 (December, 1967).
4. In a sidewalk survey on New York's Lower East Side, the author found that only three people out of 100 residents had heard of the neighborhood mayor's office, known as the Urban Action Task Force. Fifty of those interviews were conducted within a three-block radius of the government office. Several residents who were interviewed lived on the same block as the Task Force Office and still were not aware of its existence.

Chia-ling Kuo: COMMUNITY CONTROL AND THE ENCAPSULATING POLITICAL STRUCTURES

1. Percy E. Sutton, *A Plan for Localizing Government in New York City* (1972), p. 2.
2. New York City government, *Office of Local Neighborhood Government, 1973* (Forest Hills, New York).
3. Sutton, *A Plan.*
4. *China Post,* July 19, 1976.
5. Hart, Krizatsy, and Stubee, "Chinatown: A Report on the Conditions and Needs of a Unique Community." Mimeographed. New York, 1968.

Hoover and Vernon: HOW NEIGHBORHOODS EVOLVE

1. The Standard Metropolitan Area used by the Census Bureau, it will be recalled, covers all of the New York Metropolitan Region except five outlying counties: Fairfield, Dutchess, Putnam, Orange, and Monmouth.
2. Calculated from data in Bureau of the Census, *1956 National Housing Inventory, Components of Change, 1950 to 1956: New York–Northeastern New Jersey Standard Metropolitan Area* (Washington, 1958). The other causes of housing

inventory change, including mergers, did not appear on balance to affect the number of nonwhite-occupied units between 1950 and 1956. It should be borne in mind that the 1956 inventory survey was based on a sample, leaving a considerable margin of error, particularly in findings involving relatively small numbers of dwelling units.

3. A suggestive indication of the importance of conversions in the older neighborhoods of the Region prior to 1950 can be derived from the Census reports on housing by age of structure and the estimated number of households. Thus, the *1950 Census of Housing* reported that 3,080,865 dwelling units in the 22 counties of the New York Metropolitan Region in 1950 were in structures built prior to 1930 (almost certainly a substantial under-estimate, since it may be presumed that a high proportion of the 200,000-odd units for which no building date was reported were in old structures). It has been estimated by the Regional Plan Association (Bulletin 87, Tables 19 and 22, pp. 26 and 39) that the number of households in the Region in 1930 was about 2,860,000. The number of dwelling units exceeded the number of households (occupied dwelling units) by only 3 percent in 1940. It seems to follow that (despite all the demolition of old structures that must have occurred between 1930 and 1950 in the Region) there were actually a few more dwelling units in pre-1930 structures in 1950 than 1930, the increase representing the excess of gains by conversion over losses through demolition and all other causes.

4. The highest migration and moving rates are characteristically found in the 20–24 age group in both sexes. Compare Bureau of the Census, Current Population Reports, Series P-20, No. 85, *Mobility of the Population of the United States, March 1957–March 1958* (Washington, October 13, 1958), Table 4, p. 11.

5. The remaining Health Area showing a significant increase in population was at the lower tip of Manhattan, where fluctuations in the transient population of seamen play a major role in population change and the total population does not exceed 12,000.

Warner: TREMONT STREET DISTRICT

1. For the purposes of this book the mile square of Roxbury from Washington Street to Blue Hill Avenue, from Dudley Street to Franklin Park, has been called Roxbury highlands. In the 1870's the hilly character of this part of town lent all of Roxbury the temporary name of Boston highlands.

The remainder of Roxbury has been lumped together under the name lower Roxbury to distinguish it from West Roxbury and Roxbury highlands. Only relatively small amounts of building went on in the Back Bay parts of Roxbury during the nineteenth century, principally on the streets off Massachusetts Avenue. Therefore, for all practical purposes, lower Roxbury comprises all of the former town excepting the highlands and the large Back Bay tract west of Huntington Avenue.

2. The author's analysis of the "Tenement House Census" shows wards 19, 20, and 22 in lower Roxbury to have had 7,703 structures. There were 4,381 multiple dwellings and 3,322 singles. Of these, 53.4 percent of the singles and 12.6 percent of the multiple structures had resident owners. The building habits of a representative sample of 361 builders and 122 of the largest builders indicates that local landlordism must have been a very common pattern for rental units.

This analysis included only 60–80 percent of the rental units so that many small suites of one and two rooms were omitted. If these rentals were included, probably two-thirds of the total dwelling units of the area would appear in multiple structures.

3.   From 1885 on, fire regulations required brick construction in all of Roxbury below the Ruggles and Ward Street line. This part of lower Roxbury therefore continued in row housing of the old kind long after such practice had been abandoned elsewhere. City of Boston, *Revised Ordinances of 1892* (Boston, 1892), pp. 99–100.

Osofsky: HARLEM

1.   There is no legally definable modern community of Harlem. The first settlement was made in the area in 1636, and the town of New Harlaem created in 1658. The last Harlem colonial patent was made in 1686. Its boundaries ran roughly from present-day Seventy-fourth Street to One Hundred and Twenty-ninth Street, East River to Hudson River. Subsequent grants made in the general area of New Harlaem in colonial times outside these boundaries were also often referred to as Harlem grants. Sometimes the name Harlem was used to designate all upper Manhattan. Harlem in the late nineteenth century was part of the Twelfth Ward, which included all Manhattan above Eighty-sixth Street. At the turn of the nineteenth century, its residents generally defined the community as bordered by One Hundred and Tenth Street on the south, One Hundred and Fifty-fifth Street on the north, East River on the east, and present-day Morningside and St. Nicholas Avenues on the west, but were never rigid in applying this definition. The same holds true today. This absence of legally designated boundaries presents no significant difficulty for this study, because after this chapter I shall use an ethnic definition—the specific sections within the general area of Harlem occupied by Negroes, and these can be traced in the greatest of detail. In the 1920's Negro Harlem was most often called Central Harlem or North Harlem.

Simon: HOUSING AND SERVICES IN AN IMMIGRANT NEIGHBORHOOD
Milwaukee's Ward 14

1.   Since Poland did not exist as an independent country, the Census Bureau did not list it as a possible country of birth. A valuable surrogate, however, is the data on mother tongue of the foreign white stock.
2.   The occupational categories in Table 3 and 4 differ because they are based on different tabulations. Table 4 is based on the sample data from the 1905 census manuscripts.
3.   The census tract analysis is based on the four census tracts which most closely approximated the Ward 14 area. . . . The housing data from the block census was tabulated from all the city blocks actually in Ward 14.

Stone: ATLANTA'S NEIGHBORHOOD RENEWAL

1.   The number of temporary units remained at 60 until a new wave of large-scale clearance was begun in the 1970's after the close of the present narrative. By the summer of 1973, when the city had reached the point of disposing of a 78-acre tract for residential reuse, the Planning and Development Committee recommended that rebuilding be oriented toward middle-income (that is, "nonsubsidized") housing. On an adjacent tract at that time, the Housing Authority had newly completed or had in the planning stage 283 public housing units for the elderly and 168 units for families. Thus public housing was being built in the numbers originally agreed on although not on the schedule or with the relocation

arrangements agreed on; but the plans to build 221 (d)3 housing were being scotched in favor of a new policy of maximizing "housing possibilities for all income levels" (*Atlanta Constitution,* June 28, 1973).

2.   The CAIA was the principal backer of the idea put forth in 1973 that re-development in the area should include middle-income housing.

BIBLIOGRAPHIC ESSAY

1. SOURCES FOR BAYOR'S "THE NEIGHBORHOOD INVASION PATTERN"

For ease of reading, the extensive notes to this article have been replaced by the following essay on sources.

The main parts of the article are based on population statistics and social surveys of the areas. The 1920 and 1930 census tract population data is drawn from Walter Laidlaw (ed.), *Population of the City of New York, 1890-1930* (1932) and *Statistical Sources for Demographic Studies of Greater New York, 1920* (1922). See Ronald H. Bayor, *Neighbors in Conflict: The Irish, Germans, Jews and Italians of New York City, 1929-1941* (1978), pp. 214-15, for a discussion of the technique used to secure this data. For 1930 see also William B. Shedd, *Italian Population in New York,* Casa Italiana Educational Bureau, bulletin no. 7 (1934); Jewish neighborhood statistics come from C. Morris Horowitz and Lawrence Kaplan, *Jewish Population, New York Area, 1900-1975* (1959).

All voter registration material is from various volumes of the City Record, City Record Supplement, *List of Registered Voters* (see Bayor, *Neighbors,* p. 215, n. 11.)

Neighborhood social surveys also provided information on population movements. See Mayor's Committee on City Planning, *East Harlem Community Study* (1937); Jewish Welfare Board, *Study of the Changes in the Population of East Harlem with Special Reference to their Effect on the Federation Settlement* (1931); Jewish Welfare Board, *Supplementary Study of the Federation Settlement, New York City and the East Harlem Area* (1932); Jewish Welfare Board, *Study of the*

Uptown Talmud Torah and Jacob H. Schiff Center (1937). The economic survey of Harlem can be found in New York Times, Daily News, and Herald Tribune, *New York City Market Analysis* (1934).

Interviews with Leonard Covello in 1969 and 1972 (principal of Benjamin Franklin High School in East Harlem from 1934 to 1956) and Alfred Santangelo in 1972 (district leader, state senator and, congressman from the East Harlem area during the 1940s and 1950s) were also useful for determining population shifts and neighborhood attitudes.

For the Harlem area other important sources used, both primary and secondary, were: *First Report of the Tenement House Department of the City of New York* (1902-1903); *Harlem Magazine; New York Age; Opportunity; New York Times;* Harry Shulman, *The Slums of New York* (1938); Gilbert Osofsky, *Harlem: The Making of a Ghetto* (1966). Francesco Cordasco and Rocco G. Galatioto, "Ethnic Displacement in the Interstitial Community: The East Harlem Experience," *Phylon* (fall, 1970); E. Franklin Frazier, "Negro Harlem: An Ecological Study," *American Journal of Sociology* 43 (July, 1937); James Ford, *Slums and Housing,* vol. 1 (1936); Jeffrey S. Gurock, *When Harlem Was Jewish, 1870-1930* (1979).

For Washington Heights, see Bayor, *Neighbors,* pp. 150-55, 214-16.

The discussion on population succession theories is drawn from: Paul Frederick Cressey, "Population Succession in Chicago," *American Journal of Sociology* 44 (July, 1938); Richard Ford, "Population Succession in Chicago," *American Journal of Sociology* 56 (September, 1950); William F. Whyte, "Race Conflict in the North End of Boston," *New England Quarterly* (December, 1939); Humbert S. Nelli, *The Italians in Chicago, 1880-1930: A Study in Ethnic Mobility* (1970); Karl E. and Alma F. Taeuber, *Negroes in Cities* (1965); Otis and Beverly Duncan, *The Negro Population of Chicago* (1957).

2. GUIDE TO FURTHER STUDIES

The intent of the following essay is to offer the interested reader a guide for delving further into neighborhood studies. The list is not comprehensive but rather points to some of the major works in an ever growing field.

Scholarly community analysis begins with the early publications of the Chicago School of Sociology. These books and articles provided the framework for the field. Especially notable are Robert E. Park, "The City: Suggestions for the Investigation of Human Behavior in the Urban

Environment," *American Journal of Sociology* (1915), and Ernest W. Burgess, "The Growth of the City: An Introduction to a Research Project" (1923). Both can be found in Robert E. Park, Ernest W. Burgess, and Roderick D. McKenzie, *The City* (1925); see also Roderick D. McKenzie, *The Neighborhood: A Study of Local Life in the City of Columbus, Ohio* (1923). and Louis Wirth, *The Ghetto* (1928). These studies should be read in conjunction with Walter Firey, *Land Use in Central Boston* (1947), Sidney Wilhelm, *Urban Zoning and Land-Use Theory* (1962), and Albert Hunter, *Symbolic Communities: The Persistence and Change of Chicago's Local Communities* (1974), which serve as critiques of and additions to the concentric zone model. Also, as alternative models of urban structure the following should be consulted: Homer Hoyt, *The Structure and Growth of Residential Neighborhoods in American Cities* (1939), and Chauncy Harris and Edward Ullman, "The Nature of Cities," *Annals of the American Academy of Political and Social Science,* 242 (November, 1945).

Discussions on the definition, role, and development of neighborhood can be found in Jane Jacobs's and Suzanne Keller's works but also in M. Leanne Lachman and Anthony Downs, "The Role of Neighborhoods in the Mature Metropolis," in *The Mature Metropolis,* ed. Charles L. Leven (1978); Donald I. Warren, "The Functional Diversity of Urban Neighborhoods," *Urban Affairs Quarterly* 13 (December, 1977); Gerald D. Suttles, *The Social Construction of Communities* (1972); Scott Greer and Ann Lennarson Greer, eds., *Neighborhood and Ghetto: The Local Area in Large-Scale Society* (1974), a collection of articles which first appeared in the *American Sociological Review;* and David R. Goldfield, "The Neighborhood: Islands in the Urban Mainstream," *South Atlantic Urban Studies* 4 (1979).

The fourth issue of *South Atlantic Urban Studies* is primarily devoted to the topics of decentralization, community control, and the neighborhood power movement (see articles by Milton Kotler, Robert A. Rosenbloom and Dick Simpson), for which there is already a voluminous and still growing body of literature. Other important works to consult are Douglas Yates, *Neighborhood Democracy: The Politics and Impacts of Decentralization* (1973), which focuses on the decentralization issue in New York and New Haven; Milton Kotler, *Neighborhood Government: The Local Foundations of Political Life* (1969). Kotler is executive director of the National Association of Neighborhoods and offers his arguments for strong local control; Joseph F. Zimmerman, *The Federated City: Community Control in Large Cities* (1972), discusses the origin and implementation of neighborhood government, concentrating on New York and Detroit, analyzes its role and function, and suggests decentralization models; David J. O'Brien, *Neighborhood Organization and Interest-Group Processes* (1975), provides a theoretical and empirical analysis of neighborhood organizing for low income communities; Allen H. Barton et al., *Decentralizing City Government* (1977), offers an evaluation of the decentralizing district manager program within the community planning districts of New York City; Alan Altshuler, *Community Control: The Black Demand for Participation in Large American Cities* (1970), an analysis of the local control issue for black communities and leaders; Herbert Kaufman, "Administrative Decentralization and Political Power," *Public Administration Review* 29 (January–February, 1969), which suggests a cycle of urban political institutions to explain the present neighborhood movement. Also, the entire issue of *Publius* 6 (1976) is devoted to the topic of neighborhood control, with analysis, for example, of the Office of Neighborhood Government in New York. For a historical view of this topic see Samuel P. Hays, "The Politics of Reform in Municipal Government in the Progressive Era," *Pacific Northwest Quarterly* 55 (October, 1964), an influential essay which discusses the basis for the Progressive era municipal centralization movement; Joseph L. Arnold, "The Neighborhood and City Hall: The Origin of Neighborhood Associations in Baltimore, 1880–1911," *Journal of Urban History* 6 (November, 1979), which notes the historical development of middle class community associations; and Michael J. Austin and Neil Betten, "Intellectual Origins of Community Organizing, 1920–1939," *Social Service Review* 51 (1977).

On the issue of community control of schools, see Maurice R. Berube and Marilyn Gittell, eds., *Confrontation at Ocean Hill-Brownsville* (1969), an anthology which explores the important 1968 New York City school decentralization controversy. Nicholas Mills, "Community Schools—Irish, Italians, and Jews," *Society* 11 (March–April, 1974), reviews the issue of community schools in New York's ethnic neighborhoods from a historical perspective.

Another topic on which much has been written is neighborhood renewal and rehabilitation. Some studies concentrate on specific neighborhoods. For example, Paul R. Levy, *Queen Village: The Eclipse of Community: A Case Study of Gentrification and Displacement in a South Philadelphia Neighborhood* (1978), focuses on a northeast section of South Philadelphia; and Judith Martin, *Recycling the Central City: The Development of a New Town-In Town* (1978), looks at the Cedar-Riverside section of central Minneapolis. Others look at a number of cities. Good here are Bernard J. Frieden, *The Future of Old Neighborhoods: Rebuilding for a Changing Population* (1964), which considers urban renewal policies and the economics of neighborhood renewal in

New York, Los Angeles, and Hartford; Jeanne R. Lowe, *Cities in a Race with Time: Progress and Poverty in America's Renewing Cities* (1967), a view of urban renewal policies and programs in various cities such as Washington, D.C., Philadelphia, Pittsburgh, and New Haven. Also to be considered are: Harold Kaplan, *Urban Renewal Politics: Slum Clearance in Newark* (1963), a look at renewal during the 1949–1960 period, concentrating on the political process; Roger Ahlbrandt and Paul Brophy, *Neighborhood Revitalization: Theory and Practice* (1975), which analyzes and provides a theoretical overview of inner city neighborhood revitalization programs and stresses the theme of neighborhood preservation; Charles Abrams, *The City Is the Frontier* (1967), which ably discusses the assets and liabilities of urban renewal; Martin Anderson, *The Federal Bulldozer* (1967), which criticizes the federal government's urban renewal policies; Herbert J. Gans, "The Failure of Urban Renewal: A Critique and Some Proposals," *Commentary* (April, 1965), which offers his suggestions for changes in the urban renewal system. Scott Greer, *Urban Renewal and American Cities* (1965), provides a good discussion of this topic. An alternative response to the renewal issue can be found in Eileen Zeitz, *Private Urban Renewal: A Different Approach* (1979).

Studies of single neighborhoods have often emphasized the ethnic groups residing there. Among the important studies in this area, see Jacob Riis, *How the Other Half Lives* (1890); Moses Rischin, *The Promised City: New York's Jews, 1870–1914* (1962), a penetrating analysis of this group but also an excellent view of the Lower East Side neighborhood in New York; Alter F. Landesman, *Brownsville: The Birth, Development and Passing of a Jewish Community in New York* (1969), which provides the entire history of the Jews within this Brooklyn community; Jeffrey S. Gurock, *When Harlem Was Jewish, 1870–1930*, which does the same for Harlem; Herbert Gans, *The Urban Villagers: Group and Class in the Life of Italian Americans* (1965), on the life of the Italian community in Boston's West End. Gerald Suttles, *The Social Order of the Slum: Ethnicity and Territory in the Inner City* (1968), on Chicago's Near West Side community offers an excellent study of life in a multi-ethnic slum neighborhood; Caroline Ware, *Greenwich Village, 1920–1930* (1935), is a fine sociological study of this famous New York area; see also Joseph P. Lyford, *The Airtight Cage: A Study of New York's West Side* (1968), and Patricia Cayo Sexton, *Spanish Harlem: Anatomy of Poverty,* which also contains a good chapter on the impact of urban renewal on this community.

Other significant works which include discussions of specific neighborhoods in a broader study include Thomas Kessner, *The Golden Door: Italian and Jewish Immigrant Mobility in New York City 1880–1915*

(1977); Jay P. Dolan, *The Immigrant Church: New York's Irish and German Catholics, 1815-1865* (1975); Humbert S. Nelli, *The Italians in Chicago 1880-1930: A Study in Ethnic Mobility* (1970); Ronald H. Bayor, *Neighbors in Conflict: The Irish, Germans, Jews and Italians of New York City, 1929-1941* (1978); David M. Katzman, *Before the Ghetto: Black Detroit in the Nineteenth Century* (1973); Robert A. Caro, *The Power Broker: Robert Moses and the Fall of New York* (1974); Kathleen Neils Conzen, *Immigrant Milwaukee, 1836-1860: Accommodation and Community in a Frontier City* (1976); Robert Ernst, *Immigrant Life in New York City, 1825-1863* (1949); Thomas Lee Philpott, *The Slum and the Ghetto: Neighborhood Deterioration and Middle Class Reform, Chicago 1880-1930* (1978). See also the excellent discussion on ethnicity and neighborhoods in Kathleen Neils Conzen, "Immigrants, Immigrant Neighborhoods, and Ethnic Identity: Historical Issues," *Journal of American History* 66 (December, 1979).

Other works that should be consulted on a variety of neighborhood topics are Howard Aldrich, "Ecological Succession in Racially Changing Neighborhoods: A Review of the Literature," *Urban Affairs Quarterly* 10 (March, 1975), which offers a good synthesis of the literature on transitional neighborhoods; Reynolds Farley, Suzanne Bianchi, and Diane Colasanto, "Barriers to the Racial Integration of Neighborhoods: The Detroit Case." *Annals of the American Academy of Political and Social Science* 441 (January, 1979) discusses the problems of neighborhood integration in Detroit; Charles L. Levin et al., *Neighborhood Change: Lessons in the Dynamics of Urban Decay* (1976), concentrates on changing neighborhoods in St. Louis; Bruce Wilkenfeld, "New York City Neighborhoods, 1730" *New York History* 57 (April, 1976), looks at neighborhood clustering in the eighteenth century; Robert B. Zehner, "Neighborhood and Community Satisfaction in New Towns and Less Planned Suburbs," *Journal of American Institute of Planners* 37 (1971), studies Reston, Virginia, and Columbia, Maryland, and offers an analysis of neighborhood attitudes in these new towns.